AMERICAN INDIANS IN THE LOWER MISSISSIPPI VALLEY

D1617469

Indians of the Southeast

American Indians in the Lower Mississippi Valley: Social and Economic Histories

DANIEL H. USNER JR.

University of Nebraska Press
Lincoln and London

Earlier versions of three chapters were previously
published: chapter 4 as "The Frontier Exchange Economy
of the Lower Mississippi Valley in the Eighteenth
Century," *William and Mary Quarterly*, 3d ser., 44 (April
1987): 165–92, reprinted with permission of the
Omohundro Institute of Early American History and
Culture; chapter 5 as "American Indians on the Cotton
Frontier: Changing Economic Relations with Citizens and
Slaves in the Mississippi Territory," *Journal of American
History* 72 (September 1985): 297–317, reprinted with
permission; and chapter 8 as "The Noble and the Savage:
Nineteenth-Century Images of Lower Mississippi Valley
Indians," *Louisiana Cultural Vistas* 7 (winter 1996–97):
32–39, reprinted with permission of the Louisiana
Endowment for the Humanities.
First Nebraska paperback printing: 2003
Library of Congress Cataloging-in-Publication Data
Usner, Daniel H.
American Indians in the lower Mississippi Valley: social and
economic histories / Daniel H. Usner Jr.
p. cm. – (Indians of the Southeast)
ISBN 0-8032-4556-4 (cloth: alk. paper)
ISBN 0-8032-9563-4 (paper: alk. paper)
1. Indians of North America – Mississippi River Valley –
Social conditions. 2. Indians of North America –
Mississippi River Valley – Economic conditions.
3. Indians of North America – Mississippi River Valley –
Government relations. 4. Natchez Indians – Social
conditions. 5. Natchez Indians – Economic conditions.
6. Natchez Indians – Government relations.
I. Title. II. Series.
E78.M75.U75 1998
305.897'077–dc21 98-20925
CIP

For Rhonda Seals Usner

Contents

PLATES

Series Editors' Introduction

From the Natchez chiefdom and the emergent Choctaw confederacy to the "petite nations" of the Gulf Coast, the Indians of the Lower Mississippi Valley demonstrate a remarkable and not well understood diversity in social and economic organization, population, and political and military power. Daniel Usner's theory of a "frontier exchange economy," developed in an earlier book, works well for bringing some order to this history. Enmeshed in the French empire by the end of the seventeenth century, the Indians of present Mississippi and Louisiana created ways to profit from and defend against the imperial presence. Usner's perspective, primarily social and economic, permits an examination of the coping strategies of southern Mississippi Valley Indians that emphasizes their attempts to preserve and maintain control, to influence their destinies, and to survive. Agency, an interpretive focus well adapted to an ethnohistorical methodology, thus becomes visible and conducive to scholarly explanation. Usner, well recognized as a leading student of Lower Mississippi Valley Native history, excels in analyzing the nuances of agency. This collection of essays both fills gaps and presents a coherent picture that extends to nineteenth-century New Orleans, explores the vitally important problems of regional demographic change, and vigorously addresses the problems of the historiography of southern Indian history. We are thus proud to present *American Indians in the Lower Mississippi Valley: Social and Economic Histories* as the most recent addition to the Indians of the Southeast series.

Theda Perdue

Michael D. Green

Preface

In this book on the Lower Mississippi Valley, I offer essays that focus on various dimensions of American Indian society and economy. After completing a previous study that encompassed the wide scope of interethnic relations in this region before 1783, I continued to research the Indian experience in what became the states of Mississippi and Louisiana more intensively and over a longer span of time. The chapters of this book represent various lines of inquiry and argument, suggesting approaches that might be applicable to other groups of people in comparable historical situations. But altogether they constitute, I hope, a coherent exploration into important changes and challenges endured by American Indians from the beginnings of European colonization through the emergence of the Cotton South. A consistent emphasis is placed on Indian strategies of adaptation and resistance, although non-Indian policies and perceptions are also included in my analysis. I call the essays "Social and Economic Histories" in order to convey the variety of directions taken by different Lower Mississippi Valley Indian groups as they struggled for survival during the eighteenth and nineteenth centuries.

Chapter 1 is a review of the historiography on American Indians in the early South, examining how the study of Indian-colonial relations has changed during the twentieth century and situating my own work on the Lower Mississippi Valley within the framework of contemporary scholarship. Although the Natchez Indians' relationship with French Louisiana has been studied extensively over the years, my reexamination in chapter 2 attempts to rescue long-term Natchez struggles from historians' preoccupation with their final war against the colony. Chapter 3 explores the wider struggle of Lower Mississippi Valley Indians against adversity and even catastrophe by tracing changes in their population size and location over the eighteenth century. No understanding of Indian life since the beginnings of European colonization can ignore the destructive effect of epidemiological disease and the hazardous influence of alcohol upon health and livelihood. Even in the face of colonial domination and demographic decline over the eighteenth century, however, the Lower Mississippi Valley's native peoples managed to forge durable social and economic relations with Louisiana settlers and slaves. The spheres of interaction and the means of exchange that went into the formation of this multicultural economy are surveyed on a regional scale in chapter 4.

Chapters 5, 6, and 7 explain how Indian people contended with new social and economic changes during the early nineteenth century, as their familiar network of interaction with non-Indians was rapidly displaced by the cotton economy. Finding themselves surrounded by the newly created states of Mississippi and Louisiana, American Indians faced escalating pressures on their livelihood and territory. In effectively weaving together old and new forms of economic activity, however, they expressed a resourceful determination to survive in their homeland. The final chapter discusses pictorial images of Lower Mississippi Valley Indians in locations and settings usually considered marginal to both Indian and non-Indian societies in nineteenth-century America. These drawings, paintings, and photographs generally reflected a racial ideology that eventually shaped the United States government's policy of Indian removal. But when examined closely with other sources, they nonetheless help document Indian strategies of resistance and adaptation both before and after most Lower Mississippi Valley Indians were uprooted from their native land.

Acknowledgments

Three of these chapters are revisions of previously published articles. The original version of "American Indians in a Frontier Exchange Economy" appeared in the *William and Mary Quarterly* and "American Indians and the Early Cotton Economy" was published in an earlier form by the *Journal of American History*. An abridged version of "Images of Lower Mississippi Valley Indians in the Nineteenth Century" appeared in *Louisiana Cultural Vistas*. I thank Michael Sartisky, executive director of the Louisiana Endowment for the Humanities, for helpfully editing the latter article and making it available to many readers across Louisiana. My appreciation goes to the editors of all three journals for granting permission to publish these essays in revised form here.

I presented earlier drafts of other chapters at various professional conferences and colloquia. Presentations of my work on Natchez-colonial relations at the 1992 meeting of the American Historical Association and Louisiana Historical Association received useful comments from Karen Kupperman, James Merrell, and Mathé Allain. The Colonial Workshop at the University of Minnesota's Department of History provided me with an opportunity in 1994 to discuss my essay on the economic strategies of Louisiana Indians in the early nineteenth century. I thank the participants of this workshop for their warm hospitality and thoughtful comments. I benefited from careful readings of the entire book manuscript by Mary Beth Norton, Donald Birchfield, Patricia Galloway, and Michael Green. Peter Wood will recognize portions of this work dating back to my studies with him at Duke University. Peter's formative contribution to chapters 2, 3, and 4 was especially important, and his formidable example as teacher and scholar will always be appreciated.

Several organizations deserve my gratitude for the support provided me during the writing of this book. Cornell University's Department of History helped allay costs of research and conference travel through the Return

J. Meigs Fund. My colleagues in the history department continue to influence my studies through their encouragement and inspiration. The American Indian Program at Cornell University has also enriched my work over the years. In their determination to balance tradition with change, communities with careers – in the face of attitudes that continue to thwart and belittle their efforts – friends and students in the program have taught me a cherished lesson. Research funds provided by the American Indian Program helped me acquire most of the illustrations featured in chapter 8 of this book.

A Williams Research Fellowship awarded by the Historical New Orleans Collection was used to examine pictorial and literary sources found in that important research center. I thank its former director, John Kukla, for his friendly assistance whenever I visited the collection either for my research in Lower Mississippi Valley history or for my Cornell University alumni programs in New Orleans. I owe deep appreciation to Berndt Ostendorf of the Amerika Institut at the Ludwig-Maximilians-Universität München. One of the most knowledgeable scholars of New Orleans history and culture that I have ever met both inside and outside my home city, Berndt invited me to teach at the University of Munich and proved to be a generous host. I spent a splendid year teaching and writing in Munich, thanks to a 1994–95 J. William Fulbright Fellowship.

I dedicate this book to Rhonda Seals Usner, who shared fully the many pleasures and frustrations of its completion. Because of her loving friendship and graceful cooperation, our efforts to blend work with family life continue to be gratifying.

AMERICAN INDIANS IN THE LOWER MISSISSIPPI VALLEY

But the third old lady had books, though she was the one that was a little crazy, and she waited till the others had done and then explained that Floyd had the blood of a Natchez Indian, though the Natchez might be supposed to be all gone, massacred. The Natchez, she said – and she nodded toward her books, "The Queen's Library," high on the shelf – were the people from the lost Atlantis, had they heard of that? and took their pride in the escape from that flood, when the island went under. And there was something all Indians knew, about never letting the last spark of fire go out. What did the other ladies think of that?

Eudora Welty, "At the Landing"

Onatima nodded. "Don't be vulgar, Luther. But I see what you mean. That white writer thought change only meant death. And you could tell he loved death better than life. That's what they've been writing about for a long time. Even that boy in the novel I gave you, the one about the boy and the slave. Remember how the boy kept making up stories and they were always about death? They have a romance going with death, they love it, and they want Indians to die for them."

Luther nodded. "Lucky thing most of us Indians wasn't reading their stories."

"Lucky thing some of us were. But don't change the subject. It's a mess, old man. You'd better do something."

Louis Owens, The Sharpest Sight

ONE

The History of American Indians
in the Early South

The study of American Indians in the early South is finally gaining on the busier and richer scholarship of Indian-colonial relations in the Northeast. Following the work of John R. Swanton, Verner W. Crane, and a few others, the mid–twentieth century saw very little progress in scholarship on southern Indian culture and history for the formative centuries of European contact. Anthropologists and historians paid much closer attention to Iroquois- and Algonquian-speaking Indians and their interaction with northeastern colonies. Southern Indian history, meanwhile, centered on the early nineteenth century. The obvious importance of removal as a defining experience for a large number of southern Indian people had something to do with this emphasis. But the concentration on the antebellum South among American historians in general played an important role in the overall neglect of the South for the sixteenth, seventeenth, and eighteenth centuries.

Now we are witnessing an efflorescence of scholarship on American Indians of the colonial South. Recently acclaimed works by M. Thomas Hatley, Kathryn Braund, Charles Hudson, and Patricia Galloway demonstrate that southern tribes and colonies are a vital area of interest in the new American Indian history. Important studies of slavery in the long-neglected seventeenth and eighteenth centuries, published during the 1970s, helped pave the way for historians of Indian-colonial relations in the South. Archaeological and documentary evidence from early encounters in the Southeast also attracted renewed attention from anthropologists. Deepening interest in the experiences and policies that led to the U.S. government's removal of the largest southern tribes also pulled scholars backward through time.

As these various lines of inquiry currently converge on American Indians of the early South, it might be useful to review old and new areas of scholarship. Understanding how the literature on southern Indians has evolved over the twentieth century helps us identify strengths and weaknesses in established works as well as opportunities and possibilities for future research. Before the 1950s only a few historians and anthropologists ventured into sources dating before the removal era. John Swanton of the Smithsonian Institution dominated the field for a long time. Since the 1950s more and more scholars have turned to American Indians of the early South. Although their purposes and perspectives vary, all must begin with the bountiful legacy of Swanton.

As a student at Harvard University, John Swanton apprenticed under the Peabody Museum's F. W. Putnam before receiving his Ph.D. in anthropology in 1900. Swanton probably grew tired of digging artifacts in Ohio and washing human remains in the museum basement, as suggested by A. L. Kroeber, and so he abandoned archaeology to take up ethnography. Studying linguistics with Franz Boas in New York, Swanton began to work on Pacific Northwest Indians but soon turned to the Southeast. During his half-century career at the Smithsonian's Bureau of American Ethnology, Swanton produced a host of works that largely constituted all of southeastern Indian studies.[1] For anthropologists of Swanton's time, American Indians in the Southeast were less interesting than those in other regions. Kroeber's revealing explanation for the vacuum that Swanton so energetically filled is worth quoting in full:

The Southeastern United States differed from most other native American ethnic areas in its conditions and opportunities. The first contacts go back to Hernando de Soto. All the tribes have been under strong European influences, or at least impingements, for two centuries or more. The contacts and encroachments were multiple: Spanish, English, French, later American also. The smaller tribes have long been extinct – either outright or merged in the more and more composite larger groups that have survived, partly through absorption of such remnants and of White and Negro blood. Here and there, hidden away and overlooked, there remained dwindling little communities of the tribes that had long since ceased to count as entities. In the pre–Civil War days, good memory-ethnology could have been obtained from many of these. When the first ethnologists arrived – Gatschet and J. O. Dorsey – and still more so a generation later in Swanton's time, little could be got beyond the speech, sometimes already broken down or half-forgotten, and scraps of folk tales, customs, and beliefs. The larger groups mostly had bitterly resisted eviction from their homelands. When they finally yielded, it was to set up in Indian Territory semi-autonomous, powerless, miniature imitations of American political forms and economic ways, or blends of these with what was left of their former but already modified institutions. Even these compromises were necessarily transient and gave way to the semiabsorption of citizenship. Field work by direct inquiry and observation, such as was and still is largely possible in the Plains and Plateau, Southwest and California, Northwest and Arctic, was enormously diluted in its possibilities for the Southeastern tribes. It was like working over tailings instead of following a fresh vein. The cultural material available in some ways resembled that obtainable in Latin America – it is imbedded in a matrix of long acculturation; and, as there, it is so firmly imbedded that dissociation is possible only through knowledge of the absorbing culture; and the most authentic data are often to be found in the written records of preanthropological centuries.

Such a field discourages and repels the average American ethnologist. It uncovered a streak of historical genius in Swanton. What informants could not give, good documents did yield, in many cases; and the information was one, two, three, and even four centuries nearer the purely aboriginal.[2]

Most of Kroeber's assumptions about southeastern Indians are now dubious. The very conditions that discouraged and repelled ethnologists of his time, in fact, make the Southeast an especially interesting field for anthropologists and other scholars today. Nevertheless, John Swanton's archival talents resulted in an incomparable body of historical studies that examined much of the South from the sixteenth century into the nineteenth century. The indifference exhibited by contemporaneous historians toward the sources explored by Swanton makes his contribution even more important. In mastering the documentary sources, synthesizing and interpreting them, and even fusing them with some fieldwork, Swanton indeed produced, in Kroeber's words, "something as permanent and fundamental as it is unique."[3]

During the first half of the twentieth century, John Swanton enjoyed little company among anthropologists as well as historians in his study of southeastern Indians. Frank G. Speck, James Mooney, and David I. Bushnell Jr. produced some important works but devoted their careers only partly to the South.[4] Perhaps the best signpost of anthropology's neglect toward American Indians in the South was the fact that among thirteen essays published in a collection celebrating Swanton's fortieth year at the Smithsonian, only one was about the Southeast, David Bushnell's "Virginia before Jamestown."

Meanwhile, professional historians almost completely neglected the South as a region for studying Indian-colonial relations. Fortuitously, the higher visibility of both colonial history and of contemporary Indians in northeastern and Great Lakes states meant that much more work would be produced in Indian history for those regions.[5] Such prominent southern historians as Thomas Abernethy, Ulrich Phillips, and Avery Craven explored some features of the backcountry South early in their careers, but American Indians and their relations with colonists received little notice from them. Thanks mostly to Herbert E. Bolton and Verner Crane, two historians seldom associated with the South, some influential works on Indians in the colonial Southeast were written during the early twentieth century.

Best known for his seminal influence on the study of Spanish Borderlands in North America, Herbert E. Bolton himself researched Spanish missions in both Texas and Florida while encouraging students at the University of California at Berkeley also to examine the Spanish colony of Louisiana. John W. Caughey's collection of documents pertaining to Alexander McGillivray, including a sixty-page introduction to the life of this important Creek leader, became the most widely recognized publication on southeastern Indians produced by a student of Bolton.[6] But also under the tutelage of Bolton, John Tate Lanning wrote two important books on Spanish missions and diplomacy in Georgia before turning to the intellectual and educational history of colonial Latin America.[7]

Another historian influenced by Bolton was Anna Lewis, an Oklahoman of Choctaw descent who earned her B.A. in 1915 and M.A. in 1918 at the University of California. Born in 1885 in the Choctaw Nation, Lewis became the first woman to receive a Ph.D. degree at the University of Oklahoma and taught history at the Oklahoma College for Women from 1917 to 1956. For her 1930 doctoral dissertation, published two years later as *Along the Arkansas*, Lewis examined French and Spanish manuscripts in order to describe colonial exploration and settlement in the Arkansas district of Louisiana. Lewis later applied her exceptional interest in the eighteenth- and early-nineteenth-century Lower Mississippi Valley to writing a book-length biography of Pushmataha, the Choctaw leader best known for assisting Andrew Jackson at the Battle of New Orleans.[8]

Verner W. Crane spent 1911–12 at Harvard University, where he earned an M.A. in history. A seminar with Frederick Jackson Turner and a spring research trip to South Carolina launched Crane into a study of Indian trade in the lower South, which became the topic of his Ph.D. dissertation at the University of Pennsylvania. The final outcome of his studies was *The Southern Frontier, 1670–1732*, published in 1929. As Peter Wood has explained, Crane's scholarship on Indian-colonial relations in the South was anomalous on at least two grounds. Following the publication of *Southern Frontier*, Crane himself shifted to subjects far removed from the early South and eventually became best known as a biographer of Benjamin Franklin. More importantly for the field of southern Indian history, no one else during Crane's early career took a comparable interest in American Indians and their relations with southern colonies before the Revolutionary Era. Like Swanton's studies in anthropology, Crane's work on southern Indians stood alone for a long time.[9]

Crane's scholarship and the subsequent works of Helen Shaw, Chapman Milling, and John Alden were largely histories of diplomacy and policy.[10] Further refinement and expansion of this line of inquiry came steadily in the works of Louis De Vorsey, David Corkran, J. Leitch Wright, and James O'Donnell. These later scholars recognized more than their predecessors the importance of American Indian interests and objectives in international relations, but studies focusing on other forms of intercultural contact or on earlier periods of colonization were slow in coming.[11] Douglas L. Rights, pastor of the Trinity Moravian Church, included a significant amount of material on the colonial era in his 1947 book on North Carolina Indians. A student of Bell Irvin Wiley at Emory University, Henry Thompson Malone published a study of social change among the Cherokees that focused on the early nineteenth century. The Catawbas' experiences during and after the colonial period received some notable attention from Douglas Summers Brown, a woman who wrote local history and children's literature.[12]

With the publication of *The Southern Indians: The Story of The Civilized Tribes before Removal* in 1954, Robert S. Cotterill contributed a major work to southern Indian history in what he called an act of "self-defense." As a university professor teaching southern history, Cotterill felt that he "needed a knowledge of Southern Indians and failed to find it in the books then in print."[13] Cotterill's early scholarship had focused on frontier Kentucky, and in 1936 he published a study of the antebellum South. But some twenty-five years of reading source materials in archives and libraries across the South went into the making of *The Southern Indians*, his last book.[14]

The lack of literature that induced Cotterill to publish his own book in 1954 reflected the neglect toward Indians in the early South over the previous half-century. Cotterill's approach to the subject, however, signaled a persistent tendency among contemporary and subsequent scholars to neglect the sixteenth, seventeenth, and early eighteenth centuries. His overview of southern Indians concentrates heavily on the period from the American Revolution to Jacksonian Removal. The era before 1775 is only briefly treated as background. Cotterill's emphasis on the Creeks of the late eighteenth and early nineteenth centuries resulted in an important interpretation of Indian-white relations in the Deep South and generated additional interest in Alexander McGillivray, Indian trade, and the Creek War among younger scholars. Earlier periods and other topics continued to be neglected.

Historians based in Oklahoma, meanwhile, turned to the removal of southern Indians and their fate in Indian Territory. Grant Foreman was an attorney who had worked on the Dawes Commission, responsible for negotiating and implementing allotment agreements with the Choctaws, Chickasaws, Cherokees, Creeks, and Seminoles. He devoted the last thirty years of his life to studying Oklahoma history and wrote a series of books on Indian Territory. In *Indian Removal: The Emigration of the Five Civilized Tribes of Indians*, published in 1932, Foreman chronicled the injustice and misery suffered by southern tribes as they were relocated to the West. The preremoval history of these Indians, however, was briefly examined only in order to demonstrate how they had become "civilized" in their homelands before the government forced them out.[15] Angie Debo was an Oklahoman who earned her M.A. at the University of Chicago in 1924 and her Ph.D. at the University of Oklahoma in 1933. Debo went on to write many important books on western and Indian history, even though discrimination against women prevented her from acquiring a faculty position at a university or college. *The Rise and Fall of the Choctaw Republic*, a revision of her Ph.D. dissertation, was published in 1934. Its treatment of Choctaw history and culture before the removal era was thin, relying heavily on the works of Swanton. Debo was primarily interested in the struggles of the Choctaw people during the time between their removal from Mississippi and the admission of Oklahoma to statehood. Her later book on the Creeks followed the same pattern.[16]

Many of these works on southern Indians were published by the University of Oklahoma Press through its "Civilization of the American Indian" series. The common format of books written for this series tended to collapse time before the nineteenth century into a relatively brief background. Most volumes also selected single Indian nations as the subjects. In what might best be called a "before-and-after" approach to American Indian history, there is usually an opening chapter depicting the group's culture before European contact. Here the historian calls upon the work of anthropologists and archaeologists to paint a static ethnographic picture. A summary of the tribe's interaction with colonies and of changes in its culture usually follows in one or two chapters. Then each book focuses on relations with the United

States, usually during the nineteenth century. The emphasis here is usually placed on conflict, treaties, policy, and leadership.[17]

At the 1953 meeting of the Ohio Valley Historic Indian Conference, organized by Erminie Wheeler-Voegelin, a new professional organization was founded. Called the American Society for Ethnohistory, this national group included both historians and anthropologists. Like Wheeler-Voegelin, an anthropologist at Indiana University, many of these scholars were employed as expert witnesses for cases presented to the Indian Claims Commission. Through its annual conferences and quarterly journal, the American Society for Ethnohistory provided a setting for interdisciplinary work that significantly advanced scholarship on American Indians in the colonial era. For the South, anthropologists still led the way as historians continued to shy away from the early period. Raymond Fogelson, William Sturtevant, and Charles Hudson produced cultural studies of southern tribes that included some research into colonial sources.

As a professor of anthropology at the University of Georgia, Charles Hudson became instrumental in encouraging and coordinating studies of southern Indians. Nearly half of his own *Catawba Nation* covered the colonial period, and he edited important collections of essays that included other scholars' work on American Indians in the early South. "It is shocking to contemplate that the native people of the southern United States have been a part of our history for over four centuries," Hudson wrote in the introduction to one of these anthologies, "and yet for all the pages that have been written about them, they remain to us as strangers, or even worse, as caricatures."[18] In 1976 he published *The Southeastern Indians*, a graceful introductory text that conveyed the importance and excitement of studying southern Indian cultures. With this up-to-date survey, Hudson joined Swanton as an influential guide for future students of southern Indians. Hudson's greatest contribution to the history of American Indians in the early South has been to recover the sixteenth-century South from obscurity, as he has devoted the past two decades of his scholarship to exploring both the archaeological and documentary records of early Spanish encounters.[19]

Several important contributions to the history of southern Indians originated in a variety of projects since the 1950s. Wilcomb E. Washburn's study of Bacon's Rebellion sparked interest in Indian-colonial relations in the Chesapeake Bay region. Mary Young's work on Creek, Choctaw, and Chickasaw allotments during the removal era set a new standard for closely examining Indian experiences and, even more significant for preremoval historiography, led her to study social and political change among the Cherokees.[20] Interesting approaches to the Cherokees during the colonial period were taken by Frederick Gearing, John Reid, and Rennard Strickland on government and law and by Gary Goodwin on economy and environment.[21] By the 1970s a new generation of historians approached southern Indians with a stronger self-consciousness about the field. Although focusing on nineteenth-century topics, Michael Green's exploration into the causes of Creek removal, Theda Perdue's study of slavery in Cherokee society, and Daniel F. Littlefield's work on Indian-black relations effectively demonstrated the importance of reaching back into earlier times.[22]

Two historians with successful careers outside American Indian history meanwhile produced significant landmarks in the field by turning to Indians in the early South. Having already achieved distinction as a historian of American religion, William McLoughlin devoted the last decade of his life to publishing major works on the Cherokee Indians. McLoughlin applied his thoroughness in both archival research and informative narrative mainly to the nineteenth century, but many of his most original insights enhanced our understanding of the Cherokees' formative relations with the United States during the 1780s and 1790s.[23] After devoting many successful years to the history of international relations on the Gulf of Mexico, J. Leitch Wright Jr. shifted to an emphasis on southern Indians. Published in 1981, *The Only Land They Knew* offered a provocative overview of American Indian history before the removal era. Through Wright's able synthesis, long-neglected information about the enslavement of southern Indians during the colonial period, the importance of Indian trade, and the influence of southern Indians on African Americans reached a wide audience. Just before his fatal accident in 1986, Wright completed *Creeks and Seminoles: Destruction and Regeneration of the Muscogulge People.* This bold analysis of ethnic diversity among the Muscogulge people set a new standard for the study of southern Indians during the colonial and early national periods.[24]

J. Leitch Wright's *Creeks and Seminoles* was the first book published by the University of Nebraska Press in its new series called "Indians of the Southeast." Since 1986 this series, edited by Theda Perdue and Michael D. Green, has constituted an important venue for current scholarship on American Indians in the South. As represented by a few books already published in this series, a growing amount of solid work is being done for the twentieth and nineteenth centuries. Much of this new attention to the post-removal period derives from greater interest in contemporary Indian communities all across the eastern United States. It also reflects a deepening awareness of the new insights into race relations and ethnic identity that can be gained from analysis of American Indians in the post–Civil War South. Perusal of this new literature, however, impresses the reader with wonder over what remains to be learned from and about the endurance of southern Indian communities through the painful experiences of political disruption, economic marginalization, and social discrimination.[25]

Meanwhile, scholarship on southern Indians from the beginnings of European colonization to the removal era began to flourish. Many scholars acquired an interest in American Indians of the colonial South along one of three paths. The escalation of work during the 1970s on Indian-colonial relations in the Northeast, led by such scholars as Francis Jennings, James Axtell, Bruce Trigger, and Neal Salisbury, naturally awakened interest in comparable work for the Southeast. A second trajectory taken by curious students was the exciting new work on slavery in the colonial South. Edmund Morgan's *American Slavery, American Freedom* and Peter Wood's *Black Majority* opened new windows to the dynamic and multifaceted features of intercultural relations in the early South.[26] Gary Nash's *Red, White, and Black: The Peoples of Early America*, first published in 1974, provided an inspirational vista of what awaited younger scholars. By 1989 James Merrell's *The Indians' New World*, a prize-winning study of the Catawbas, reflected the best work in a field that was fast improving. Essays edited and written by Peter Wood, Thomas Hatley, and Gregory Waselkov in their 1989 collection, *Powhatan's Mantle*, offered a rich sample of just some of the important work then in progress.[27]

The third important and productive approach to American Indians in the early South originated with new interest in the Spanish missions of Florida and in the Spanish explorations across the region. Several recent works on the sixteenth century, including those of Charles Hudson already mentioned, have contributed to our understanding of early Spanish relations with southern Indians.[28] Demographic studies have demonstrated the catastrophic impact of diseases carried by early European explorers on the population of American Indians in the Southeast.[29] Plenty of archaeology and history has been devoted recently to the Spanish origins of Florida. Amy Bushnell, Kathleen Deagan, John Hann, Jerald Milanich, and others have closely examined Spanish Indian policy and American Indian life in and around Spanish missions.[30] Thanks to this scholarship, the South during the sixteenth and early seventeenth centuries is finally coming into focus.

Essays published in *The Forgotten Centuries: Indians and Europeans in the American South, 1521–1704*, edited by Hudson and Carmen Chaves Tesser, feature this development. They also show how interest in southern Indians over these forgotten centuries can help bridge studies of English, Spanish, and French colonies of North America, which for too long have been written in virtual isolation from one another.[31]

General themes emerging from this new history of American Indians in the early South depart boldly from understandings that prevailed in earlier scholarship. No longer are Indian tribes portrayed as static groups of people unable to withstand the inexorable force of European invasion. European viewpoints, motives, and policies are no longer privileged over those of American Indians. Whenever featured in the new literature, colonial objectives appear less blunt and uniform than they did in earlier works. The metaphor of a downward spiral once commonly used to characterize all kinds of change in Indian society has been replaced by a sense that erratic motion on an unpredictable course more accurately captures the experiences of American Indians in the early South. A better understanding of the multiple dimensions of both change and continuity should improve our ability to define more precisely real turning points and transformations in southern Indian history during the colonial era.

The diversity of native encounters with colonial peoples across the South is striking but not surprising when one considers the span of time and breadth of space encompassed. Contributing specifically to the wide variation and sometimes erratic rhythm of Indian-colonial interaction were intratribal and intertribal relations, intracolonial and intercolonial relations, and shifting interests of both Indian and colonial societies. The new scholarship also reveals that many Indian nations in the South were in a state of flux as they faced early European colonial efforts. The origins of specific tribes dated to fairly recent changes in population size, political organization, and geographic location. Epidemics triggered by the arrival of Europeans at the beginning of the sixteenth century played a prominent role in decentralizing Mississippi chiefdoms and reconfiguring political associations among survivors.

The responses of native societies to European colonization were as complex and dynamic as this immediate background. Many groups merged in order to withstand new pressures. Individual tribes sought trade alliances with particular colonies in order to protect or bolster themselves vis-à-vis other tribes or colonies. Acceptance of missionaries as well as traders into one's territory, according to the new history, was a form of adaptation to rapidly changing circumstances, securing close ties to colonial societies and stable access to foreign goods. Resistance to European domination also took versatile forms. Wars waged against colonies by tribes and intertribal alliances occurred frequently across the South but were not the only means of asserting independence and self-determination. Historians now see more subtle, everyday manifestations of resistance in diplomacy, trade, and even conversion as American Indians attempted to make relations with colonists suit their own beliefs and serve their own needs.

Once overshadowed by an emphasis on political and military features of Indian-colonial relations, social and economic exchange has come under brighter light in the new scholarship. Historians now appreciate the importance of the deerskin trade to colonies and tribes alike. They pay closer and more nuanced attention to the various and incongruent effects of trade on Indian life. The informal exchange of goods and ideas beyond the more commercialized channels of the deerskin trade is also coming into view. And we are beginning to realize the many different forms that Indian interaction with African Americans took over the long colonial era.

Most of this work on American Indians in the early South has occurred strictly inside the academic world, with little participation by southern Indians themselves and with little impact on the general public. Curriculum projects sponsored by the Mississippi Band of Choctaw Indians and the Eastern Band of Cherokees have concentrated on history and culture since the removal era, understandably more accessible and interesting to young Indians.[32] This cultivation of historical learning will perhaps motivate an increasing number of American Indian students to pursue their own investigations into the colonial era. Widespread interest in American Indians of the early South waits for the all-too-slow incorporation of new scholarship into public museums and popular writings. Works recently written for a wider audience by Peter Wood and Mary Ann Wells are splendid examples that will be followed, it is hoped, by other efforts.[33]

Within this new scholarship on American Indians in the early South, there are important areas that await further study as well as weaknesses and gaps in our understanding. Methodological and conceptual problems evident in much of American Indian history today are shared by works on southern Indians.[34] Closer investigation of population change is necessary for establishing more firmly the location, size, and identity of Indian communities as they confronted colonial peoples and forces between the sixteenth and nineteenth centuries.[35] A project like Helen Tanner's *Atlas of Great Lakes Indian*

History is also needed for the Southeast in order to depict on maps the dynamic and complex experiences of its native population.[36] Since most of the new scholarship has busily focused on particular colonial or native subregions of the South, with heavy emphasis on social and economic change, analysis of broader diplomatic relations across the entire region would also help present new insights into political change on the scale of Crane's *Southern Frontier*. History of the early South that focuses on American Indians should eventually improve our understanding of the imperial contests among England, France, and Spain in North America, since many Indian nations interacted with two or more empires at one time or another.

Shifting attention from the regionwide to the group-level perspective, the new Indian history of the early South could benefit furthermore from closer attention to cultural dimensions of change and continuity. In reacting against the ethnographic framework of earlier studies, recent work has tended to concentrate more on social and economic dimensions of Indian-colonial relations — with, as already noted, much-needed results. But now greater attention to culture is required in order to advance our understanding of what this all meant to the participants themselves. Joel Martin's *Sacred Revolt* and Frederic Gleach's *Powhatan's World and Colonial Virginia* stand out because of their exceptional attempts to balance historical context with cultural perspective. Stronger textual analysis of the ritual and language of Indian diplomacy and greater attention to change and continuity at the village level are just two specific approaches that will enhance knowledge about native world views.[37]

The importance of focusing historical analysis on American Indian women is becoming evident in the work of a growing number of scholars.[38] There is still a great need for this line of inquiry in the study of southern Indian societies during the colonial period. Kathryn Braund's and Thomas Hatley's integral treatment of women's experiences and perspectives in their respective books on the Creeks and Cherokees effectively demonstrates the understanding gained through such analysis.[39] The publication of Theda Perdue's *Cherokee Women: Gender and Culture Change, 1700–1835* in 1998 marks a major breakthrough in thinking about the construction of gender as well as the experience of women in southern Indian societies over the eighteenth and early nineteenth centuries. This book will serve as a model for students interested in the history of American Indian women across all regions of North America.[40]

James Merrell's *Indians' New World* was a landmark study because of its impressive emphasis on the active and versatile role that the Catawbas played in their ever-changing struggles against colonialism. More scholars who are now exploring the wide range of subjects that constitute the history of American Indians in the early South need to emulate Merrell's skillful recovery of Indian agency and voice from a variety of sources. This need is especially urgent in studies of Florida missions in the seventeenth century and in works about southern Indian relations with the United States at the beginning of the nineteenth century. Much of the investigation in both of these areas offers new insight into official policies and practices but with only minimal attention given to native initiatives and responses.[41] Whether examining Indian livelihood and trade, diplomacy and warfare, or mission and town life, historians must seek to understand more fully how Indian people themselves influenced the American South and shaped their own future within the region – before they confronted perhaps their greatest challenge in the U.S. government's removal policy.

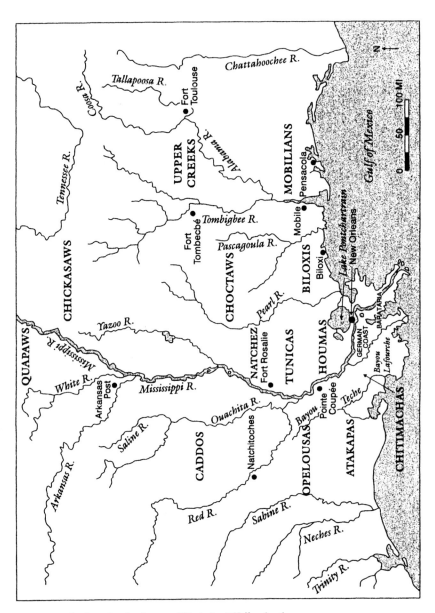

American Indians in the Lower Mississippi Valley in the 1720s.

TWO

French-Natchez Borderlands in Colonial Louisiana

During the heyday of ethnological inquiry into the social organization of American Indians, the Natchez were the object of great curiosity and controversy. A caste system of lineage and government, which had amazed early French observers, confounded modern anthropologists debating a so-called Natchez paradox.[1] John Swanton attributed the fact that two-thirds of his 1911 publication, *Indian Tribes of the Lower Mississippi Valley*, was devoted to the Natchez largely "to its strongly centralized system of government, to the sanguinary mortuary rites of its ruling classes, and finally to the spectacular massacre perpetuated by it upon the French settlers of Natchez in the year 1729 and the bloody war which followed." "The Natchez are, therefore, practically extinct," Swanton concluded, "but thanks to their peculiar manners and customs and the romance and tragedy surrounding their last war with the French they have probably attained a fame which many existing tribes will never enjoy."[2]

In the field of colonial history, meanwhile, the Natchez shared the neglect toward all Lower Mississippi Valley Indians who fell into the French sphere of colonization. French Louisiana was long perceived as an anomalous colonial province in North America. With attention fixed on British provinces, American colonial historians ignored French and Spanish colonial regions. Within the list of French colonies in the Western Hemisphere, Louisiana also fell into a somewhat enigmatic slot. Unlike Canada and the Caribbean in significant ways, it was classified as a hybrid between fur trade and slave societies and considered less successful than other colonies.[3] Surrounded by other Indian societies that had become more dispersed and decentralized than their Mississippian predecessors, the Natchez were one of the few centralized chiefdoms left in the Lower Mississippi Valley by the eighteenth century. The Natchez Indians earned the distinction, therefore, of being an anomaly within an anomaly – seeming to be an exceptionally powerful native society within an exceptionally weak colonial region.[4]

In light of current shifts in both anthropology and history, it is time to reexamine the Natchez Indians and their relations with colonial Louisiana. Less interested in reconstructing "authentic" aboriginal cultures and more interested in understanding cross-cultural exchange, we can return to the Natchez experience with new questions. In tracing the erosion of "classic norms of social analysis" since the 1960s, anthropologist Renato Rosaldo explains how "cultural borderlands" have moved to the center of current inquiry. The myriad crossroads and borderlands where people have encountered cultural differences were too easily reduced to simplistic patterns of conflict or acculturation as long as cultures themselves were defined as unified wholes with rigid boundaries. Now we are more attentive to the borderland spaces in which individuals and groups forge intercultural relationships out of necessity or convenience. Adaptation and resistance to colonialism might even require border crossings of one kind or another.[5]

In their relatively short-lived but well-documented relationship with the French, the Natchez illustrate important dimensions of Indian-colonial borderlands and border crossings that deserve close attention. Recent scholarship in American Indian history for various regions of the Western Hemisphere demonstrates that patterns of adaptation and resistance predating European colonialism played a significant role in shaping Indian relations with empires.[6] So instead of treating the Natchez chiefdom like some static or prototypical political organization, it is more informative to consider its dynamic borderlands with other Indian nations as well as with the French colony. The fateful decision by Natchez leaders to revolt against the French in 1729 should not be viewed as the inevitable result of some linear process of conquest by more advanced or more powerful Europeans. Indian relations with European colonies took many different paths, as emphasized in the new Indian history, each path involving a mixture of tradition and innovation, resistance and adaptation, which cannot be easily broken down into phases or stages. Making the Natchez War even more complicated and less predictable to Louisiana natives and newcomers alike was its connection to wider borderlands among Indians, settlers, and slaves. Finally, it is worth noting that colonial victory over Indian enemies did not completely stop their resistance. Long after the French empire destroyed the Natchez chiefdom, dispersed groups of Natchez people resisted French colonialism in intercultural borderlands across time. These groups warrant discussion.[7]

From their first encounter with René-Robert Cavelier, Sieur de La Salle, the Natchez Indians relied on ready responses to new challenges that had worked for them on earlier cultural borderlands. French explorers and traders introduced new kinds of unpredictability to a world already familiar with instability. The Natchez descended from Muskhogean migrants who traveled down the Mississippi River sometime between A.D. 1000 and 1500 and integrated with older Gulf Coastal cultures. The high bluffs located about 250 miles (as the crow flies) from the mouth of the river provided protection against natural flooding and human invasion. Amidst abundant wildlife and fertile soil, the Natchez established villages along St. Catherine Creek. When La Salle descended the Mississippi in 1682, they lived in some nine or ten different towns numbering approximately six thousand people.[8]

The Grand Village of Natchez centered around the temple of the eternal fire and the cabin of the highest chief, who was called the Great Sun. This sacred ruler maintained absolute authority over his people, who worshipped the heavenly sun through a perpetual fire. Many years ago, according to Natchez tradition, a man and his wife descended from the sun to "teach us to live better and live in peace among ourselves." On becoming the people's sovereign, he ordered them to move to another country, maintain a perpetual fire, and acknowledge only his descendants, who would be perpetuated by women.[9] The grand chief's residence and the sacred temple were built on mounds situated around a plaza, an architectural feature that the Natchez preserved long after other Mississippian societies had dissolved or dispersed. When the French arrived at Natchez, in fact, the Grand Village included two plazas; an older one had apparently been replaced by a newer one as the central axis between temple mound and chief's mound.[10]

The peculiar caste system that continues to fascinate scholars probably evolved among the Natchez during their assimilation of other tribes along the lower Mississippi in a borderland predating French arrival. Natchez society at the beginning of French contact consisted of four classes of people: Suns, Nobles, Honored People, and Commoners. The first three classes, considered nobility, propagated themselves through rules of exogamous marriage and matrilineal descent. Ambiguous descriptions of Natchez social structure prevent conclusive understanding, but a conjectural organization can be made. Suns were children of Sun mothers and Commoner fathers. Nobles included the children of Noble mothers and Commoner fathers or of Sun fathers and Commoner mothers. Honored People were the offspring of Honored women and Commoner men or of Noble men and Commoner women. Commoners were born to Commoner mothers and Honored fathers or to Commoner fathers and Commoner mothers.[11]

As migrants into the region, the Natchez might have devised a form of social organization that legitimized dominance while facilitating incorporation of indigenous groups. The classification system suggests that social instability would have resulted from a diminishing Commoner class. Anthropologists have offered a number of hypothetical solutions to this "Natchez paradox," including assimilation of outside tribes, status differentiation of brothers and sisters, and differential fertility. Despite anthropological controversy over its actual mechanics, however, the Natchez's social structure managed to unify different peoples during migration and conflict. The marriage rule of exogamy also helped resolve tension between social differentiation and political unity within the evolving nation.[12]

La Salle's encounter with the Natchez in 1682 foreshadowed the complex borderland that developed between the French and the Natchez over the ensuing years. The Great Sun met La Salle in "wooden canoes to the sound of the tambour and the music of the women." He offered the calumet, or peace pipe, and expressed pleasure at the arrival of the French. On his return visit from the mouth of the Mississippi, La Salle faced unexpected hostility. After offering the Natchez some scalps of Quinipissas killed in combat by La Salle's party of Frenchmen and Indians, the explorers were suddenly surrounded by an estimated fifteen hundred warriors. The ensuing scene confused Henri de Tonti, the expedition's most experienced guide. "They brought us something to eat, and we ate with our guns in our hands. As they were afraid of fire-arms, they did not dare to attack us. The chief begged M. de la Salle to go away, as his young men had not much sense, which we very willingly did – the game not being equal, we having only 50 men, French and savages."[13] This ambivalent response to the disruptive presence of intruders, common in early Indian encounters with Europeans, probably reflected a predictable degree of uncertainty and disagreement within Natchez society over appropriate strategies of engagement.

When the French began to colonize the Gulf Coast some seventeen years later, Louisiana officials immediately recognized the prestige and power of the Natchez head chief. Successful alliance with local Indian nations against English expansion and their conversion to Catholicism – two of France's initial goals in the region – might hinge on friendship with such a powerful ruler. In 1700 missionary Paul Du Ru, accompanying Pierre Le Moyne d'Iberville's exploration upriver, commented on the Great Sun's "somewhat Spanish" manners. The absolute respect and obedience that he received from the villagers resembled the "air of an ancient emperor."[14] The Natchez never approached their chief directly and always saluted him with a howl.

Female chiefs, whose sons or brothers became Great Suns, also bore great influence. Father Gravier was struck by the genius of the woman chief, whose brother, Ouachilla, seemed less intelligent and less tolerant. The Great Sun always maintained a company of guards, through whom French colonial officials appealed for services and favors.[15]

The French at first placed high hopes on using the Great Sun to inspire religious conversion among the Indian populace at large, but Natchez leaders demonstrated a recalcitrance that had facilitated their own dominance in the past. The arrival of Iberville in 1700 coincided with the illness of Ouachilla. The death of a Sun chief required the sacrifice of nearly a hundred lives in what might have been the Natchez's most sacred ceremony. Father Du Ru rushed to baptize Ouachilla but lacked knowledge of the language to explain the procedure to him. He then tried to persuade his wife to prevent any killing if the chief died. Relieved by her promise to do so, Du Ru sent some medicine and a rosary to Ouachilla. The chief's subsequent recovery convinced the Jesuit that "the Holy Virgin gave her blessing to the remedies that we sent." Despite Du Ru's optimistic assessment of their disposition to "accept a missionary's teaching," other colonists quickly realized that Natchez chiefs "have too much interest in passing among their people for spirits to embrace Christian humility very soon."[16]

The persistence of their death ritual indicates the strength of Natchez resistance to such direct cultural interference by the French. While living among the Natchez in 1704, ship carpenter and interpreter André Pénicaut witnessed this "most horrifying tragedy that could be seen." After the grand female chief died, her son strangled her husband. His body was placed beside her on "a kind of triumphal chariot," around which were laid twelve strangled infants. During the next four days, fourteen people descended scaffolds every quarter hour and danced in the village square to the howling and singing of the chief's kinsmen. These sacrificial victims had honored their families by offering their death while the Dead One was alive; they would lovingly serve her in the next world. Following the march of the corpses, in which the dead infants were trampled on by their fathers, the victims undressed and sat outside the temple. Cords, made by their own hands, were then placed around their necks. With deerskins over their heads, they swallowed three tobacco pills and lost consciousness. The Dead One's kinsmen then tightened the slipknots until the victims died.[17]

The death ritual and more seasonal ceremonies endured in the face of new threats posed by the French empire. At communal feasts and dances, or during the annual renewal of the temple roof, all classes of the Natchez gathered on the public square between the mounds of the sacred temple and the Great Sun's cabin.[18] "The fathers of families do not fail to carry to the Temple the first of their fruits, their corn and vegetables," reported Father Le Petit in 1730. "They never plant their fields without having first presented the seed in the Temple with the accustomed ceremonies."[19] The unity of Natchez life rested upon the sacredness of their ancestors' land and the continuity of their kinship system from one generation to the next. French colonists eventually affected both land and lineage but hardly altered Natchez government and society. Missionaries gained permission to baptize those children sacrificed by their fathers. In explaining such limited success, André Pénicaut argued that "this nation is too stubborn in its religion, which humors the wicked inclinations of their depraved natures so that there has been no progress in converting them and in establishing Christianity among them."[20]

During the early nineteenth century, the Natchez Indians became the exotic and tragic medium of François René Chateaubriand's popular stories *Atala*, *René*, and *The Natchez*. Their revolt against the French in 1729, however, was not as predictable or as inevitable as romantic representations in literature over the years have made it seem.[21] As the Natchez people forged borderland relations with French colonists, they chose from a number of possible paths taken by other Indian groups in the Lower Mississippi Valley – none of which led automatically to violent confrontation. In some ways the Natchez resembled other large, interior tribes because of their strategic location along the Mississippi River. Like the Choctaws and Chickasaws, the Natchez communicated with Louisiana through formal channels. For Louisiana's defense against English encroachment from Carolina, Jean-Baptiste Le Moyne de Bienville encouraged diplomatic and trade ties with these Indian nations. Carolinians scattered among Choctaw, Chickasaw, and Natchez villages were offering valuable merchandise in return for Indian slaves. Indians now demanded the same presents, especially firearms, ammunition, and alcohol, from the newly arrived French.[22] But financial deficiency and profiteering at first thwarted Louisiana's efforts to recruit Indian allies. In 1713 three Englishmen and Price Hughes, a Welshman hoping to establish an English colony on the river, purchased Chaouacha slaves from the Natchez. The Chaouachas, a coastal nation already decimated by the European presence, had been attacked by a Yazoo and Natchez raiding party.[23]

The Natchez benefited early from competition between English and

French traders but not without suffering some stress from the contest. Villages divided into factions, weakening the Great Sun's authority and threatening national solidarity in what might be called a domestic borderland. Internal tension violently surfaced in 1715, when Governor Antoine de La Mothe Cadillac traveled upriver without offering presents or accepting the Natchez calumet. Uneasy over the establishment of a trading post two years earlier, the Natchez interpreted the governor's negligence of the sacred exchange ritual as a sign of impending aggression. They assassinated four passing voyageurs and raided the Crozat Company's storehouse. Bearded One, chief of the hostile, pro-English village of White Earth, pillaged all its arms, powder, and bullets for the anticipated conflict. Bienville led an expedition of only thirty-four men to avenge these hostile acts. Up against a force of about twelve hundred warriors and without sufficient arms, the French were forced to accept an offer of peace largely on Natchez terms. Tattooed Serpent, war chief and the Great Sun's brother, offered the heads of three hostile warriors, returned stolen merchandise, and promised to execute the Bearded One – probably in order to undermine the pro-English faction.[24]

Disagreement within colonial society also emerged during this conflict, revealing the advent of ambitious economic plans. Bienville argued against Cadillac's assertion that the Natchez were the most docile and friendly nation along the Mississippi River. He began to distrust the Natchez "more than any other" and insisted that a fort be built there. He also refused to continue scattering his small garrison among Indian huts. Pressure from investors and officials to find an exportable agricultural staple for Louisiana sparked interest in Indian land, and the Natchez area looked promising for such a development. General Commissioner Jean-Baptiste Duclos went so far as to declare it "necessary according to their principles to destroy the Natchez entirely or at least, according to our laws . . . to tomahawk all those who killed or participated in the murder of the Frenchmen."[25]

Over the first two decades of colonization, however, trade and sexual relations engendered an interdependency between Indians and Frenchmen that proved to be a resilient borderland inviting border crossings. A census of August 1708 recorded 146 men, 28 women, 25 children, and 80 Indian slaves, "plus 60 Canadian backwoodsmen who are in the Indian villages situated along the Mississippi River without permission from any governor, who destroy by their wicked, liberated lives with Indian women all that the missionaries . . . teach them about the divine mysteries of the Christian religion."[26] Troubled by frequent desertions and the constant lure of native concubinage, General Commissioner Bernard Diron d'Artaguette demanded that Frenchwomen be shipped to Louisiana to attract Canadians from Indian companions. Louisiana officials in the Superior Council regretted that "newcomers have Indian women as slaves who are always with child or nursing." They feared that Louisiana was becoming a colony populated with "half-breeds who are by nature idle and loose."[27]

Both the continuing scarcity of European women and dependency on Indian trade in the Lower Mississippi Valley ensured that French relations with Natchez and other Indians would remain difficult to govern. General Commissioner Marc-Antoine Hubert complained in 1717 that "inhabitants are too accustomed to trade with Indians who supply their needs abundantly and will not bring themselves to work unless they are on the mainland and have negroes for this work who are more laborious than the Indian slaves, who desert when they are hard pressed."[28] Many soldiers deserted to Spanish Pensacola, English Carolina, and enemy tribes in order to escape famine, disease, or work. Canadian voyageurs and young settlers often chose to live among friendly Indian nations rather than suffer from inadequate rations on the coast. Pénicaut reported that in 1704 a group of twenty men, "young and passionately fond of rambling," stayed in Natchez villages.[29]

This intimate border crossing by colonists complemented the Natchez Indians' sexual norms without undermining their social order, as long as the French population remained small. When Natchez boys and girls reached puberty they were encouraged to indulge in sexual intercourse. Young women sold their favors to form their trousseaus. Marriageable men rated future spouses' merit by the wealth that women accumulated through sexual activity. But once married, wives maintained strict fidelity to their husbands. In satisfying the sexual passions of Louisiana colonists through prostitution, Natchez women also prepared themselves for marriage. Sexual contact on the colonial frontier actually involved white adoption of Indian cultural traits. Frequent abortions of interracial offspring tormented French missionaries. In their encounters with Natchez women, some Frenchmen acquired their soft and smooth pronunciation of the language to the great amusement of Natchez men.[30] In 1717 Father François Le Maire urged that France establish a settlement on the Mississippi as a "buffer against English expansion" and to prevent "all the disorders and scandals" in Indian villages.[31]

The fertility of Natchez land and its natural protection from the river's inundation did indeed begin to attract Louisiana officials and settlers. After the first importation of African slaves by the Company of the Indies in 1719, two large land concessions were established adjacent to the Grand Village. The introduction of commercial agriculture among the Natchez suddenly pushed them in a direction shared by smaller Indian tribes along the Mississippi River and Gulf Coast. Like the Houmas, Chitimachas, and Chaouachas downriver, the Natchez found themselves in closer and looser contact with French colonists.[32] As concessions at Natchez became promising tobacco plantations, the arrival of European indentured servants and African slave laborers had devastating effects on the Natchez population. Descending the river to depart for St. Domingue, Father Pierre de Charlevoix observed in 1721 that the great village of the Natchez, which stood halfway between the St. Catherine and White Earth plantations, was "at present reduced to a small number of cabins." Except for the eternal fire, the grand temple lacked the ornaments and relics that were publicized by earlier French travelers. The Jesuit priest speculated that "the neighborhood of the French made the Natchez apprehensive of losing the dead bodies of their chiefs, and whatever was most precious in their temple," so the Indians carried them to another location.[33] "Some contagious diseases," especially smallpox and colds, ravaged the Natchez and reduced the nation to only five villages. Their military force decreased from four thousand warriors in 1715 to two thousand warriors in 1721.[34]

The intrusion of plantation agriculture, however, did not immediately dissolve older forms of interaction across the cultural borderland. Frenchmen still depended on the Natchez for trade in deerskins and for knowledge about the environment. Beginning with Fort Rosalie itself, the Natchez assisted the French in clearing land and constructing buildings.[35] They hunted for the new settlement, providing colonists with food and furs. In exchange for products of their own fields and of the forests, Indians received fusils, gunpowder, lead, linen, and brandy – European goods on which they increasingly depended. The Natchez's understanding of local flora also provided Frenchmen with invaluable health care. Conjurers used many plants to cure various ailments among the French. Boiled ground ivy eased women's labor pains, cured ulcers, and relieved headaches. Desiccated sassafras induced sweating and cured venereal disease. Antoine Le Page du Pratz, a Dutchman who lived among the Natchez for eight years, often observed their use of balm from the bearded creeper to reduce fever.[36] The Natchez were even known to exert themselves spiritually on behalf of the French. The Great Sun once vigorously fasted, according to Le Page du Pratz, to aid some colonists "who had been complaining that it had not rained for a long time." He consumed nothing but corn and water and abstained from the company of his wives for nine days "to invoke the spirits of the air for rain."[37]

A crisis in 1722 exposed new stresses and strains on the French-Natchez borderland as the region rapidly became more ethnically and economically volatile. That summer a Fort Rosalie guard killed a White Apple villager in a dispute over a debt. A St. Catherine director named Pierre Guenot enchained and imprisoned an honored man of that Natchez village. After an unsuccessful attempt to kill Guenot, White Apple warriors began raids on the St. Catherine plantation on 22 October. Skirmishes broke out when the Indians, while "talking to the negroes who had stopped to eat," opened fire and killed a slave. Within a week the Natchez killed eleven cattle, injured one black and one white laborer, and stole three horses, sixteen pigs, six quarts of flour, fifty quarts of corn, fifty quarts of potatoes, and forty quarts of Appalachian beans. Tattooed Serpent once again mediated peace between the French settlement and the hostile villages of White Apple, Gray, and Jenjenque.[38]

Colonial officials downriver at New Orleans treated this hostility as a serious breach in French-Natchez relations. Bienville mobilized a punitive expedition of 150 colonial troops and promised rewards to Choctaw and other allies for Natchez scalps and captives. His initial policy of peace and cooperation rapidly gave way to war and enslavement. Louisiana's Superior Council had already placed a bounty on Chickasaw scalps and slaves because of their increasingly pro-English position. During the winter of 1722–23, French soldiers and Indian allies attacked White Apple village with intentions of killing all men and enslaving their women and children for sale to the West Indies. Soldiers found the hostile village abandoned and burned it with assistance from the Tunicas. These destructive measures ran counter to official colonial policy but reflected changes in the colony's economic and demographic conditions. Dependence on local Indians diminished as the importation of African slaves increased. With preparations in mind for establishing a company plantation and tobacco factory at Natchez, Jacques de La Chaise expressed "hope that with the aid of the Tunicas [Bienville] may be able to destroy the Natchez Indians, but he has gone there rather late for that."[39]

Efforts to destroy hostile Natchez villages were hindered by a shortage of provisions, sickness among the troops, and the elusiveness of enemy warriors. Fearing that these fugitives would incessantly threaten the safety of French settlers and travelers, the council granted peace provided that the

Natchez execute several named rebels and "that they bring in dead or alive a negro who has taken refuge among them for a long time and makes them seditious speeches against the French nation and who has followed them on occasions against our Indian allies."[40] The security of European colonists, surrounded by African slaves and various Indian nations, increasingly depended on their ability to divide and control racial majorities. Colonial officials escalated efforts to separate Indians from settlers and slaves and to generate conflict among Indian nations. On 18 September 1723 the Superior Council denied peace to the Chickasaws and declared "that the Choctaws be left free to continue the war against the Chickasaws since the losses that these two nations may inflict on both sides can only be advantageous to us."[41]

The Natchez had managed to resist French cultural intrusion more than some other nations along the Mississippi River but now were confronting serious dilemmas. The chief of the neighboring Tunicas had early adopted French ways and imposed them on his people, even outlawing the eternal fire. He practiced Catholicism, wore French clothes, and hoarded French currency. Cultural perseverance among the Natchez, however, did not prevent political disruption. Accommodation and resistance to the French became antithetical approaches as colonial pressure mounted, widening the gap between pro-English and pro-French factions. At a deeper level the infiltration of unfamiliar European commodities, especially firearms and alcohol, into Natchez society threatened spiritual belief. Leaders like Tattooed Serpent had hoped to accommodate traditional life to the new relations with French colonists, but after 1723 the French-Natchez borderland rapidly deteriorated.[42]

Discontent over specific abuses and general influences of French colonization deepened among Natchez villagers. Warriors raided livestock on the concessions, hunting them like a new species of game and taunting their owners at the same time. Lieutenant Dumont at Fort Rosalie observed that the Natchez considered it "brave and valiant" to mangle or kill horses, cows, and pigs, detecting in their harassment of colonial property a sporting test of Indian manhood. Irritated by repeated incidents of costly pillage, French officials imposed penal taxes on Natchez villages by demanding payments in produce for damages. Natchez leaders, especially the older generation, resented not only the burdens imposed on the tribe's economy by colonial demands but, moreover, the toll being taken on the people's cultural autonomy by European goods. Shortly before his death in 1725, Tattooed Serpent complained to Le Page du Pratz how, before the French arrived, "Did we not live better than we do, seeing we deprive ourselves of a part of our corn, our game, and fish, to give a part to them?" Pointing to the men's reliance on guns and the women's recourse to blankets, the war chief reminded him that earlier "we lived like men who can be satisfied with what they have; whereas at this day we are like slaves, who are not suffered to do as they please."[43]

A rapid succession of three French commandants at Fort Rosalie after 1723 only exacerbated French relations with the Natchez. When Captain de Merveilleux finally received the position, he briefly restored confidence among inhabitants and amity with Indian villagers. But in 1728 Étienne Boucher de Périer, who replaced Bienville as governor two years earlier, appointed Sieur de Chepart to the commandant post at Natchez. De Chepart, already known as a drunkard and a brash person, immediately "tyrannized the people and abused his power," as recalled by Lieutenant Dumont. When he removed a company of soldiers from the White Earth concession and thereby endangered its inhabitants, De Chepart was summoned before the Superior Council. The council found him guilty of "some acts of injustice," but Governor Périer pardoned De Chepart and restored him to his command.[44]

De Chepart actually returned to Natchez with African slaves and ambitious plans to establish concessions there for both himself and Périer. In line with the tobacco designs of the Company of the Indies, De Chepart's immediate interests imminently clashed with the concerns of the Natchez Indians. The deaths of Tattooed Serpent in 1725 and of his brother, the Great Sun, in 1728 strengthened the influence of anti-French leadership; the new grand chief was closely related to one of the White Apple chiefs whose skull went to the French in 1723. With intentions of building a plantation at the White Apple village, De Chepart insolently ordered its chief to relocate his people. Looking for time and discerning the commandant's greed, the village council asked that their people "be allowed to stay in their village till harvest, and till they had time to dry their corn, and shake out the grain; on condition each hut of the village should pay him in so many moons . . . a basket of corn and a fowl." De Chepart predictably accepted the proposition.[45]

The village chiefs and elders assembled to plan their revenge. With the French increasing the number of African slaves in their midst, some Natchez leaders dramatized their rhetoric with images of colonial slavery. "Before the French came amongst us," exclaimed one elder, "we were men, content with what we had" and "we walked with boldness every road." "But now," he continued, "we go groping, afraid of meeting thorns, we walk like slaves, which we shall soon be, since the French already treat us as if we were such." Warning that for the least fault the French would tie young Natchez people "and whip them as they do their black slaves," the stirring orator asked, "Is not death preferable to slavery?" Within a week of deliberation the council settled on a plot to "cut off the French to a man, in one day and one hour" – that day and hour fixed by the French commandant for the payment of their tribute. Several warriors were to "carry him the corn, as the beginning of their several payments, also carry with them their arms, as if going out to hunt: and that to every Frenchman in a French house, there shall be two or three Natchez; to ask to borrow arms and ammunition for a general hunt-ing-match, on account of a great feast, and to promise to bring them meat; the report of the firing at the Commandant's, to be the signal to fall at once upon, and kill the French: that when we shall be able to prevent those who may come from the old French village [New Orleans], by the great water [Mississippi] ever to settle here."[46]

With all the villages consenting to this plan, the Natchez began their elaborate preparations for war. In each town the war chiefs erected two poles painted red and ornamented with red feathers, arrows, and toma-hawks. Warriors enlisted by smearing their faces with various colors and de-claring their desire to die for their nation. They then drank kettles of "war medicine," an emetic made from boiled roots. The ceremony, as described by Father Le Petit, was "to swallow them with a single effort, and then to throw up immediately by the mouth, with efforts so violent that they can be heard at a great distance." After they danced before the sacred temple, sang their death songs, and boasted of their previous war feats, warriors marched from the village in single file.[47]

Rumors of attack spread among settlers during the autumn months of 1729. But De Chepart confidently disregarded all warnings and, as reported by Diron d'Artaguette, even "put in irons seven colonists who had asked to assemble to forestall the disaster with which they were menaced." One colo-nist wrote to Governor Périer requesting arms for his slaves, while the Natchez themselves recruited "several negroes, among others those of the White Earth at the head of whom were two foremen who gave the other ne-groes to understand that they would be free with the Indians." On the morning of 28 November 1729, the Natchez implemented their plan with deliberate speed. They deceived De Chepart and his wards with generous quantities of tribute and friendly promises of meat and furs. A familiar pat-tern of frontier exchange now served to veil the Indians' rebellious design. Within hours Natchez warriors killed 145 men, 36 women, and 56 children and captured nearly 300 Negro slaves in addition to some 50 white women and children.[48]

Over the months of conflict that followed this Natchez attack, colonial authorities suppressed collaboration across the borderland between Indians and slaves with extreme force. Hoping to allay the fear stirred in the New Orleans area by news of an Indian massacre and to generate antagonism between Africans and Indians, Governor Périer dispatched a group of armed black slaves downriver from the capital on 5 December 1729 to destroy the Chaouachas, a neighboring village of only thirty warriors. This expedition, according to his report, "kept the other little nations up the river in a respectful attitude." Commending the slaves for their prompt and secret mission, the governor boasted, "If I had been willing to use our negro volunteers I should have destroyed all these little nations which are of no use to us, and which might on the contrary cause our negroes to revolt." He did not further employ these black soldiers "for fear of rendering [them] . . . too bold and of inclining them perhaps to revolt after the example of those who joined the Natchez." Defying customary practices more than once during his troublesome governorship, Périer was criticized for his genocidal assessment of local Indians, who, in fact, were very useful to colonial Louisiana.[49]

As feared by slaveowners, many of the African-American slaves taken from the upriver concessions during the 28 November attack did serve as allies, more than as hostages, of the Natchez rebels. On 27 January 1730 five hundred Choctaws under Sieur Jean-Paul Le Seur besieged the Natchez, killing about one hundred warriors and recovering most of the white women and children and about a hundred slaves. But as later discovered by Périer, "this defeat would have been complete if it had not been for the negroes who prevented the Choctaws from carrying off the powder and who by their resistance had given the Natchez time to enter the two forts." Three slaves "who had taken the most active part in behalf of the Natchez," reported Father Le Petit, were given to the Choctaws and "burned alive with a degree of cruelty which has inspired all the Negroes with a new horror of the Savages, but which will have a beneficial effect in securing the safety of the Colony." On 8 February the Choctaws were joined by two hundred troops from New Orleans, including fifteen blacks, and a protracted bombardment of the Natchez forts with cannons soon began. By 25 February the Natchez agreed to return the remaining hostages to the French, who promised to stop the siege. Within a few days the Natchez managed to slip by the French and cross the Mississippi. The colonial army pursued them into the Ouachita River basin.[50]

Under heavy criticism in France, Governor Périer attempted to avert responsibility for the Natchez revolt by magnifying it into a conspiracy with

Chickasaws and Choctaws. Trepidation over Indian and slave conspiracies and suspicion of English interference fueled this belief among many Louisiana colonists, but officials both in the colony and at home recognized Périer's ambitions for a plantation at Natchez and refuted his justification for negligence and repression. A second military campaign against the Natchez over the winter of 1730–31 did little toward reversing his disrepute. Numerous colonial troops and Indian allies trudged through the Black River wetlands with limited results. Some five hundred prisoners, mostly women and children, were captured when only one of three Natchez forts was seized. In what proved to be the waning months of its dominion in Louisiana, the Company of the Indies shipped these Natchez captives as slaves to the Caribbean. The question pronounced by one of their elders at the war council – "Is not death preferable to slavery?" – must have echoed through their minds during this painful exodus from their homeland.[51]

The Natchez chiefdom was destroyed, but survivors of the war contributed on some significant cultural borderlands to continuing native resistance in the South. Immediately after the war, Natchez refugees lived in small bands not far from their homeland. One group hid in the upcountry woods behind the Tunicas. Probably in retaliation for the Tunicas' contribution to the French campaigns against the Natchez, these refugees attacked the Tunica village in June 1731, killing at least twenty men and capturing about eight women.[52] Their vengeance might have been directed at an even more specific act, however. Sometime before this episode, Governor Périer had permitted Tunica warriors to torture a Natchez woman to death in New Orleans. She was slowly burned on a frame outside the government house in order to display French power over Indian rebels. But as recorded by one French officer, this tortured Natchez woman "seemed to deride the unskillfulness of her tormentors, insulting them, and threatening that her death would soon be avenged by her tribe."[53]

For some time to come, embittered Natchez refugees waged guerrilla warfare against French traders and travelers along the banks of the Mississippi River. One group attacked the French fort at Natchitoches in October of 1731.[54] The bases of Natchez resistance were located in remote lowlands along the Yazoo and Ouachita Rivers. From an elderly Natchez woman captured during the summer of 1733, Bienville learned that as many as two hundred warriors were still hiding out near their old territory. The largest group of Natchez survivors found refuge among the Chickasaws, forming their own village within an Indian nation firmly allied with the English. Together with the Chickasaws as well as in separate forays, Natchez warriors continued to antagonize French Louisiana.[55] Another group of Natchez migrated into Upper Creek country, where at first their hosts apparently treated them as a subordinate people. In the early 1750s Philippe de Rigault de Vaudreuil was informed that some twenty or thirty Natchez at the Creek village of Abikudshis wished to return to their people's homeland. The governor of Louisiana seemed willing to permit these Natchez to move back to the Mississippi but reported that "they are not entirely free to do so because of the proximity of the Abihkas and Talapoosas, who are keeping them in slavery among them."[56]

The Natchez actually secured for themselves a distinct identity within the Creek nation, occupying a separate village on Tallasseehatchee Creek for a while and maintaining a sense of ethnic pride well into the nineteenth century. Born into this Natchez community in 1788, George Stiggins wrote a rare insider's account of Creek culture and history sometime during the 1830s. His mother was a Natchez woman with the English name of Nancy Grey, and his father was a Virginia trader of English descent named Joseph Stiggins. Although George's treatment of Creek history, particularly the Creek War of 1813–14, criticized native traditionalism, he offered some interesting information about Natchez resistance and survival. Stiggins reported that the Natchez language was still spoken throughout his lifetime and that he was entitled to inherit from his mother's uncle the title of Natchez chief. George's family had moved outside the Creek nation when he was young, so he abandoned traditional ways and never assumed that leadership role. Nevertheless, Stiggins recorded an important Natchez interpretation of their war against the French a century earlier. The Natchez had revolted against the French because "without a previous compact with the natives to insure their good will, they pitched on a site in the vicinity of the town, though much against the will of the Indians." Also according to Natchez memory, they had successfully surprised the French because "as was expected, their lewd practices soon caused a relaxation of their vigilance and discipline." Stiggins identified other groups of Natchez survivors among the Chickasaws and Cherokees but emphasized that "the greater part headed by the royal family made a compact of assimilation with the Abekas, or Creek tribes." "This remnant of the Natchez tribe to this day," Stiggins boasted, "are unfriendly to the French people."[57]

Among the other refugee groups mentioned by Stiggins were some Natchez who established a new borderland with Cherokee Indians. In 1736 a delegation of twenty-six Natchez successfully applied to the British for emigration to South Carolina. A Frenchman captured by the Cherokees was told by a group of Natchez in April 1742 that "they were going hunting among the Chicachas, to seek 15 of their men who were still there; that on their return they were to have a village of 75 men."[58] By the 1750s these Natchez were inhabiting a distinct town within Cherokee territory, on the north bank of the Hiwassee River. Near the end of the nineteenth century, anthropologist James Mooney met some descendants of these refugees among Cherokees in both North Carolina and Oklahoma. A few still spoke the Natchez language. A Natchez identity also endured in the role that some played as dance leaders.[59] During the late 1890s in Oklahoma, a group of Natchez revived their ceremonial ground and hosted all-night dances in the southwestern part of the Cherokee nation's territory, where a rebellious political organization regularly met. In 1907 a Natchez man named Creek Sam was among the visionary leaders of a revitalization movement gripping many Cherokees during that nation's latest ordeal – the transformation of Indian Territory into the state of Oklahoma.[60]

Like major Indian wars in other North American colonial regions – Powhatan's War in Virginia, the Pequot War in New England, the Pueblo Revolt in New Mexico, and the Tuscarora and Yamassee Wars in Carolina – the Natchez War in Louisiana marked a significant breakdown on an Indian-colonial borderland. With mounting anxiety colonial officials warned their superiors about the need for more colonists and troops to overcome the province's vulnerability to native demands. "The least little nation thinks itself our protector," Périer reported in August 1730, "whereas if we had forces to sustain ourselves by our own efforts the greatest nations would respect us and would very carefully seek an alliance with us, which would be as honorable as it would be useful for them."[61] The obstinate governor's appeal, however, had little chance of improving Louisiana's capacity to dominate all Lower Mississippi Valley Indians. While Chickasaw and Creek enemies kept this fringe of the French empire unstable, the colony continued to depend heavily on trade and alliance with the powerful Choctaw nation.

Some Choctaws even expressed defiance against French authority by adopting, for at least a while, a ritual of rebellion improvised by the Natchez. Before Choctaw men launched their January 1730 attack against the Natchez on behalf of the French, they had apparently carried the calumet (peace pipe) into the village only to be received in what Father Le Petit called "a very novel manner." The Natchez adorned themselves and their horses with priests' garments and altar drapes, while drinking brandy from chalices and ciboria. When the Choctaws later acquired these items in their raid against the Natchez, they "renewed this profane sacrilege, by making the same use of our ornaments and sacred vessels in their dances and sports." Le Petit further complained that "we were never able to recover more than a small portion of them."[62]

As a result of the Natchez War, a troubled Company of the Indies returned its monopoly over Louisiana to the French government. Louis XV reappointed Bienville, who had been away from the colony for seven years, as governor to replace the disreputable Périer. In the eyes of French officials the commercial potential of Louisiana took a backseat to its geopolitical function. But the turbulence at the end of the 1720s left people living in the Lower Mississippi Valley with a more enduring legacy. Although Indian trade continued to be economically and politically important to Louisiana, some Indian trade partners could suddenly be sacrificed for the sake of other interests. When the Natchez rebelled against encroachment by Louisiana's most promising settlement, they became a nuisance to the colony. So their violence was met by a colonial retaliation amounting to near extermination, and the complex interplay of adaptation and resistance that had characterized this cultural borderland was long forgotten.

THREE

A Population History of American Indians in the Eighteenth-Century Lower Mississippi Valley

Trade and military alliances, colonial policies and rivalries, and native strategies of resistance and accommodation influenced the lives of American Indians in important ways – as illustrated in the case of the Natchez Indians in French Louisiana. But there were more drastic changes, less conspicuous in the historical evidence, that profoundly affected the size and composition of the Lower Mississippi Valley's Indian population. A calamitous decline among the region's native inhabitants occurred with the arrival and growth of a colonial populace. The rapid depopulation of American Indians has finally come into its own as a subject for scholarly investigation. The unevenness and unreliability of documentary sources can no longer justify negligence of the information that does exist regarding demographic change in Indian societies.[1] Some debates among historical demographers over the means and implications of studying this evidence have been fierce, signaling perhaps that the population history of American Indians is undergoing predictable growth pains.[2]

The following approach to the population history of American Indians focuses on a particular colonial region instead of on any single tribe or what anthropologists call a culture area. The objectives are to explain in a general way the wide range of changes in both size and location experienced by Indian societies during the colonial period and to create a framework for future analysis of cultural and socioeconomic change. A fuller understanding of the innumerable causes and consequences of the decline suffered by the Lower Mississippi Valley Indian population will take years of close-up biological and historical analysis.[3] An overview of patterns and variations of population change, meanwhile, might help guide future research in this and other colonial regions. As this study will demonstrate, movement by Indian people was an important dimension of population change. Less tragic than death and decline, decisions made about when and where to migrate underscore the agency of American Indians in shaping their future.[4]

From the beginnings of French colonization in 1699 to the end of the American Revolution in 1783, the two most significant demographic processes of Indian population change were epidemics caused by exposure to foreign viruses and migrations caused by the intrusion of colonial powers. Native peoples in the Southeast and other regions of North America had long relied on relocation and amalgamation as a means of adapting to sudden political, economic, or environmental challenges.[5] The absorption of smaller groups by Natchez migrants exemplifies one form of this pattern. Epidemics that struck upon initial contact with Europeans caused the collapse of most chiefdoms and the consolidation of surviving people into new political formations.[6] During the eighteenth century many Indian villages migrated into, within, and from the Lower Mississippi Valley, and one must be conscious of these movements in order to keep track of the numbers and identities of the region's native inhabitants. While few Indian nations actually disappeared (although a cursory look at smaller areas might suggest otherwise), many changed their location and even combined with others into single towns.

Instead of a village-by-village or tribe-by-tribe account of demographic change, this study divides the region into five different population areas delineated by differential experiences in the eighteenth century.[7] The tribes in the Gulf Coast Area experienced the earliest regular contact with Louisiana colonists at Biloxi and Mobile. The Inland Area includes the larger nations east of the Mississippi River who developed the most extensive trade and military involvement in the Lower Mississippi Valley, the Chickasaws mainly as foes and the Choctaws and Upper Creeks mainly as allies of French Louisiana. Throughout most of the eighteenth century, Indian tribes along the banks of the Mississippi below the mouth of the Red River, or the Lower River Area, had the most intimate contact with colonial settlements, especially the town of New Orleans. Between the Red and Arkansas Rivers, in what is here designated the Central River Area, another group of Indian nations found themselves at a crossroads of colonial expansion from literally all directions. The final subregion to be considered is the Red River Area, where the colony of Louisiana extended its influence up the Red River into the western interior of the Lower Mississippi Valley (see table 1).

Nearly every reference to Indian populations in the Lower Mississippi Valley estimated only the number of guerriers, or warriors, reflecting colonial authorities' principle concern with how many men of fighting age belonged to each nation. A general populace-to-warrior ratio, therefore, must be used to reach total population figures. The application of such ratios is

Table 1. Estimated American Indian Population of the Lower Mississippi Valley in the Eighteenth Century

	1700	1725	1750	1775
GULF COAST AREA (Biloxis, Pascagoulas, Moctobis, Capinas, Mobilians, Tohomés)	3,500	1,700	900	—
INLAND AREA				
Choctaws	17,500	14,000	12,600	13,400
Chickasaws	7,000	3,500	2,000	2,300
Upper Creeks	13,300	7,000	3,000	9,200
LOWER RIVER AREA (Ouachas, Chaouachas, Mongoulachas, Bayogoulas, Chitimachas, Atakapas, Opelousas, Houmas, Acolapissas)	10,000	3,000	700	1,200
CENTRAL RIVER AREA (Quapaws, Taensas, Natchez, Upper and Lower Yazoos, Tunicas)	11,500	4,400	1,900	2,100
RED RIVER AREA (Avoyelles, Natchitoches, Doustionis, Yatasis, Kadohadachos)	4,200	1,500	1,000	4,200
TOTAL INDIAN POPULATION	67,000	35,000	22,000	32,200

Note: Names in parentheses represent those groups occupying each area in 1700. Population figures were reached by deriving the most reliable estimates made by observers for each of the nations in an area, nearest the quarter-century year. In the few cases where actual figures are not available, the population size has been approximated through comparison with previous and subsequent estimates. Since most numbers in the records are of warriors, a factor of 3.5 was used to reach total population figures for each group. Tribal figures were then added into their respective area populations, excepting the large groups in the Inland Area, and total area population estimates were finally rounded to the nearest hundred. The blank under 1775 for the Gulf Coast Area indicates the migration of all Indian communities from this area by then.

the most problematic step in computing the size of Indian villages and tribes. Family and household sizes naturally varied according to time and place. But since counts of both the number of warriors and of total inhabitants for the same group are so scarce, a general ratio must be applied to the entire region and period until further research discloses more specific information. Ratios from a very small sample of such sources, which provide numbers for warriors and populace together, indicate the presence of from three to four total inhabitants for each warrior in a village. The extremes of this range would produce widely different totals, a population in 1700 of 57,000 resulting from a 3:1 ratio and one of 76,000 from a 4:1 ratio. The most detailed census from the eighteenth century, that of 11,447 Choctaws in 1795, suggests that the midpoint in this range would serve as a representative and convenient populace-to-warrior ratio.[8] The totals in the table, therefore, were reached by multiplying the most reliable estimate of warriors by a factor of 3.5. The chronic illnesses and epidemic diseases that plagued their villages after contact probably reduced the rate of birth and the size of families among Indians, and if so the ratio of 3.5:1 derived from the middle- to late-eighteenth-century sources will produce a conservative total population for the beginning of the century. Whether or not their families were larger in 1700 than in 1775, there is no question that Indian mortality rates loomed far above birth rates during the intervening years.

Among the many epidemic diseases that decimated the native population of the Lower Mississippi Valley from more than sixty-six thousand people in 1700 to scarcely twenty-two thousand people by 1750, smallpox had the most extensive and fatal influence. Transmittable by an infected person or even by a piece of cloth, smallpox could spread rapidly from village to village following a single Indian's exposure to the virus. As in cases from other colonial regions, the mobilization of military personnel and the transportation of people or products through a native population most frequently sparked the outbreak of smallpox epidemics.[9] Within a week an infected person experienced fever, chills, and headaches. Boils subsequently erupted on the skin like large blisters and then festered into putrid sores, leaving recovered survivors with pockmarks on their bodies. European and African contact with this virus over preceding centuries had reduced its fatality among immune settlers and slaves, who nonetheless carried the disease to people never before exposed. Smallpox infection brought catastrophic rates of death to Indian populations, and the awesome and sudden mortality had immeasurably traumatic effects on community life. Those who lived through the second and third week of infection experienced a very slow recovery from both the physical and psychological devastation of the illness. Surviving the infection, however, made a person immune to further contact with the virus, contributing to the gradual accumulation of a village's general immunity in the course of periodic epidemics. A Choctaw woman who managed to survive her infection in the epidemic of 1731 would have lived through that of 1742, but she most probably would have lost her newborn child to the disease. Other infectious diseases, less documented for the eighteenth-century Lower Mississippi Valley but common killers of American Indians, included typhus, influenza, measles, yellow fever, dysentery, and cholera.[10]

Even before Iberville's small fleet – the *François, Badine* and *Marin* – reached the Gulf Coast in January 1699, the Indian populace in the Lower Mississippi Valley had already been drastically reduced by smallpox. The presence of European infectious diseases among the region's native inhabitants dates back to the coastal reconnaissance and interior expeditions carried out by Spanish explorers in the sixteenth century and helps explain the disappearance of the populous and centralized chiefdoms encountered by Hernando de Soto in 1540.[11] Comparative demographic data from other postcontact regions in the Western Hemisphere suggest that by 1682, when La Salle traveled down the Mississippi River to its mouth, the population of the valley had already been cut in half. During the last quarter of the seventeenth century, the growing interest of Europeans in this region set off a new wave of decimation among its Indian societies.

By the time the French built their first post on Biloxi Bay in the spring of 1699, the Indian villages in the vicinity of the Gulf Coast were already familiar with the demographic effects of European expansion. Slave raids supported by Carolina traders had reduced their numbers by warfare, captivity, and sickness. The establishment of a Spanish garrison at Pensacola Bay only a few months before the French arrived exposed these people to an even closer source of new infectious diseases. By 1699 there were six groups of Indians living within a few days' reach of the earliest French settlement. The Biloxis, Pascagoulas, Moctobis, and Capinas occupied separate villages on small bluffs overlooking the Pascagoula River, situated near enough to the coast to take advantage of its rich fishing resources but far enough to be protected from spring floods and autumn hurricanes. To the east of Biloxi Bay, clusters of Mobilian and Tohomé villages enjoyed similar positions along the Mobile River.

In considering early approximations of this and all other native population groups, we must keep in mind the fact that Europeans were trying to count people whose decimation their very presence was causing. Traveling up the Pascagoula River in April 1700 and up the Mobile two years later, Iberville noticed several deserted villages and found signs of epidemic sickness within the villages still occupied.[12] Recalling these early years of contact later in his career, Bienville reported that the Tohomés "have been almost annihilated by the plague that a vessel of the King brought to us in 1704." This particular "plague" was probably yellow fever carried by the *Pelican* from its stopover at Havana, where that disease was then rampant.[13]

Estimates made during early reconnaissance and in later accounts indicate that the Gulf Coast villages numbered about thirty-five hundred men, women, and children in 1700. On 29 April of that year Iberville visited the "Pascoboula," a village of "some twenty families." Bernard de La Harpe estimated that the Pascagoulas, Biloxis, and Moctobis altogether "numbered about 130 warriors." Bienville recalled having seen two hundred men among the Pascagoulas and Capinas but provided no estimates for the other villages.[14] Indian communities along the Mobile River were visited during the summer of 1700 by Charles Levasseur, who figured that about five hundred men, women, and children lived in five Mobilian villages and that another three hundred people comprised the neighboring Tohomés. Together these same two tribes received estimates of six hundred men by Iberville and of "more than seven hundred men" by Bernard de La Harpe.[15] Given this mixed series of figures and the decimation going on at the beginning of the century, a total approximation of one thousand men seems appropriate for the Gulf Coast Area in 1700.

Over the next twenty years other causes of population change were added to epidemics among Indians around Mobile. English raids against native towns in Spanish Florida drove Apalache and Chahto refugees into the French colony. Numbering about four hundred and two hundred persons, respectively, the Apalaches and Chahtos established two new villages on Mobile Bay by 1704. The already diminishing Mobilians suffered a severe blow in 1709 when a large force of Alibamon warriors burned their village and captured some thirty women and children.[16] Warfare along the lower Mississippi River during these years caused the survivors of the Taensa nation and a group of Chaouachas to migrate to Mobile Bay. By 1725 there were nine Indian villages in the Gulf Coast Area: Biloxi and Pascagoula-Capina along the Pascagoula River and Mobilian, Grand Tohomé, Petit Tohomé, Apalache, Chahto, Petit Taensa, and Chaouacha situated around Mobile Bay and the Mobile River. Altogether these communities included approximately 480 warriors or a total population of seventeen hundred people.[17]

Throughout the French period these villagers maintained close relations with colonial settlers and slaves, often at great risk to their health. They regularly provisioned Mobile and Biloxi with venison, corn, and other necessities without which these posts could not have been constructed and garrisoned. A number of Canadians settled around the thirty or so cabins of the Pascagoula village, and according to one observer "they live together like brethren."[18] Interaction increased as the men from these Indian villages performed such wage-earning services as rowing pirogues, carrying trade merchandise, and delivering messages between posts.[19] Having been converted to Catholicism by the Franciscans in Florida, the Apalaches insisted that a priest live in their town. The Indians of this Gulf Coast Area, in fact, became the only native group in the entire colonial region to adopt Christianity collectively before the end of the French period.[20] By the middle of the eighteenth century, smallpox and other viruses contracted during their varied involvement in colonial life reduced this populace to only 250 men. Finally, when Great Britain assumed control over the Gulf Coast in 1763, most of these people decided to abandon the area and move to the banks of the Mississippi River. The few families that remained eventually intermarried with both white and black settlers, leaving this part of the Lower Mississippi Valley virtually vacant of its native inhabitants. Itinerant camps of Choctaw people, however, would frequent Mobile for trade and work well into the nineteenth century.[21]

The larger tribes living upriver from the coastal villages experienced a somewhat different population history between the beginning of foreign settlement and the end of the American Revolution. Their deeper political entanglement in intercolonial conflict caused the Choctaws, Chickasaws, and Upper Creeks to lose a larger percentage of their people to warfare, especially during the early years of colonization. With the development of trade relations and military alliances during the first decade of the eighteenth century, disease and alcohol began to spread throughout their villages. Because of the pivotal role of these tribes in European competition for the Southeast, colonial authorities took a particular interest in the changing size of their populations.

At the first major council held with Choctaw and Chickasaw leaders in 1702, Iberville asked them to count the men of their nations "family by family." The delegates from the Chickasaws reported that their eighteen villages included 588 cabins, and the Choctaws named thirty-eight villages with 1,146 cabins. Told that three to four men lived in each cabin, the French derived population estimates of two thousand warriors among the Chickasaws and five thousand warriors among the Choctaws.[22] Negotiations at this meeting also revealed that in the course of ten years of warfare, stirred by slave dealers from Carolina who had already armed at least seven hundred Chickasaws with muskets, more than eighteen hundred Choctaws had been killed. Another five hundred Choctaws were taken captive, while the Chickasaws themselves lost "more than 800 men, slain on various war parties."[23] The estimated total populations of 7,000 Chickasaws and 17,500 Choctaws at the beginning of the eighteenth century, therefore, were considerably smaller than those in 1670, before the permanent intrusion of foreign microbes and munitions began its spiraling effect.

The Alibamons, Tallapoosas, and Abehkas, those tribes living up the Alabama River and its tributaries who became known as the Upper Creeks, numbered approximately thirteen thousand people during the first few years of the eighteenth century. An Alibamon informant from the town of "Maugoulacho" named thirty-six villages along the Coosa, Tallapoosa, and Alabama Rivers for Charles Levasseur in 1700. In 1701 Iberville estimated that four hundred families comprised the Alibamons alone.[24] Twenty-five years later Bienville reported that the population of the Alibamons included "Four villages in which there are still certainly three hundred men very brave and very devoted to the French." Located just east of these people, the Tallapoosas had six hundred "very warlike and very good hunters, divided into six villages which cover ten leagues of country." The Abehkas lived in a cluster of eleven villages along the Coosa River and numbered one thousand men "more skillful in hunting than in war." All three of these nations had lost an undetermined number of people during the years preceding Bienville's 1726 report, which unfortunately offers no estimate of their earlier populations. His calculation of nineteen hundred warriors for 1726 along with earlier references to the Alibamons, however, indicate that altogether the Upper Creek villages contained more than two thousand warriors at the time of French contact. Given an average rate of 50 percent decline among other Indian populations in the region over the first quarter of the eighteenth century, a figure of 3,800 warriors, or 13,300 persons, has been applied to the Upper Creeks for the year 1700.[25]

Bienville's assertion that the Choctaws numbered eight thousand warriors seems to be the most questionable estimate in his memoir of 1726. Possibly an attempt to inflate on paper the size of France's most important military ally in the region, this figure lacks support from contemporaneous accounts. General knowledge among officials as well as actual censuses taken in 1730 and 1732 suggest a warrior population of four thousand among the Choctaws around 1725.[26] On the other hand, Bienville's approximation of eight hundred warriors for the Chickasaws, firm allies of the British by then, may have underestimated their strength. By 1725 the Chickasaw nation had probably been reduced by half, as had most tribes on both sides of the Mississippi, to approximately one thousand warriors.

Maps and censuses made by both French and English observers provide us with much more precise information about the Choctaws, Chickasaws, and Upper Creeks during and after the 1730s. The Natchez War and the continuous Choctaw raids against Chickasaw towns took a heavy toll on the Chickasaw population, even forcing groups of people to migrate out of the region to the Savannah River.[27] The Choctaws very noticeably suffered epidemics of smallpox and measles over the second quarter of the eighteenth century. In 1730 Father Mathurin Le Petit reported that "every year disease diminishes this Nation, which is now reduced to three or four thousand warriors."[28] Many Choctaws were killed in a divisive revolt against the French between 1746 and 1750.

Epidemic disease often struck inland Indian nations following the arrival of trade parties or diplomatic missions at their villages. This correlation was neither unnoticed by tribal leaders nor unused by colonial rivals. When a Choctaw from the town of Yellow Canes reported to Regis du Roullet on 4 January 1731 that "there were many sick and dead in the nation," the French officer "showed him that that came from nothing else than the medicine that the English put into their limbourg cloth, and he agreed to it." By February word was spreading among the Choctaws that "the sickness which was current in the nation came from a medicine that the English made with sugar cane and put in the limbourg that they had sent to trade by way of the Chickasaws for the purpose of making all the Choctaws die."[29] The Alibamons and other Upper Creek villagers undoubtedly experienced similar hardships, as both the French and English competed for their allegiance. Sometime after 1735 an anonymous Frenchman compiled a village-by-village count of these interior tribes and produced the following numbers: 3,610 warriors in forty-five Choctaw villages, 560 warriors in eleven Chickasaw villages, 475 warriors in fifteen Tallapoosa villages, 230 warriors in six Abehka villages, and 160 warriors in six Alibamon villages.[30]

Within fifty years of interaction with French and English traders, the total population of the Choctaws, Chickasaws, and Upper Creeks declined from nearly forty thousand people in 1700 to less than twenty-five thousand by 1750. The impact of smallpox became less devastating with time, due to the immunity among survivors from prior epidemics, but other sources of sickness and disruption increasingly encroached upon village life. Shortages of food occurred more frequently, especially among the Chickasaws whose fields were repeatedly the object of a scorched-earth policy devised by colonial officials and implemented by Choctaw warriors.[31] The deerskin trade and, especially in the case of the Choctaws and Chickasaws, warfare took more and more men away from food-producing activities and made villages increasingly dependent on women's labor in the cornfields. Sometimes Choctaw spokesmen requested the French to either postpone or hurry military expeditions so that their crops could be planted at the proper time. When Regis du Roullet requested military assistance from the village of Boukfouka in May 1732, the men "begged me please to ask for people from the neighboring villages, since they could not furnish me all I needed on account of their planting."[32]

Growing alcohol consumption threatened Indian communities with even greater illness and poverty. English naturalist and cartographer Bernard Romans witnessed a scene in Choctaw country during 1771 that dramatized the effects of "spiritous liquor" upon village life. It also illustrates one resourceful way that Indian women tried to regulate this perilous commodity:

They are extravagant in their debauches; when met for a drinking match some women attend them, when these find the men beginning to be heated with liquor they will take away all the weapons found near them and return with a calabash under their wrappers, then mixing with them, the men offer them their bottles, they take a draught and when not observed they empty into bottles brought for that purpose, and thus they will accumulate two or three bottles full, and with the help of a little water, still make them more; after a while rum fails among the men, and the women acquaint them, that they have got some; they are told to fetch it; they refuse, saying it cost them much and they cannot give it for nothing; a bargain ensues, they receive the consideration first, and then bring it; in this way of trade they will often get all the effects the men can command for such a delicate nectar.[33]

The responses of Indian leaders to the rising consumption of alcohol within their villages ranged from the unhealthy addiction of some to the militant protest of others. Operating at a disadvantage in their competition with English commerce, because of a chronic shortage and an inferior quality in merchandise, Louisiana officials grappled with their reliance on alcohol as a trade commodity. On the death in 1737 of an Alibamon chief, "who thought himself stronger than the drink which killed him," the other chiefs of that tribe implored the commandant at Fort Toulouse not to deprive them of brandy "since they never drank [it] before night for fear of the sun's rays, to which they attribute his death." Referring to the Alibamons, Tallapoosas, and Abehkas in 1750, Governor Vaudreuil reported to Minister Rouillé, "it is regrettable that some of them are perishing every day because of the illness that is caused them by the trade in liquor, which cannot be suppressed because of the want of merchandise of the qualities [that we have] long asked for without being able to obtain them."[34]

After Great Britain assumed jurisdiction over the area in 1763, pressures to expand Indian production of deerskins continued to obstruct efforts made by both Indian and colonial leaders to reduce the flow of alcohol into interior villages. Aggressive trading by Englishmen made regulation increasingly difficult in the new province of West Florida. Among his many complaints voiced to the colonial government during the 1770s, Mingo Emmitta of the Choctaw town of Bouktouchoulouchito requested that "the Traders be allowed to Carry no more than a Small Quantity Sufficient to procure some Provisions and pay for the building Stores or Houses." He went on to describe vividly the effects of alcohol on his people: "When the Clattering of the Packhorse Bells are heard at a Distance our Town is Immediately deserted young and old run out to meet them Joyfully crying Rum Rum; they get Drunk, Distraction Mischief Confusion and Disorder are Consequences and this the Ruin of our Nation."[35]

Despite a high mortality rate and a myriad of new health hazards, the population of these interior tribes began to stabilize by the last quarter of the eighteenth century. A decline in warfare between the Choctaws and Chickasaws, the migration of a few hundred Shawnees into Upper Creek country, and a stronger immunity to smallpox all contributed to a slowdown in depopulation and eventually to a phase of population growth. According to a French census, 2,625 warriors inhabited thirty-nine different Upper Creek towns in 1764.[36] The Choctaws and Chickasaws, whose number had fallen below four thousand and five hundred warriors, respectively, also began to increase in population.[37] During the winter of 1764–65 all three groups of Indians suffered another smallpox epidemic.[38] But by 1780, according to a report compiled by cartographer Joseph Purcell, the Choctaw nation numbered 13,423 people and the Chickasaw nation 2,290 people. Of his total figure of 17,280 Creeks in general, the Alibamons, Tallapoosas, and Abehkas, as indicated by the earlier census of 1764, probably accounted for more than nine thousand people.[39]

The Indian tribes settled along the Mississippi River between the Gulf of Mexico and the lower Arkansas River experienced the worst rate of decimation in the entire colonial region. A population of over twenty thousand people in 1700, already reduced from a much larger number during the late seventeenth century, declined to fewer than three thousand people by 1750. The French war against the Natchez in 1730–31 destroyed this area's largest and most centralized nation. Villagers of the smaller tribes who managed to survive the wars and epidemics became known as the *petites nations*. Like the "praying towns" in New England, "tributary tribes" around the Chesapeake Bay, and "reductions" in Spanish Florida, these people lived in close contact with the colonial populace but maintained separate cultural and political identities throughout the eighteenth century.

Below the mouth of the Red River, in the Lower River Area, reconnaissance by the French identified nine different tribal groups in 1699–1700. The Ouachas and Chaouachas inhabited the southernmost banks of the Mississippi, maintaining their villages on the natural levees formed by sediment deposited during annual flooding. Early colonial observers noticed the exceptional mobility of these people, who numbered an estimated 250 men.[40] These delta inhabitants followed a productive round of seasonal activities in pursuit of a diversity of wetlands resources. Abundant fishes were trapped in backwater lakes after the spring floods receded. Summer corn was planted in small fields situated on narrow levees along the bayous. During the fall months, nuts and berries were harvested in hardwood forests located on scattered spots of higher ground. Deer and bear were hunted throughout the lowland forest into the winter.

Upriver from the Ouachas and Chaouachas, the Mongoulachas and Bayogoulas also lived by hunting and fishing across a widespread area. But at the beginning of the eighteenth century they occupied a single village above the mouth of Bayou Lafourche on the west bank of the Mississippi. Numbering about 250 men, or a total population of nearly a thousand residents, the town of Bayogoula-Mongoulacha included a number of refugees from villages already destroyed by foreign viruses or warfare.[41] The Quinipissas had inhabited their own village in the vicinity of present-day New Orleans, a "fairly good" stretch of land along the Mississippi, according to Iberville on 18 January 1700, "part of it being a country of canes and fine woods, suitable to live in." Virulent disease, however, had already killed most of these people and forced the survivors to seek refuge among the Bayogoulas, who had also taken in the Mongoulachas.[42]

This pattern of village consolidation and intertribal assimilation, although contributing to the spread of infection, was a rational response to the disruption of life being caused by epidemics and wars. As early as 15 March 1699, when he first visited the Bayogoulas, Iberville reported that "smallpox, which they still had in the village, had killed one-fourth of the people." All around this town, which consisted of 107 cabins, two temples, and a large square, stood platforms covered with the bodies of their dead.[43] Arriving at Bayogoula a year later to establish a short-lived mission, Father Paul Du Ru observed that these villagers seemed unwilling to hunt, fish, and plant. The lingering physical and psychological effects of smallpox upon people who narrowly escaped death were arrogantly judged by the Jesuit priest as "the dominant preference of these tribes for indolence." The inhabitants of Bayogoula-Mongoulacha, however, did not neglect their guest and even managed to entertain him with dances and games. Inside the town's two dome-shaped temples, Du Ru saw "many rows of packages piled one on the other" containing the bones of dead chiefs "carefully wrapped in palm mats."[44]

Located behind Bayogoula-Mongoulacha along the Atchafalaya basin were the Chitimachas. In 1706 a decade-long conflict with the French began when a missionary was killed by a band of Chitimachas. Bienville later remembered that "they had more than six hundred men when I had war declared on them by all nations that were allied with us." Many Chitimachas died in combat during the early eighteenth century. Many more, especially women and children, were captured and sold as slaves.[45] The Atakapas and Opelousas, who lived farther westward between the Atchafalaya and Sabine Rivers, remained largely unknown to the French until the 1720s and were simply considered nomadic allies of the Chitimachas.[46] Their population in 1725, according to Bienville, included 130 Opelousa warriors and 200 Atakapa warriors. These inhabitants of the rich prairies and wetlands of southwestern Louisiana must have numbered at least twice as many men at the beginning of the century, so a combined warrior population of one thousand is roughly estimated as their size in 1700.[47]

The Houmas and Acolapissas occupied the territory between the Mississippi River and the Pearl River, now known as the Florida parishes of Louisiana. Shortly before the arrival of the French on the Gulf Coast, the Acolapissa villages on the Pearl River had been destroyed and at least fifty of their residents captured by a force of Chickasaw warriors, who according to Du Ru "had two Englishmen at their head." Numbering about three hundred warriors in 1700, the Acolapissa refugees along with some surviving Tangipahoas established two villages just above Lake Pontchartrain. "Living in cabins made of bark until they erect their dwellings," these displaced and disease-struck people were struggling to "raise enough Indian corn to maintain life" but seemed to lack "enough spirit" to kill the very animals that ate their crops for food.[48]

When Iberville first visited the Houmas in March 1699, they inhabited a village on the east-bank bluff overlooking the large bend in the Mississippi just below its junction with the Red River. Then numbering about 350 men the town was struck during the following winter by what the French called "la maladie du flux de ventre," or diarrhea, which "had killed more than half the people." This particular epidemic, probably either dysentery or cholera, killed the chief of the Houmas and caused the women, heard by Paul Du Ru, to "bewail their dead day and night."[49]

During the first quarter of the eighteenth century, the native population in this Lower River Area went through a series of changes in both size and composition. The in-migration of the Taensas and the Tunicas, driven south from the Central River Area by Chickasaw raids, set off costly intertribal conflicts throughout the first decade of the century. The Taensas quickly moved away, most of them migrating to Mobile Bay, but the Tunicas settled permanently at the village of the Houmas, from which the latter people fled and moved downriver. The Natchitoches from the Red River Area relocated themselves among the Acolapissas for a while, clashed with their hosts, and returned to their home village sometime around 1712.[50] By the 1720s the Indians of this volatile area had reorganized their lives around the colonial population, which began to spread along the lower banks of the Mississippi. The overall Indian population of what is known today as south Louisiana in 1725 consisted of some 830 warriors or an estimated 3,000 men, women, and children, only a fraction of its seventeenth-century size but not yet outnumbered by settlers and slaves within that part of the colonial region.[51]

The villages of Chaouacha, Bayogoula, Houma, Acolapissa, Chitimacha, and Tunica – the names of once larger tribes – were all situated within a hundred-mile radius of New Orleans and participated heavily in the evolving colonial economy. As early as 1722 the chief of Tunica looked like a colonial entrepreneur to Father Pierre Charlevoix, who observed that this Indian had already acquired "fashion" and "the art of laying up money" from the French in the course of "supplying them with horses and poultry."[52] Acolapissa hunters became regular suppliers of fresh meat to New Orleans, while the Houmas raised abundant surpluses of corn at their new location below Bayou Lafourche for the city's early grain market. Charlevoix was welcomed at the Acolapissa village, situated by 1722 on the east bank of the Mississippi about thirty miles above New Orleans, with music played by a drummer "dressed in a long fantastical parti coloured robe." Inquiring into the origin of this custom, he "was informed that it was not very ancient; that a governor of Louisiana had made a present of this drum to these Indians, who have always been our faithfull allies; and that this sort of beadle's coat, was of their own invention."[53] Charlevoix called the Acolapissas' village "the finest in all Louisiana," but they and all of the *petites nations* continued to decline in population as European colonists established farms at the abandoned village sites of their ancestors. Counting as few as 210 men in 1758, Governor Kerlérec suggested that the villages along the lower Mississippi River were "greatly reduced by the quantity of drink that has been traded to them" and reported on the disappearance of the Acolapissas, Bayogoulas, Chaouachas, and Ouachas, "which the proximity of the French and the trade in drink have likewise destroyed." The destruction of the village of Chaouachas ordered by an earlier French governor in December 1729, as seen in the preceding chapter, also had something to do with the virtual disappearance of Indians downriver from New Orleans by midcentury.[54]

The diminishing Indian population below the Red River, however, was revived during the mid-1760s when villagers from the Gulf Coast Area moved to the banks of the lower Mississippi River. After Great Britain occupied West Florida, the Apalaches, Biloxis, Pascagoulas, Chahtos, Mobilians, and Taensas abandoned their old villages around Mobile in order to resettle themselves on French territory. Also joining this exodus were some Alibamons and Koasatis who departed the Alabama River for Louisiana.[55] But as these Indian migrants and their new white and black neighbors suddenly learned, the island of New Orleans and the west bank of the river actually belonged to Spain. Now English and Spanish officials vied for the loyalty of both old and new Indian communities along the lower Mississippi River, still serving as food provisioners and military auxiliaries for the colonies. In the early 1770s there were at least eight Indian communities interspersed among colonial plantations and farms between New Orleans and the mouth of the Red River. Together with the Atakapas and Opelousas, who still inhabited the interior of southwestern Louisiana but interacted regularly with the river settlements, the Indian population along the lower Mississippi in 1775 included 331 men or an estimated total of 1,200 people.[56] From this area the Biloxis, Pascagoulas, and Chahtos migrated northwestward and concentrated around the Rapides trading post by the early 1780s, while Houmas and Chitimachas eventually shifted their villages in a southwest-

ward direction toward Bayous Lafourche and Teche. This small but heterogeneous group of people became the nucleus of the state of Louisiana's
present-day Indian population.[57]

The area along the Mississippi River between the mouth of the Red River
and the lower valley of the Arkansas River underwent an extremely long and
severe process of depopulation which, as in other parts of the Lower Mississippi Valley, actually began during the 1680s. The southward extension of
Canadian trade led by La Salle and Henri de Tonti coincided with the pene-
tration of the southern interior by Carolina traders. The Quapaws, situated
at a critical nexus of various Indian trade routes, were especially vulnerable
to the transmission of European diseases.[58] In 1686 Tonti established his
own private post near the mouth of the Arkansas River, pulling nearby
Quapaw villagers, called the Arkansas by their northern neighbors, temporarily into the Great Lakes sphere of trade and disease. During the last decade of the seventeenth century, Shawnee trade parties acted as intermedi-
aries between the English and Quapaws, carrying contagious microbes as
well as merchandise from the Atlantic coast into the central Mississippi Valley. In 1700 Tonti estimated that since his earliest visit in 1682 the Quapaw
Indians had lost twelve hundred men "by disease and war" and now numbered only three hundred men.[59]

The Taensas inhabited about eight different villages around Lake St. Joseph, located some 150 miles down the west bank of the Mississippi from the
Quapaws. Hostile toward their northern neighbors since the 1680s, the
Taensas resembled the more southerly Natchez and Tunicas in their political
organization. According to early French observers, each of these tribes was
governed by a chief who possessed absolute power over his people. In the
wake of unprecedented sickness and death, lightning struck the sacred temple of the Taensas in March 1700. Interpreting this calamity as the ultimate
sign of their great spirit's anger, the temple guardian ordered several women
to offer their youngest children into the burning remnants of the building in
order to appease him.[60] By that time the Taensas still numbered more than
four hundred warriors and had been joined by some Ouachitas, refugees
from a rapidly diminishing tribe on the Ouachita River (near present-day
Monroe, Louisiana).[61]

Downriver from the Taensas, the Natchez Indians inhabited a large pine-
forested bluff on the east bank of the Mississippi. Following La Salle's initial
encounter in 1682, the densely populated Natchez villages suffered heavily
from the spread of disease. By the time the Le Moyne brothers launched the

French colony of Louisiana, traders and missionaries were making frequent visits to Natchez country. In 1700 large numbers of Indians flocked to the French camp along the river which, according to Father Du Ru, "looks like one of our ports in France, or like a Dutch fair."[62] Such large-scale contact with outsiders and passersby exposed the Natchez and other tribes up and down the Mississippi River to an even greater degree of epidemic destruction than the inhabitants of the southeastern interior. Bienville approximated their number in 1699 at twelve hundred men, but on 4 March 1700 Tonti reported to his brother that the Natchez nation "counts 8 to 900 men." Of the fifteen hundred warriors estimated by Tonti back in 1686, it seems that approximately a thousand still inhabited the nine or ten villages comprising the Natchez tribe at the beginning of the eighteenth century. This population included some Tioux and Grigra Indians, who in keeping with the Natchez pattern of assimilating neighboring groups had recently left their backcountry villages to join the highly centralized tribe along the Mississippi River.[63]

In the fertile delta of the Yazoo River, which enters the Mississippi from the east above Natchez, at least seven different groups encountered the French in 1700. The people living on the upper Yazoo – Chachiumas, Ibitoupas, and Taposas – and those of the lower Yazoo – Yazoos, Ofogoulas, and Koroas – numbered at least a thousand warriors or about thirty-five hundred villagers altogether. The Tunicas, occupying villages on the Big Black River just below these Yazoo tribes, totaled about another two thousand people.[64] Like the Natchez, Tunicas received a great deal of attention from both French missionaries and English slave dealers at the beginning of the eighteenth century. Intense contact made Tunica villagers extremely vulnerable to foreign disease; Father La Source noted in 1700 that "sickness was among them when we arrived there" and that "they were dying in great numbers."[65]

From 1700 to 1730 village life in the Mississippi Valley between the mouths of the Red and Arkansas Rivers changed drastically. Chickasaw war parties drove the Taensas and Tunicas downriver and, along with disease, attenuated the population of other tribes. On 2 December 1721 Father Charlevoix found the Quapaw village of Ouyapes "in the greatest desolation." From a passing Frenchman infected with smallpox, the entire town was immobilized by the disease. All night in his tent, the priest "heard nothing but weeping, in which the men joined as well as the women, incessantly repeating the word *nihahani*." Reduced to only "about twelve hundred souls" by 1727, according to one missionary, the Quapaws congregated into three villages near the French post. The Quapaw village of Sotouris, where soldiers and travelers regularly purchased corn, contained forty-one cabins and 330 inhabitants. It stood on a bluff thirty feet high when the Arkansas River was low and three feet high when it rose during the spring.[66]

American Indians along the Yazoo River likewise consolidated into fewer towns as their population plummeted over these years. This strategy of adaptation and survival, however, faced a countervailing French policy of disruption and dispersal. Fear of English influence in the area and conflict with the Natchez led Louisiana officials to drive violent wedges between Indian groups in the Central River Area. By 1725 Yazoo valley tribes were united into only two villages. The Ibitoupas, Taposas, and Chachiumas lived in a single town called Chachiuma, which now numbered about two hundred warriors. The town of Yazoo included Ofogoulas, Koroas, and Yazoos and counted only 120 warriors.[67] But with the outbreak of the Natchez War, Ofogoula allies of the French joined the Tunicas, while the Yazoos and Koroas – allies of the Natchez – were scattered and reduced to fewer than forty men. In June 1731 the Tunicas suffered a blow when some Natchez fugitives seeking refuge suddenly attacked their hosts, killing at least twenty men and capturing some eight women. The Natchez themselves had declined to six hundred warriors before their revolt and, as we have already seen, were nearly extinguished by combined French and Indian forces during the early 1730s.[68]

By midcentury the total Indian population in the Central River Area numbered fewer than two thousand men, women, and children – most of them Quapaws.[69] Suspected of favoring English alliance and trade, the Chachiumas were attacked in 1736 by a force of French troops and Tunica warriors. The latter were coerced into this action by Governor Bienville's demands that they demonstrate their allegiance to the French. The Chachiumas lost twelve warriors killed and an equal number of women and children captured during the assault.[70] Some Chachiumas were later adopted into a rebel Choctaw village and played a prominent role in the civil war against pro-French forces during the 1740s. But they were virtually eliminated when that town, Nushkobo, was completely destroyed in the Choctaw Revolt. Meanwhile, a small group of Ofogoulas, refugees of the earlier Natchez War, had moved just outside the French fort at Natchez, providing it with game and defense against marauding Chickasaws. On 5 November 1748 Governor Vaudreuil mentioned "eight or ten Ofogoulas who have their homes there," those numbers probably referring to men.[71]

After 1762 English migrants to West Florida began to settle the eastern bank of the Mississippi at Natchez and other points between the mouths of the Red and Yazoo Rivers. As will be seen in chapter 5, Choctaw and Chickasaw hunting parties began to cross the Mississippi in order to hunt in the Ouachita basin during this same period of time. The indigenous Indian population of the Central River Area, meanwhile, continued to decline. The Quapaws still lived along the lower Arkansas River, near the now Spanish garrison, and remained the largest group in this once heavily populated section of the Lower Mississippi Valley. As reported by Philip Pittman in 1770, "they are divided into three villages, over each of which presides a chief, and a great chief over all: they amount in all to about six hundred warriors."[72]

The population history of the Red River Area, which fanned out in a northwestward direction from that river's junction with the Mississippi, involved four distinct phases of change between the 1680s and 1780s. The ill-fated landing of La Salle's colony on the Texas coast in 1685 and the subsequent extension of New Spain's mission network toward the Red River set off a deadly epidemic that spread throughout the area. By the end of the 1690s an estimated three thousand Indians had died in the course of this initial phase of depopulation. With colonization of the Red River well underway by 1720, the remaining Caddo villages concentrated around either the settlement of French Natchitoches or the bend upriver. Caddos and their downriver neighbors, the Avoyelles, became important participants in the frontier exchange economy of colonial Louisiana, trading buffalo robes, deerskins, and even livestock for European merchandise. This second phase of population change, characterized by steady decline, ended during the 1750s when large bands of Wichitas migrated into the periphery of this area and initiated a third phase – one of native population growth. The fourth phase began during 1777–78 when a massive smallpox epidemic struck the Caddos and Wichitas, repeating another process of sudden depopulation.

Located near the Red River's junction with the Mississippi, the Avoyelles were more closely related to the Natchez and Tunicas than to the Caddos upriver. In 1700 they numbered more than two hundred warriors. Traveling up the Red River from the Avoyelle villages, one encountered the first of three confederacies that constituted the Caddo people. The villages of Natchitoches, Doustionis, and Yatasis comprised the Natchitoches confederacy. These villagers scattered their cabins along the banks of the Red River, which flooded their fields before each planting season. Annual flooding also drove deer and other wildlife into easily hunted herds on adjacent oak- and pine-forested hills. Bienville visited the Natchitoches in 1700 and later estimated that this cluster of Caddo villages included at least four hundred men altogether. Villages of the Kadohadacho confederacy were situated at the bend of the Red River and, according to Bienville, "had five or six hundred men" at the beginning of the eighteenth century.[73] The third Caddo confederacy was the Hasinai. Hasinai villages were located around the upper Sabine, Neches, and Angelina Rivers. A Canadian voyageur who had already spent several years among these people reported in 1699 "that they do not exceed six hundred or seven hundred men."[74]

In tracing changes in the native population of the Red River Area, it is necessary to exclude the large Hasinai populace from calculations of Caddo numbers. Hasinai villages were more strongly influenced by Spanish missionary efforts in Texas than by French advances from Louisiana, although many Hasinai people managed to trade frequently within the frontier exchange economy of the Lower Mississippi Valley.[75] In 1700, therefore, approximately twelve hundred warriors or forty-two hundred people constituted the Indian population that would deal integrally with the colony of Louisiana. The economy and material culture of these villagers closely resembled those of their woodland neighbors in other parts of the Lower Mississippi Valley. As observed by early Spanish missionaries and French explorers, the Caddos planted two crops of corn each year, one at the end of April and another in June. During the autumn and winter months, they dispersed into hunting camps and produced abundant supplies of meat, hides, nuts, and oil. Rivers and lakes also provided an important source of fish, fowl, and even salt.

As the Red River became a major trade route in the eighteenth century, contact between villagers and colonists intensified and drastically undermined the number of native inhabitants throughout the valley. Within a quarter of a century, this population declined to fewer than five hundred men.[76] The people who participated most actively in the colonial economy, as seen in other areas, seemed to suffer most from disease and alcoholism. The Avoyelles, for example, served as horse and cattle dealers and therefore traveled extensively along the Red River and traded directly with Europeans. By the 1750s their one remaining village was abandoned, its inhabitants apparently debilitated by overexposure to viruses and brandy.[77] Depopulation upriver from the Avoyelles caused surviving Indian villagers to migrate into a few compact, but never secure, towns between the colonial settlement of Natchitoches and its outpost at Nasonite on the bend of the Red River.[78]

The in-migration of the Wichitas from the upper Arkansas River between 1740 and 1760 created a new group of Indian villages to the west of the Kadohadachos. Attracted into the region by French trade and alliance opportunities, these newcomers became part of the Natchitoches trade sphere. By the mid-1770s the Wichitas occupied four separate villages along the Red River – Taovaya, Wichita, Iscani, and Tawakoni – which altogether included one thousand warriors.[79] Another in-migration of Indians occurred in 1763, when approximately eighty Apalaches from Mobile Bay resettled themselves near the newly emerging post of Rapides on the lower Red River. Within a decade their population consisted of an estimated twenty-six warriors.[80]

When visited by Monsieur J. Gaignard in 1773–74, the Caddo population along the Red River consisted of the following villages: about seventy-five miles above Natchitoches stood Natassee, where "there are three warriors"; Petit Cadohadacho was located another seventy-five miles upriver and was said to have sixty warriors; another ten warriors occupied Preiry d'est Ennemy, situated between Petit Cado and Grand Cado; the latter village stood at the bend of the Red River about ninety miles above Petit Cado and consisted of ninety more warriors. Adaes, an autonomous Caddoan-speaking village, stood about twenty miles west of Natchitoches (near present-day Robeline, Louisiana) and numbered only about thirty families.[81] The total Indian population of this area by 1775, moving up the Red River, can be summarized at 91 Apalaches, 105 Adaes, 543 Caddos, and 3,500 Wichitas.

In 1777–78 this population of the Red River Area, much larger than it had been in 1750 because of in-migration, suffered another devastating smallpox epidemic. According to the commandant of Natchitoches, more than three hundred people perished in the Caddo and Wichita villages. As reported by Athanase de Mézières in February 1778, the Adaes became "almost extinct since the last epidemic" and were by then "given extremely to the vice of drunkenness."[82] Indian villagers throughout the Lower Mississippi Valley were combating a new wave of illnesses introduced into the region by the mobilization of European troops during the American Revolution. For the Caddos as well as their neighbors, recovery from this latest demographic setback would come only at a slow rate.[83]

Emphasis on the changing size and location of American Indians, group by group, allows us to recognize that their lives centered around real communities. Indian-colonial relations and the impact of colonization on native societies are discussed too often in abstract ways that lose sight of actual people with their own homes and identities. It is hoped that this demographic survey provides a framework for identifying all of the many specific Indian groups living in the Lower Mississippi Valley over the eighteenth century. The population changes experienced by each group form an important context for closer and fuller analyses of culture and society. It helps to know, in other words, approximately how many Indian people in a particular community were engaged in adapting to and resisting European colonialism and roughly where they lived and moved at a given time.

By examining population changes within specific areas, the wide variety of American Indian experiences also comes to light. Within the Lower Mississippi Valley, as in other colonial regions, uneven demographic patterns were related to different geographical, political, and socioeconomic situations. Coastal groups situated near the Gulf of Mexico and along the banks of the Mississippi River suffered very early and rapidly from their greater exposure to settlers and soldiers. Following the initial wave of epidemics through their villages, survivors lived in greatly attenuated communities in close association with colonists. Lacking diplomatic and military leverage between colonial powers, people like the Biloxis and Houmas traded freely with non-Indians but only within the colonial region. Many were even employed at specialized tasks such as rowing and construction. But their immediate access to alcohol and their higher visibility in towns and along waterways made these coastal Indians easy targets of abusive treatment and disparaging commentary. "Debauched" and "miserable" were commonly used by insensitive observers to describe conditions in Indian settlements located near colonial settlements. And as will be seen in later chapters, the size and location of Indian communities would continue to affect both their livelihood and image well into the nineteenth century.

Although their populations were also cut down by epidemics, the greater distance of interior tribes from early colonists and their more advantageous position in the continental rivalry of European powers helped mitigate the demographic impact on their power and their image. Trade with colonies operated through more formal, regulated channels, and military prowess earned them greater respect from outside commentators. A lasting capacity to damage settlements and switch allegiance made groups like the Choctaws and Wichitas appear in colonists' eyes to be "superior" and "braver" than coastal Indian peoples.

Finally, at the broadest level of analysis, there was the drastic decline in the American Indian population of the Lower Mississippi Valley from sixty-seven thousand at the beginning of the eighteenth century to scarcely twenty-two thousand by midcentury. The overall impact of smallpox and other diseases was demographically reversed during subsequent decades only by the in-migration of other Indian groups and some indigenous recovery by older regional inhabitants. But the declining Indian population was not simply replaced by a colonial population during the eighteenth century. When general regions like the Lower Mississippi Valley are examined as demographic wholes, the word "settlement" fails to capture accurately the direction of population change. While population grew in coastal New England over the seventeenth century because of European colonization, total population for some time actually declined across the wider region of New England as Indians died from disease and war. The same can be said about the Chesapeake Bay region, New Mexico, and other North American colonial regions. An especially slow growth in the number of settlers and slaves inhabiting Louisiana, also marked by disease and disruption, meant that much of the Lower Mississippi Valley was being vacated or thinned during most of the eighteenth century – to be reoccupied only in the nineteenth century.

FOUR

American Indians in a
Frontier Exchange Economy

For a long time American Indian history followed anthropology's ethnographic preoccupation with single tribal groups, reconstructing precontact societies and then tracing predictably deleterious effects of European colonialism and American expansionism upon them. These older tribal histories emphasized diplomatic relations and military conflicts with particular colonies but oversimplified social and economic dimensions of interaction. Under the influence of social history and historical geography, new students of Indian-colonial relations are more interested in the everyday lives of natives and newcomers within wider regional contexts. We are consequently discovering that, in many different places over various lengths of time, Indians interacted with Europeans and Africans more openly and mutably than imperial policies officially permitted.

Over the last several years the historical study of American Indians has departed dramatically from earlier scholarship. The works of James H. Merrell, Peter C. Mancall, Richard White, and Ramon A. Gutiérrez, among others, focus on previously ignored dimensions of intercultural relations.[1] Phrases like "Indians' new world" and "the middle ground" are deployed as conceptual insights into processes of interaction and invention shared by different groups of Indians and non-Indians. An emphasis on either interethnic or intertribal relations across regions transcending discrete colonial provinces, as demonstrated by Joel W. Martin and Gregory E. Dowd, can also shed new light on political and religious movements during the eighteenth and early nineteenth centuries.[2]

These new works in Indian history recover important periods and places from North America's past that became obscure or forgotten because of their transitory nature. The very forces that eventually displaced or destroyed earlier worlds of cross-cultural interaction also inhibited later understanding of the non-Indians as well as Indians who occupied them. More careful examination of those "middle grounds" is now revealing that the

American Indian experience has been more integral to, and less separate from, the main story of American history. My own discovery of the eighteenth-century Lower Mississippi Valley, an especially remote world to many scholars and laymen alike, proves this point.[3]

Over the eighteenth century, American Indian villagers across the Lower Mississippi Valley forged a network of social and economic relations with European settlers and African slaves along the Gulf Coast and lower banks of the Mississippi that I call a frontier exchange economy. The term *frontier exchange* is meant to capture the form and content of economic interactions among these groups, with a view to replacing the notion of frontier as an interracial boundary with that of a cross-cultural network. For this conceptualization of an interethnic web of economic relations, I am indebted to a variety of works in anthropology, political science, and history that emphasize the prosaic features of livelihood in ordinary people's struggles for survival.[4] Small-scale, face-to-face marketing in North American colonial regions must be taken as seriously as the more impersonal forces of transatlantic commerce if we are to understand how peoples of different cultures related to and influenced one another in daily life.

In order to underscore this sphere of exchange, the Lower Mississippi Valley is here defined as an economic region that was shaped by common means of production and by regular forms of trade among its diverse inhabitants. Upper Louisiana, the area known as Illinois country, is not examined, therefore, because economic connections between the upper Mississippi Valley and lower Louisiana were more impersonal and less predictable before the last quarter of the eighteenth century. The inhabitants of the Illinois settlements, numbering 768 French settlers, 445 black slaves, and 147 Indian slaves at midcentury, belonged to Louisiana politically but were more closely integrated economically into the Great Lakes region. The standard image of Louisiana as a vast territory spread along a thousand miles of the meandering Mississippi and sparsely occupied by Frenchmen and their Indian allies not only exaggerates the boundlessness of life in the Mississippi Valley but distracts attention from the substantial intraregional connections that differentiated lower Louisiana from upper Louisiana.[5] In 1762–63 the Lower Mississippi Valley was partitioned into the Spanish province of Louisiana and the English province of West Florida. The latter colony, therefore, must be included in any study of the region's economy. The persistence of frontier exchange across the political boundary can too easily be overlooked when Louisiana and West Florida are treated separately.

As explored in the preceding chapter, the Indian population of the

Lower Mississippi Valley declined as drastically here as in other colonial regions of North America. But in contrast with the English colonies along the
Atlantic seaboard, Louisiana was colonized at a slow rate. Because Louisiana remained a low priority in the mercantile designs of both France and
Spain, sluggish immigration and population growth were accompanied by
an erratic exportation of agricultural staples to Europe. Consequently, the
Indian population of the Lower Mississippi Valley – even while diminishing
– maintained a high profile in both the demographic and economic evolution of the region. Louisiana's sparse colonial populace and tentative transatlantic commerce, therefore, can be used to the historian's advantage, allowing one to turn more attentively to social and economic dimensions of
life that were neglected in the Lower Mississippi Valley as well as in other
colonial regions.

The focus of this essay falls on the informal interstices in which people exchanged small quantities of goods in pursuit of their livelihood rather than
on the more familiar and formal economic setting of Indian-colonial relations – the commercial fur trade. A brief summary of how a network of
towns and outposts took shape is accompanied by an outline of changes in
the Lower Mississippi Valley's colonial population. Then the reader is asked
to follow more closely the multiple directions of interaction through which
deerskins and foods circulated from group to group. Over most of the eighteenth century, exchanges of these two kinds of products contributed
strongly to the notable fluidity of social relations between Indians and non-
Indians in the Lower Mississippi Valley. It must be emphasized, however,
that exchanges occurred under, and often despite, very unequal social conditions because a colonial elite worked steadily to enforce dependency on
American Indians as well as bondage on African Americans and subordination on a mixed lot of white settlers.

Sent by France late in 1698 to establish a military post near the mouth of the
Mississippi River and to forestall Spanish and English advances in the region, naval captain Pierre Le Moyne d'Iberville encountered dismal prospects for what he hoped would become a colony. Already overextended im-
perially and facing shortages of food at home, France was not prepared to
deliver supplies with any regularity to the Gulf Coast. Like many other nascent colonial ventures before it, Iberville's isolated outpost therefore depended heavily on trade with neighboring Indian villages for its survival.
Soldiers and sailors either purchased food directly from Indians or acquired
peltry from them to exchange for imported grains and meats.[6] During the

second decade of the eighteenth century this trade expanded from localized exchange with villages near the Gulf into an extensive network of interior posts that not only facilitated the movement of deerskins to the coast but functioned as marketplaces for the exchange of food. In 1714 the French built a storehouse at Natchez in order to acquire deerskins from the up-country villages and to counteract English intrigue and commerce. Joining the Yamassees in war against South Carolina, the Alibamons, Tallapoosas, and Abehkas – who eventually became known as the Upper Creeks – ousted English traders from their villages. In 1715 they began to carry deerskins to Mobile and in 1717 allowed Jean-Baptiste Le Moyne de Bienville, Iberville's brother, to build Fort Toulouse near the junction of the Coosa and Tallapoosa Rivers. Fort Rosalie was built among the Natchez Indians in 1716, following execution of some hostile chiefs at Bienville's order. In 1719 a garrison was established at Fort St. Pierre on the Yazoo River.[7]

To advance trade up the Red River, a French garrison occupied a post near the Caddo village of Natchitoches in 1716, and a subsidiary trade station was established at an upriver Indian town called Upper Nasoni in 1719. Only twenty miles southwest of Natchitoches, the Spanish, who had been gradually edging toward the Red River, constructed a military post at Los Adaes in 1721. Louis Juchereau de St. Denis, who became commandant of French Natchitoches in 1719, had already been trading in this area for several years – with both Spaniards and Indians. In 1721 a small detachment of soldiers from the Yazoo River garrison joined a group of about one hundred settlers at the lower Arkansas River, where, in 1686, the Quapaws had allowed Henri de Tonti to situate a short-lived trade house.[8]

A decade of immigration and slave trading to Louisiana, attended by death for hundreds of Europeans and Africans, resulted by 1732 in a population of only about two thousand settlers and soldiers with some thirty-eight hundred slaves at a time when the number of Indians of the Lower Mississippi Valley, though rapidly declining from disease and war, was still in the range of thirty thousand.[9] Large-scale immigration from Europe stopped by the mid-1720s, and only about four hundred black slaves reached the colony between 1732 and the 1760s. This slow growth of population – to approximately five thousand slaves, four thousand settlers, and one hundred free people of color – meant minimal encroachment on Indian lands: most settlers and slaves lived along the Gulf Coast and the Mississippi River below its junction with the Red River. Trade relations with the Indians developed more freely because, for a time at least, the region's tribes were not markedly agitated by French pressure on their territory.[10]

At first, given the scanty and erratic supply of trade goods from France, Louisianian officials relied on distribution of merchandise among Indian leaders in the form of annual gifts. In doing so, they accommodated by necessity Indian protocols of trade and diplomacy. For the Indians, exchanges of material goods represented political reciprocity between autonomous groups, while absence of trade was synonymous with a state of war. Because commerce could not operate independently from ritual expressions of allegiance, such formal ceremonies as gift giving and smoking the calumet had to accompany economic transactions between Indians and Europeans. Conformity to these conventions recognized the leverage of such large tribes as the Choctaws and Caddos on Louisiana's commerce and defense. The tribes were essential to the initiation of the network of trade for deerskins and food – both items important to the success of Louisiana – against the threat of English competition from South Carolina and Georgia.[11]

The formation of this network, as we know from the previous chapters, did not occur without costly conflict. Only after a long war against the Chitimachas, which provided Louisiana with many of its first slaves, did the French secure the alliance of all Indian tribes in the Mississippi delta. While small tribes like the Chitimachas confronted French power directly, conflict between larger Indian nations was fueled by intercolonial competition. In the 1720s Choctaw and Upper Creek villagers helped the French thwart British expansion to the Mississippi River, while the Chickasaws and Lower Creeks fought against them to protect English traders still operating within the Louisiana hinterland.[12] The most explosive crisis came in 1729 when, after a decade of deteriorating relations with encroaching settlers, the Natchez Indians waged a desperate war against the French. Meanwhile, a push by Louisiana officials and planters for the production of tobacco and indigo provoked resistance within: as the volume of these exports rose during the late 1720s, so did the level of slave rebelliousness. An African plot was discovered in New Orleans shortly after the Indians destroyed the French plantations at Natchez, and many of the slaves taken captive there assisted the Natchez in their ensuing, but losing, defense against the Louisiana army. Dealing with a black majority within the colonial settlements, and living in the midst of an even larger Indian population, officials employed greater vigilance and harsher coercion as time went on.[13]

Toward midcentury, chronic shortages of merchandise and English intervention nearly turned the Choctaw nation, a bulwark of Louisiana's security, against the French. The benign policy of gift giving could go only so far in mitigating the effects of unreliable imports on the deerskin trade with Indians. Unable to divert the powerful Chickasaw nation from the English because of inadequate quantities of trade goods, French officials resorted to a strategy of intimidation and debilitation, employing Choctaw warriors on major campaigns and in continuous guerrilla raids against Chickasaw villages. Participation in this conflict through the 1740s, which was motivated by the need to avenge enemy hostilities as well as to fulfill obligations to the French, took its toll on the Choctaws. Rebellion by a pro-English party within the nation broke out in 1746, costing the Choctaw people much suffering and death in what became a violent civil war waged to preserve their alliance with French Louisiana.[14]

Louisiana's frontier exchange economy survived the Choctaw Revolt, with the exportation of deerskins steadily increasing alongside that of tobacco and indigo. Demographic and geopolitical changes that began in the 1760s, however, portended greater challenges to the trade-alliance network. Immigration into the Lower Mississippi Valley resumed after Great Britain drove French settlers from Nova Scotia in 1755. By 1769, seven years after Spain obtained Louisiana from France, more than a thousand of these Acadian refugees reached the colony, forming new settlements along the Mississippi about seventy miles above New Orleans and at Atakapas and Opelousas on Bayou Teche. From 1778 to 1780 two thousand "Islenos" migrated from the Canary Islands and established their own communities along the Mississippi and Bayou Lafourche below New Orleans. In 1785 seven ships carried another sixteen hundred Acadians from France to Louisiana. Slaves imported from the West Indies contributed to the growth of Louisiana's African-American population during this same period.[15]

Meanwhile, Great Britain was accelerating colonization on the eastern side of the river, having acquired West Florida by the Treaty of Paris in 1763. Settlers from the Atlantic seaboard, many with slaves, increased the colonial population of West Florida to nearly four thousand whites and fifteen hundred blacks by 1774. An even larger influx occurred after the outbreak of the American Revolution as loyalist refugees sought asylum in the Florida colony and settled mainly in the Natchez area. By 1783, when Spain gained sovereignty over West Florida and control over both sides of the Mississippi, the colonial population of the Lower Mississippi Valley approached sixteen thousand black slaves, thirteen thousand whites, and over one thousand free people of color.[16]

By the 1780s the Indian population in the region was, for the first time, becoming outnumbered by colonial inhabitants, while the colonial economy shifted toward greater dependence on expanding commercial agriculture. Consequently, Louisiana officials exerted tighter political control over interethnic exchange in order to concentrate slave labor on cash crops and to reduce the mobility of Indian villagers. The frontier exchange economy did not fade from the Lower Mississippi Valley, however, because many old and new inhabitants continued to make efforts into the nineteenth century to perpetuate small-scale trade across heightening racial divides.[17]

Before 1783 the deerskin trade had encouraged widespread participation in a network of diffuse exchange from Indian villages to colonial port towns. Indian customs and French commercial weaknesses, as already seen, required a formal sphere of trade-alliance relations, but many people across the region also relied on informal and intimate forms of cross-cultural trade. For historians the less systematic trade in deerskins that evolved in Louisiana has long been overshadowed by a sequence of frustrated French efforts to create a commercial empire in the Mississippi River Valley, beginning with the ventures of René-Robert Cavelier, Sieur de La Salle. During the 1680s La Salle had attempted but failed to expand commerce in bison robes and beaver pelts. At the threshold of the eighteenth century, while his men were barely surviving the rigors of building an outpost on the Gulf Coast, Iberville promoted a grand scheme to entrench French power in North America through a system of trading posts and tanneries around which well-armed Indian allies in the Mississippi Valley would concentrate. Antoine Crozat's plans for Louisiana's commerce in 1712 included hopes of profitably controlling the fur trade throughout the region. Paling beside these mercantile designs, the Indian trade in lower Louisiana was shaped by a complex of more pedestrian circumstances. A small number of colonial troops with minimal support from the crown had to be dispersed among a few select posts. Intertribal conflicts and English trade with Indians in the region determined when and where French stations were constructed and, furthermore, continued to be destabilizing influences on Louisiana's trade. The irrepressible eastward flow of beaver skins from the upper Mississippi Valley to Canada also affected the trade network in Louisiana, making the lower valley a separate, predominantly deerskin-producing trade region.[18]

The economic and political importance of the Indian trade to Louisiana is evidenced by the close attention that officials paid to the details of its operation. Colonial administrators' interest centered on the interference and competition of English traders, but the region's internal commerce required particular measures for regulation as well. In order to maintain stable relations between traders and villagers, governments in all North American colonies administered tariffs or rates of exchange. In 1721 the Choctaws and the French agreed to trade at the following prices: a quarter of an ell (one meter) of woolen cloth called limbourg or one axe for four dressed deerskins; one blanket or tomahawk for two dressed deerskins; and two-thirds of a pound of gunpowder or twenty gun flints for one dressed deerskin.[19] As the cost of European manufactures rose and additional goods entered the regional economy, new tariffs were negotiated from time to time by colonial and tribal leaders. Although much of the trading occurred at varying rates, depending on local conditions and individual circumstances, official tariffs represented colonial accommodation to Indian insistence that trade be contained within the political sphere of relations. Once it established rates of exchange, the Superior Council of Louisiana had to contend with complaints from traders and Indians alike about inadequate supplies or inappropriate prices. Operating between a fixed ceiling of rates set between tribal and colonial governments and a rising floor of costs charged by import merchants, the traders tended to have, as noted in the minutes of a meeting in December 1728, "a greater share in the complaints that have been made about the high price of the goods than the Indians themselves."[20] For their part, Indian representatives bargained for better exchange rates by repeatedly comparing the expense and quality of French and English merchandise.[21]

Despite attempts by groups of merchants and officials to monopolize Indian commerce, the deerskin trade involved many colonial inhabitants as well as Indians. Even during the demographic and agricultural expansion of Louisiana in the 1720s, settlers relied on deerskins, acquired directly or indirectly from Indian villagers, as a means of buying imported goods. "In order to support by this new accommodation the trade with the Indians," the Company of the Indies decided in 1729 to make its warehouse in the colony the exclusive exporter of deerskins. After 1732 officials of the king further advanced this commerce "by entrusting in small lots the merchandise that he sends to settlers who will trade it to the Indians and who will settle their accounts with his Majesty with the skins that they have taken in trade."[22] As the difficulty of finding among the traders "people of sufficiently well known integrity" continued to make it "almost impossible to avoid bad debts," the deerskin trade fell into the hands of "solvent inhabitants who have given security for the merchandise."[23] Consequently, the many anonymous individuals who traded in the Indian villages became middlemen between the Indians who hunted and processed the skins and the colonial merchants who were able to acquire and forward imported trade goods. "On their return from the Indians," as one observer described the traders, "they disperse in the city their peltries or produce, which they bring in payment to those from whom they have borrowed in order to carry on their trade."[24]

Many settlers and even slaves exchanged something for deerskins once in a while, and innumerable colonists passed in and out of the deerskin trade as a temporary means of livelihood. Others made a lifetime occupation from seasonally trading imported merchandise for peltry and other native products. The identities of some professional traders among the Choctaws offer informative glimpses into the business. Marc Antoine Huché grew up among the Choctaws, was hired in 1721 as interpreter for the company at "five hundred livres per year with two rations for himself and his wife," and traded for Mobile commandant-entrepreneur Bernard Diron d'Artaguette. As reported by General Commissioner Edmé Gatien Salmon in 1732, the Great Chief of the Choctaw nation considered Huché to be "brave, firm and faithful."[25] Another employee of Diron d'Artaguette and later an independent trader, Joseph Poupart *dit* Lafleur, sent 581 skins to the Mobile commandant in July 1729, along with a letter describing the activities of English traders among the Chickasaws. A decade later his widow, Marie Roy, ran a warehouse among the Alibamons, which had to be withdrawn in 1740 because of trouble with English traders in the area.[26] Individuals known as Gaspard, Dupumeaux, and Antoine Chauvin Des Islets traded in Choctaw country at midcentury, the last described by General Commissioner Honoré Michel de la Rouvillière in 1751 as "a Famous trader who is set forth as an oracle" by the Choctaws.[27]

With the growth of the colonial population after 1762, Indian villages in the Lower Mississippi Valley hosted an increasing number of traders whose ethnic composition became more English. By the mid-1780s Spanish officials estimated that five hundred traders, employees, and transients were living in and around Choctaw and Chickasaw towns, while nearly three hundred more operated in Creek towns. Considered "vagabonds and villains" by colonial administrators interested in orderly commerce, many of these men married Indian women and became affiliated with specific villages. A "List of Choctaw Towns and Traders" compiled by Juan de la Villebeuvre in 1787 reveals the names of an array of persons involved in the deerskin trade. Frenchmen identified as Favre, Louis, Chastany, and Petit Baptiste lived in the eastern district towns of Yanabé, Ouatonloula, Yazoo, Loukfata, and Bitabogoula, respectively. In three other villages of the same district "there are many whites, both Traders and Vagabonds." Among the people trading with particular towns in the western district of the Choctaw nation were Englishmen Alexander Fraizer and three employees at West Yazoo; Louis Mulatto, evidently employed at Cushtusha by Simon Favre; Frenchman Louis Leflore at Caffetalaya; the Pitchlynn brothers, English traders, at Tchanké; and an American, Moise Forstar, at Mongoulacha. A similar mixture of traders and employees occupied villages in the Sixtown district.[28] Children born to this generation of traders and their Indian wives belonged to the clans of their mothers, and some became important tribal leaders by the beginning of the nineteenth century.[29]

Most deerskin traders learned to speak the language of the tribe with whom they dealt. As emphasized by an anonymous chronicler of the Choctaws' trade with Louisiana, who may have been a trader sometime before the mid-1730s, "it is necessary to known their language well." Many traders probably spoke Mobilian, a trade language or lingua franca, instead of or in addition to distinct tribal languages: "when one knows it," noted Lieutenant Jean François Benjamin Dumont de Montigny, "one can travel through all this province without needing an interpreter."[30] Antecedents of Mobilian may have existed in the region before European contact, but economic relations with the colonial populace of Louisiana undoubtedly accelerated and expanded its usage – resembling the evolution of Delaware, Occaneechee, and Catawba into trade languages along the Atlantic coast. Based on the western Muskhogean grammar of the Choctaw, Chickasaw, and Alibamon languages – all mutually intelligible – Mobilian served as a second language, mixing with wide variation the lexicon and phonology derived from both Indian and European speech. Well before the mid-eighteenth century, Mobilian became familiar to colonists and Indians west of the Mississippi River. All Caddo villages, as reported by Antoine Le Page du Pratz, contained someone who could speak this "langue vulgaire." Mobilian was a convenient second language for many settlers and slaves as well as traders to use among Indians, and through the nineteenth century it continued to be spoken by American Indians, African Americans, and European Americans in southern Louisiana and eastern Texas.[31]

Among the goods exchanged for deerskins, liquor was the most volatile item. As in other colonial regions, alcoholic beverages in Louisiana functioned both as a lubricant for expanding Indian commerce and as a stimulant for satisfying military and other colonial personnel. Louisiana and West Florida governments tried to control this commerce, but the very frequency of ordinances regulating trade in liquor reveals its ever-widening use among Indians, settlers, and slaves. In 1725 the Louisiana Superior Council attempted to remedy abuses caused by the "many persons here who have no other trade than that of selling brandy and other drinks at exorbitant prices and even grant credit to all the soldiers, workmen, and sailors." Beginning in 1717, innumerable orders were issued prohibiting the unauthorized sale of liquor to Indians and slaves, whose consumption of it, officials feared, would increase chances of violent rebellion.[32] By midcentury a cheap rum called *tafia* became the region's more popular drink and a convenient medium of exchange. The English government in Pensacola attempted to restrict Indian traders to fifteen gallons every three months, which was considered a necessary amount for their purchase of food from Indian villagers. But in 1772 several Choctaw chiefs bitterly complained about the quantity of rum that "pours in upon our nation like a great Sea from Mobille and from all the Plantations and Settlements round about." Traders sometimes watered their rum, four kegs of which could buy a Choctaw pony during the 1770s, and encouraged excessive consumption among Indians in order to make more profitable bargains for their deerskins. Peddlers and tavern-keepers persistently violated their licenses by selling tafia and eau de vie to soldiers and slaves as well as to Indians.[33]

The deerskin trade operated to a large degree on credit, which facilitated frontier exchange between Indians and non-Indians in the short run while contributing to its commercialization in the long run. Indian hunters required an advance in goods before they pursued the winter season's thickly furred animals, forcing traders to wait until spring for their pay. In response to this seasonal pattern, traders acquired goods on credit from town merchants and obliged themselves to pay with interest within a year.[34] Such arrangements were essential to the trade yet made all parties vulnerable to mischance or misdoing: a poor hunting season, loss of or damage to goods in transit, death by accident, or simple evasion. Indians often postponed payment of debts because hunting conditions were unfavorable or in order to stretch their trade among different peddlers; they refused to pay interest on goods advanced; they resisted paying back debts: "Nothing so much offends an Indian," observed Amos Stoddard early in the nineteenth century, "as to be requested to pay his old debts. 'If,' says he, 'I deliver you my peltries to pay for the goods I received last season, my family must suffer, and perhaps starve.'"[35] Traders, for their part, could find themselves unable to make good their debts to merchants. Thus, on 26 December 1773, John Fitzpatrick, merchant at Manchac, lent goods worth 233 pesos to a Monsieur Valliere for trade to the Atakapas, payable the following April, but Valliere failed to pay his debt on time.[36] In another instance, Joseph Montard proposed to pay thirteen packs of skins to Juan Macarty, but the merchant refused them because the delivery came a year and a half late and during the summer, when the market value of pelts was at its annual nadir.[37] Under such circumstances, it is not surprising that traders often inflated the price of merchandise to meet their debts and interest costs.

Lower Mississippi Valley Indians also produced foodstuffs for the frontier exchange economy. Colonists in Louisiana, though ill supplied from home, were at first reluctant to labor to feed themselves by growing crops; fortunately for them, Indians were able to produce more than they needed for their own use. Thus there developed a lively trade, though one less visible to historians even than the diffuse trade in deerskins. While sailors and soldiers from France, with some Canadian coureurs de bois, were constructing the colony's first fort at Biloxi Bay, the Pascagoulas, Mobilians, and other coastal Indians eagerly swapped surpluses of corn, beans, and meat for axes, beads, and other useful items of European manufacture. During the first decade of the eighteenth century, colonial officials regularly sent parties up the Mobile and Mississippi Rivers to purchase maize from Indians. In order to facilitate their trade with the French, some villages relocated closer to the coast and planted larger volumes of grain. The Houmas, for example, abandoned their town several miles east of the Mississippi and settled downriver along the west bank near Bayou Lafourche, where they became reliable suppliers of food to both travelers and settlers.[38] In 1708, when the colony consisted of 122 military men, 80 Indian slaves, and only 77 settlers (24 men, 28 women, and 25 children), "everybody," according to special commissioner Martin d'Artaguette, was asking for gunpowder "to trade with the Indians for the things we need." Through sales of venison to these people, Indians who hunted around Fort St. Louis were acquiring guns, each musket worth ten deer by 1710.[39]

The availability of Indian produce tempted some officials and colonists to profiteer in the sale of food. Louisiana's first political conflict, in fact, centered upon accusations – not entirely false – that the Le Moyne brothers engrossed "the meat and other produce that the Indians have brought to Mobile," trading with the king's merchandise and marking up the price of food for their own profit. Far away from France, where local governments and traditional constraints still protected buyers of food from profiteering middlemen, colonial merchants and administrators tried to intercept corn and game from Indian suppliers and resell the food to consumers at exorbitant prices.[40] The Superior Council assumed responsibility for fixing the price of basic food items beginning in 1722, when buffalo beef was set at eight sous per pound, cattle beef at ten sous per pound, a quarter of a deer at four livres, poultry at three livres apiece, and eggs at fifty sous per dozen. Such regulations, however, never stopped commandants of military posts from attempting to monopolize food supplies and other goods delivered by neighboring Indian villagers.[41]

Many *habitants* of Louisiana preferred direct exchange with Indians for their subsistence, which proved easier than learning how to produce their own food from the soil and wildlife of an unfamiliar land. Trade with Indians for food also allowed a degree of freedom from the pressures inherent in colonial agriculture, causing alarm among colonial officials and merchants who hoped to build a colony that would export some profitable staple. Although general commissioner Marc-Antoine Hubert found the soil along the rivers and bayous to be "of surprising fertility," he lamented in 1716 that "the colonists of the present time will never be satisfied with this infallible resource, accustomed as they are to the trade with the Indians the easy profit from which support them, giving them what they need day by day like the Indians who find their happiness in an idle and lazy life." Another observer found in France's feeble commitment to colonizing the Lower Mississippi Valley the reason inhabitants had for two decades "done nothing else than try to get a little trading merchandise to obtain from the savages their sustenance, consisting of Indian corn, beans, pumpkins, or small round pumpkins, game and bear grease."[42] The Indian trade, by deflecting colonists from agriculture, thus helped frustrate early efforts to integrate the region into the world market for the benefit of both the colony and the mother country. What looked to officials like laziness was really a testimony to the vitality of the exchange economy.

When the Company of the Indies sent a flood of immigrants to Louisiana between 1717 and 1721, dependence on Indian supplies of food actually expanded. A food crisis was created as seven thousand settlers and two thousand slaves disembarked on the Gulf Coast without adequate provisions. Malarial fevers, dysentery, and scurvy combined with hunger to kill hundreds of French and German immigrants and Bambara and Wolof captives. Soldiers and workers employed by the company were sent to live in nearby villages, and shipments of corn were sought from interior tribes.[43]

Like the deerskin trade, food marketing with Indians followed a more open and diffuse pattern than colonial administrators desired. Although France treated Louisiana as an importer of flour, alcohol, and a few more luxurious foodstuffs, supply lines were too tenuous and shipments always too small or spoiled for *habitants* to rely upon external sources for grain and meat. Colonists accused merchants who exported flour from France of shipping inedible and short-measured supplies. The Illinois country also proved to be an unreliable source of wheat for the colonists downriver.[44] Therefore, Indian villages and colonial settlements within the lower valley came to depend upon a regional network of exchange, in which food surpluses were periodically traded in bulk to areas in short supply, and smaller-scale transactions regularly occurred among Indians, settlers, and slaves.

The presence of numerous military personnel in the region and the fact that about 25 percent of Louisiana's colonial populace lived in New Orleans by midcentury especially stimulated cross-cultural food marketing. Corn, game, and other provisions consumed at interior posts like Natchitoches and Tombecbé came from neighboring Indian villagers who bartered for such trade goods as metalware, brandy, and cloth either directly with individual soldiers or more formally through their commanding officers. The government also purchased large quantities of grain for its troops from settlers along the Mississippi River.[45] The Choctaws not only sold foodstuffs to the garrison stationed at Fort Tombecbé, beginning in 1736, but also carried corn, vegetables, and poultry to the Mobile market.[46]

Indian communities in the vicinity of New Orleans and Mobile provided food crops and meats and even such prepared items as persimmon bread, cornmeal, and bear oil to the town markets. Acolapissas, Chitimachas, and Houmas who had resettled closer to New Orleans during the first two decades of the eighteenth century regularly produced corn, fish, and game for city dwellers and travelers. On the Pearl River, between New Orleans and Biloxi, the Pensacolas, Biloxis, Pascagoulas, and Capinas furnished "an abundance of meat to all the French who are near enough to trade for it." Of a group of Chaouachas who migrated from the lower Mississippi to the Mobile River outside the town of Mobile, Bienville declared that "their sole occupation is to produce corn by means of which they obtain from the French what they need."[47] *Petites nations* who migrated to the lower Mississippi during the 1760s – Alibamons, Biloxis, Pascagoulas, and Chahtos – also participated in riverside trade and the New Orleans market. Altogether by the 1770s these ten or so villages, interspersed among plantations along the Mississippi, numbered about a thousand people. "Something similar to subdued tribes in New England," as noted by Bernard Romans, individuals from these communities "serve as hunters, and for some other laborious uses."[48] Peddling foodstuffs along with other traditional goods and providing itinerant services in Lower Mississippi Valley towns, as will be seen in subsequent chapters, continued to be important economic activities for many American Indians well into the nineteenth century.

Selling food items directly from their seasonal hunting camps was another form of Indian participation in the eighteenth-century regional economy that would last some time longer. During the winter months Indian villagers dispersed into small hunting parties of ten or so families. These mobile groups were such a regular feature of the landscape that they rarely drew special attention – except from visitors like Romans, who was hospitably welcomed in the winter of 1771–72 by more than one Choctaw hunting camp and who observed that "there only they will entertain a stranger at free cost." These Indian camps, spread along the Alabama, Mississippi, and Red River drainages, were principally occupied with producing for the deerskin trade, but they rarely neglected to exchange venison, bear meat, and tallow for ammunition, cloth, and drink with settlers and travelers whom they encountered during the hunting season.[49]

Perhaps the most remarkable contribution of American Indians to the frontier exchange economy was their involvement in livestock trade across the Lower Mississippi Valley. For a long time domestic beef was scarce and expensive in colonial Louisiana; early attempts to build herds from imported livestock proved fruitless. But a regional network of cattle trading gradually developed and, like other kinds of food exchange and the deerskin trade, involved extensive interethnic participation by Indians, slaves, and settlers. In the 1720s French traders and Indian villagers around Natchitoches began moving horses and cattle eastward, down the Red River. The Caddos, experienced horsemen since the mid–seventeenth century when Spanish livestock herded by other Indians began to reach their villages, exchanged cattle and horses with the French and other Indians.[50] The Tunicas and Avoyelles, situated near the junction of the Red and Mississippi Rivers, became important middlemen in the livestock trade; Le Page du Pratz praised the latter group "for the services they have done the colony by the horses, oxen, and cows they have brought from New Mexico."[51] The amount of beef available to Louisianians was increasing by the mid–eighteenth century, and some settlers were operating meat and dairy farms at Pointe Coupée, Barataria, and other places near New Orleans. On the prairies of southwestern Louisiana, meanwhile, Atakapa and Opelousa Indians were transporting cattle from the Trinity River area. This coastal route across grasslands and bayous was further expanded as Acadian immigrants joined Indians in the livestock trade and began raising their own herds.[52]

The participation of Indian villagers in fur and food marketing discloses closer interaction and greater cultural exchange with black slaves and white colonists than historians of colonial regions have generally portrayed. In this respect, trade in the Lower Mississippi Valley generated economic roles and ethnic relations similar in flexibility and fluidity to those discovered for African Americans in early North American colonies by historians during the 1970s.[53] Clearly, Indians did not just hunt, blacks did not just grow crops for export, and whites did not merely choose to become either subsistence farmers or staple planters. All of these groups improvised ways of securing some degree of economic autonomy while becoming increasingly entangled in the transatlantic colonial system. Many of these activities involved trade between different cultural groups. However, a complex of forces circumscribed economic and social relations and minimized the leveling potential of frontier exchange. The institution of slavery, European class divisions, racism, colonial policy, and violent conflict all contributed to the building of racial barriers in Louisiana and West Florida, especially after the demographic scale tipped unfavorably for Indians. The transformation of the Lower Mississippi Valley into an agricultural export economy, which accelerated during the last quarter of the eighteenth century, further intensified the hierarchical stratification of both race and class.

Changes in the deerskin trade implemented by Spain after 1783 signaled that the network of frontier exchange stitched by inhabitants over the previous decades was beginning to ravel. Indians of the larger interior nations, who had close ties to many traders, entered this period with high expectations of further commerce. Following the withdrawal of Great Britain from West Florida, the Choctaws, Chickasaws, and Upper Creeks negotiated new trade tariffs with the Spanish government in June 1784.[54] The deerskin trade, however, rapidly slipped under the control of a few merchant houses. The English firm of Panton, Leslie and Company, with Spanish authorization, began to monopolize trade with Indian villages east of the Mississippi. On the other side of the river, Natchitoches traders and settlers likewise gave way to better-financed and more-organized merchants.[55] Accelerated commercialization of the frontier exchange economy inexorably upset its traditional customs and patterns, as the following chapters will demonstrate. Most notably, traders carried ever-larger quantities of rum into Indian villages, the distribution of gifts occurred less often, and the tribes fell into chronic debt to merchant houses and thereby became more vulnerable to pressure against their land.

Sheer demographic force explains the gradual marginalization of Indians in the regional food market. As settlers increased in number and grew their own crops, the volume and variety of foodstuffs provided by Indian communities declined. Scattered bands of Louisiana Indians concentrated on bartering venison and bear oil with travelers and settlers mostly during winter months. The declining political power and economic importance of Indian nations also manifested itself in the formal sphere of relations, where gifts of food had customarily bound parties into a reciprocal relationship. A reduction in the level of intercolonial rivalry for Indian allegiance after 1783 diminished the willingness of Louisiana officials to share food with visiting Indians. Food thus became more strictly a market commodity just as the role of Indians in the marketplace was diminishing. Indians responded to this breakdown in food-giving protocol by committing acts of banditry against the livestock and crops of settlers, pursuing on a wider scale what the Natchez had resorted to back in the 1720s.[56]

By the end of the eighteenth century, the frontier exchange network was rapidly being superseded by the commercial production of cotton and sugar. Even so, people living in the region did not wholly relinquish older forms of economic exchange. American Indians continued to peddle foodstuffs and other goods along the waterways of the Lower Mississippi Valley and in the towns of Mobile, Natchez, and New Orleans. Subsistence and trade activities rooted in the frontier exchange economy became, as will be seen, important strategies of adaptation and resistance in face of new challenges.

The role of American Indians in the earlier economic life of the region evaded historians for a long time. Now by focusing on the Lower Mississippi Valley as a cross-cultural web of economic relations, Indian agency and versatility can be better appreciated. When one follows the movement of deerskins and foodstuffs through the extensive network of coastal and interior posts stretching from the Alabama River to the Red River, the importance of small-scale trade among diverse groups of people comes to light. Louisiana was indeed an extraordinary North American colony, imposing even less demographic and commercial pressure on the continent than did French Canada. But the backcountry of England's Atlantic seaboard provinces, as well as Canada and New Mexico, also passed through a long period of frontier exchange.[57] The form and content of interethnic relations discussed here, and made more visible by Louisiana's history, can be profitably explored at the obscure crossroads and marketplaces of other colonial regions.

1. Charles-Alexandre Lesueur,
Indian cabanne. Muséum
d'Histoire Naturelle, Le
Havre, France, no. 43129.

2. Lesueur, *James. Jamy.
Chawtas. A Petit Golphe
Mississippi. April 16, 1830.*
Muséum d'Histoire Naturelle,
Le Havre, France, no. 44123.

3. Lesueur, *Baton Rouge*.
Muséum d'Histoire Naturelle,
Le Havre, France, no. 44122.

4. Lesueur, *Jeu de peaume indian à la Nelle Orleans*. Muséum d'Histoire Naturelle, Le Havre, France, no. 44071.

5. Felix Achelle Beaupoil de Saint Aulaire, *Vue d'une Rue du Faubourg Marigny, Nlle Orleans*, lithograph by P. Langlume. The Historic New Orleans Collection, acc. no. 1937.2.2.

6. Beaupoil de Saint Aulaire, *Cours du Mississippi, au dessous de la Nelle Orleans*, lithograph by P. Langlume. The Historic New Orleans Collection, acc. no. 1937.2.7.

5

6

7. Karl Bodmer, *Billie, a Choctaw Man.* Joslyn Art Museum, Omaha, Nebraska; gift of the Enron Art Foundation.

8. Bodmer, *Tshanny, a Choctaw Man.* Joslyn Art Museum, Omaha, Nebraska; gift of the Enron Art Foundation.

9

10

9. Bodmer, *Choctaws at New Orleans*. Joslyn Art Museum, Omaha, Nebraska; gift of the Enron Art Foundation.

10. Bodmer, *Choctaws at Natchez*. Joslyn Art Museum, Omaha, Nebraska; gift of the Enron Art Foundation.

11. Bodmer, *Choctaw Camp on the Mississippi*. Joslyn Art Museum, Omaha, Nebraska; gift of the Enron Art Foundation.

12

13

12. Alfred Boisseau, *Louisiana
Indians Walking along a
Bayou*. New Orleans Museum
of Art; gift of William E.
Groves.

13. François Bernard, *Choctaw
Village near the Chefuncte*.
Peabody Museum, Harvard
University, photograph by
Hillel Burger.

14. Bernard, *Louisiana Indian
Encampment*. The Historic
New Orleans Collection, acc.
no. 1992.129.5.

15. Alfred R. Waud, *Sunday in New Orleans – The French Market, Harper's Weekly*, 18 August 1866, p. 517. Original drawing, The Historic New Orleans Collection, acc. no. 1951.68.

16. Waud, *Indian Gumbo Sellers. French Market. New Orleans.* The Historic New Orleans Collection, acc. no. 1950.56.

17. W. A. Rogers, *In the French Market, Harper's Weekly*, 30 December 1899, p. 1326. Watercolor sketch, The Historic New Orleans Collection, acc. no. 1974.25.20.58.

In the French Market.

18. Edward L. Wilson, Indian
filé vendor at French market.
Hand-colored glass slide, The
Historic New Orleans Collection, 1982.127.188.

19. Paul Hammersmith, *French
Market. N.O. Feb. 1891.* The
Historic New Orleans Collec-
tion, acc. no. 1977.79.13.

20. Unknown, photograph of
Indian women on banquette.
The Historic New Orleans
Collection, acc. no.
1974.25.20.60.

19

20

21. J. Dallas, drawing of
Indians in New Orleans
market, *Emerson's Magazine
and Putnam's Monthly* 5
(October 1857), p. 441.
Engraving, The Historic New
Orleans Collection, acc. no.
1974.25.20.53.

FIVE

American Indians and the
Early Cotton Economy

The popular view of how the Cotton South began tells us that Eli Whitney's cotton gin overcame the only real barrier to the expansion of commercial agriculture and slavery into "unsettled" parts of the Deep South. With industrialized textile factories demanding larger quantities of cotton, manufacturers and merchants indeed began during the 1790s to encourage cotton agriculture in North America as well as in Asia, West Africa, Brazil, and the Caribbean. Their demand for more cotton supplies coincided with a sharp drop in the prices of tobacco, rice, and indigo due to glutted markets and the removal of bounties by European importers. To avert financial losses from declining prices of those staples, more and more cultivators attempted to grow cotton in upland areas of the South. Influenced by the promotional campaign of English industrialists, governments in the British Caribbean, the American state of Georgia, and the Spanish colony of Louisiana rewarded experimentation with gins that could accelerate the separation of seeds from the tightly clinging fiber of green-seed, short-staple cotton – the variety that grew best in the southern interior.[1]

Little is known, however, about the less benign economic changes wrought within regions undergoing that agricultural expansion, especially those experienced by American Indians. The takeoff of cotton production in the Lower Mississippi Valley coincided with a decline in the deerskin trade still important to most Indian communities as they entered the nineteenth century. No sooner did the United States carve out the Mississippi Territory from the region in 1798 than did government officials accelerate these economic processes by manipulating trade debts of Choctaw, Chickasaw, and Creek leaders, with cooperation from merchants familiar with Indian commerce, into cessions of land from the tribes. Indian peoples coped with their diminishing land base through different economic strategies. Some groups migrated out of the territory, but most remained and tried to diversify trade with the United States, became itinerant laborers and vendors, or intensified their own horticultural production. Concentration on the territorial period of Mississippi history allows us to examine initiatives taken by Lower Mississippi Valley Indians in the face of rapid change – before they confronted the influences of Protestant missionaries or the pressures of government removal.[2]

Changing relations with American settlers and African-American slaves also shaped Indian life in the early cotton economy. With noteworthy irony many of these newcomers, who are usually cast by historians in a simplistic shove against Indians, relied on economic exchange with Indians or on other economic activities resembling Indian livelihood. Migrants from eastern parts of the United States, in other words, were following the pattern of earlier colonial immigrants to the Lower Mississippi Valley. Nevertheless, a widening separation between racial groups occurred during the territorial years as laws and patrols tried to restrict economic relations and activities among Indians and blacks. The transformation of the region into the cotton states of Mississippi in 1817 and Alabama in 1819 also involved the use of military force to quell slave rebellion and Indian resistance. Examination of Indians' economic relations with both citizens and slaves in the Mississippi Territory, therefore, reveals significant dimensions of the incipient cotton economy in the early-nineteenth-century South.

By 1793, when use of Whitney's patented gin began to spread across the southern hinterland, the region between the Chattahoochee and the Mississippi Rivers was still very much Indian country. The Indian population in that area numbered at least thirty thousand individuals, most of whom lived in the more than one hundred villages that constituted the Creek, Choctaw, and Chickasaw nations. Within the same territory were only about twenty-five hundred whites and two thousand blacks, mostly concentrated in settlements along the lower Tombigbee River and around the Natchez banks of the Mississippi.[3] In order to counteract the United States's claims to territory and its demands for navigating the Mississippi River, Spanish officials made serious efforts during the 1790s to attract American settlers to Louisiana. A generous land policy offered immigrants sizable grants of free land in proportion to the size of their families and the number of their laborers. Larger diplomatic considerations, however, compelled Spain in the Treaty of San Lorenzo in 1795 to cede to the United States all land east of the Mississippi River and above the thirty-first parallel. In 1798 the U.S. Congress organized that cession into the Mississippi Territory, which was by the turn of the century occupied by nearly five thousand whites, thirty-five thousand black slaves, and two hundred free blacks, in addition to more than thirty thousand Indians.[4]

Indian nations not only comprised the majority of the new territory's population in 1798 but held title, guaranteed by treaties with both Spain and the United States, to most of its land. Indian policy, therefore, was an integral priority in the U.S. government's territorial organization of Mississippi. The United States entered the nineteenth century with four major goals in Indian affairs. The first goal of establishing and maintaining alliances with tribes required, in compliance with Indian customs, a well-regulated, steady trade relationship. In the Mississippi Territory the task was especially difficult because Spain, which had developed strong political and commercial ties with the tribes of the area, possessed adjacent territories – Louisiana until 1803 and Florida until 1819. To enforce a second policy goal, the maintenance of peace and order among Indian peoples and between them and American citizens, U.S. agents in the Mississippi Territory entered a highly volatile world shaped by two decades of Anglo-American encroachment into Indian country and of intertribal struggle over diminishing resources. As reported by Governor Winthrop Sargent in 1799, the Choctaws already felt "that their Country once affording abundance had become desolate by the hands of a People who knew them not but to increase their Wretchedness."[5] Partially to diffuse resentment among Indians over such conditions and to make them more tractable, the government also pursued a third goal of reforming Indian societies by teaching "the Arts of husbandry, and domestic manufactures" and encouraging, as Secretary of War Henry Dearborn further suggested to Choctaw agent Silas Dinsmoor, "the growth of Cotton as well as Grain." Finally and most importantly, the goal of acquiring land cessions from Indian nations shaped policy in the Mississippi Territory. "The time will come when a cession of land may be necessary to us and not injurious to them," Secretary of State Timothy Pickering informed Sargent. Suggesting how bribery might work as a means toward effecting that end, he mentioned that when the time came "the grant of an annuity should be the consideration."[6]

An important instrument for implementing all the goals was the establishment of government trading posts among the many tribes of the eastern woodlands and midwestern prairies. The first two having been legislated into existence by Congress in 1795, those stores or trade factories provided Indians with fixed exchange rates and ample supplies of merchandise and thereby facilitated regulation of Indian trade. A factory among the Creeks began at Colerain on the St. Marys River in 1795 and moved in succeeding years to more western locations. In 1802 a Chickasaw store was constructed at Chickasaw Bluffs near present-day Memphis, and a Choctaw post opened at Fort St. Stephens on the Tombigbee River. Daily records for those trade houses reveal that on a local level Indian commerce and trading practices were important facets of life in early-nineteenth-century Mississippi. Indians daily exchanged deerskins, beeswax, and small animal skins for cloth, blankets, ammunition, and steel implements. During the first decade of the century, when the U.S. factories purchased deerskins at twenty cents per pound, the Choctaw post alone exported over twenty thousand dollars' worth of peltry each year.[7]

Although on a day-to-day basis the trade houses allowed familiar economic activities to continue, their function of extending credit to individual chiefs and traders actually facilitated the displacement in the Lower Mississippi Valley of a frontier exchange economy by a cotton export economy. Most transactions were carried out by barter, but certain persons were allowed goods in advance of payment. Chiefs, captains, interpreters, and traders – many of mixed ancestry – fell into increasing debt to the factories. In the Choctaw nation, for example, of the $3,875 due to the U.S. trade house at the end of 1809, Mushulatubbee, son of the recently deceased Mingo Homastubbee, owed $1,059; Captain Tisho Hollatlak owed $616; Mingo Pushmataha, $499; mixed-blood traders John Forbes and William Jones, $290 and $229, respectively; and interpreter John Pitchlynn, $180. Between 1802 and 1815, deerskins passed through Fort St. Stephens in abundance, but by the end of that period the Choctaws still owed $7,500 to the United States. The drop in the price paid for deerskins in 1812 from twenty to seventeen cents per pound made it even more difficult to meet their obligations: the Choctaws produced 2,317 more pounds in 1812 than in 1811, but they earned $158 less. While the literature on U.S. trade houses has tended to emphasize losses incurred by the government, the impact of a deteriorating trade position on Indian livelihood evidenced at the factories has remained poorly understood.[8]

At a time when prices for deerskins were dropping in Europe and when supplies of game were diminishing in the southeastern woodlands, the economic position of Indians was further exacerbated by the fiscal tightening exerted by their private and public trading partners. Through most of the eighteenth century, colonial officials and merchants had followed Indian trade protocol, which included the practices of offering presents, smoking the calumet, and sharing food. By the end of the century, however, the United States began to discourage outright gift giving and, through its trade houses, to replace what had been political obligations with accountable debts. Influential leaders and intermediary traders still received extra merchandise for their peltry, but each advance was now carefully recorded in the debt column of the tribe's account book. In the Mississippi Territory the results of that practice materialized first among the Creeks in the Treaty of Fort Wilkinson in 1802. Of the twenty-five thousand dollars received by the tribe for a cession of land between the Oconee and the Ocmulgee Rivers, ten thousand dollars went "to satisfy certain debts due from Indians and white persons of the Creek country to the factory of the United States."[9]

After sending the Creek treaty to Congress, President Thomas Jefferson turned his attention to that portion of Chickasaw territory "of first importance to us" and evaluated several means through which the United States "may advance towards our object." One means was to encourage plow agriculture, which would reduce the acreage of farmland needed by Indians; another was to nourish their allegiance "by every act of justice & of favor which we can possibly render them." But a third approach involved selectively extending credit to draw the Chickasaws into debt. Jefferson realized it would be beneficial "to establish among them a factory or factories for furnishing them with all the necessaries and comforts they may wish (spirituous liquors excepted), encouraging these and especially their leading men, to run in debt for these beyond their individual means of paying; and whenever in that situation, they will always cede lands to rid themselves of debt."[10] Within a few months Governor William C. C. Claiborne of Mississippi instructed agent Samuel Mitchell to sound "some of the chiefs" of the Chickasaws on whether "the nation is willing to assume and pay the debts of individuals . . . by a sale of some of their lands to the United States." In July 1805 the Chickasaw tribe signed a treaty ceding all claim to lands north of the Tennessee River in exchange for $20,000 "for the use of the nation at large, and for the payment of the debts due to their merchants and traders." Of that sum, $12,000 went to merchant Forbes, who had participated directly in the treaty negotiations.[11]

The firm Panton, Leslie and Company in Spanish West Florida, renamed John Forbes and Company in 1804, had been trading for deerskins with Indian villagers across the Gulf South since 1783. After the Treaty of San Lorenzo was made in 1795, the company initiated appeals to the United States for assistance in collecting approximately $170,000 claimed from the Creeks, Chickasaws, Choctaws, and Cherokees. As its commerce shifted to buying and exporting cotton through Mobile and Pensacola, the firm became less dependent on Indian trade and more determined to force payment of outstanding Indian debts. In 1797 partner Forbes visited Governor William Blount of Tennessee, "in order to arrange the affairs of the Panton firm and to prevent the ruin of its trade." John McKee, a confidant of Blount later to be appointed U.S. agent to the Choctaws, was welcomed at the company's houses in Mobile and Pensacola shortly after Forbes returned to the coast. In a letter to Benjamin Hawkins, U.S. agent to the Creeks, William Panton tossed out the idea of extinguishing the debts of Indians "by a sale of some part of their lands." Recognizing the federal government's prohibition against any land cession without its sanction, Panton appealed for such support. If a cession to the company proved "inadmissible," he requested that "some other means will be pointed out equally commensurate with the object."[12]

Like the Chickasaw treaty of 1805, the Treaty of Mount Dexter made with the Choctaws that same year illustrates pointedly how, to their mutual benefit, the company and the United States worked out "some other means." With the cotton boom underway at the opening of the nineteenth century, officials of the Jefferson administration sought from the Choctaw nation some of the fertile land that stretched between the Alabama and the Mississippi Rivers and discerned a convenient means of acquiring such a cession in the nearly fifty thousand dollars owed by the Choctaws to the Forbes company. In 1803 Dearborn signaled to General James Wilkinson in the Mississippi Territory that "if no other consideration will induce the Chocktaws to part with any of their lands but that of paying off the debt they owe Panton & Co.," agent Dinsmoor should inquire into the willingness of tribal divisions to pay their respective shares out of lands sold west of the Yazoo River and east of the lower Tombigbee.[13] Ephraim Kirby, first sent to the territory as land commissioner and then appointed judge, observed that lands on the east bank of the Tombigbee are fertile and not subject to inundation, "in all respects suitable for the most extensive operations of husbandry." Noting "poverty and distress" among the Choctaws due to scarce game and debauching contacts with settlers, the Connecticut Republican suggested that "through the agency of the white traders settled among them, they may be pursuaded to exchange their country for a portion of the wilderness of Louisiana."[14]

By the time the United States began to pursue aggressively a Choctaw cession, the Forbes company was already employing its influence "in procuring the assent of the Indians." As recalled by partner William Simpson, "we exerted ourselves with the Chiefs of the Nation & spent much time, labor & Money" in encouraging a sale of land to the United States. We still need to uncover more details about the company's intrigue with the federal government and its brokers in the Choctaw nation and about the dissent and discord that it incited among the Choctaw people. But we already know that during 1804 Forbes corresponded with and even visited the secretary of war, having already convinced Choctaw leaders one year earlier to request the United States to purchase land for the purpose of paying their debts to the firm. The Jefferson administration had declined that offer because portions of territory designated by the tribe were not those specifically desired. But with pressure from its creditors persisting, the Choctaw nation sent a petition to President Jefferson in August 1804 proposing a cession acceptable to the government.[15]

Of the $50,000 offered the Choctaws for those four million acres of land, $48,000 were reserved for discharging their debt to the Forbes company. The United States also promised the tribe an annuity of $3,000 in merchandise. Each of the three "great medal mingoes" – Puckshenubbee, Homastubbee, and Pushmataha – was granted $500 "in consideration of past services in their nation" and was offered an annuity of $150 "during their continuance in office." Villagers who used the ceded area directed most of their opposition to the treaty against those leaders, but to little avail. Because the Treaty of Mount Dexter produced lands in the less fertile pine barrens and swamps of southern Mississippi rather than in the rich Yazoo River delta targeted in the commissioners' instructions, Jefferson did not submit it to the Senate for ratification until 1808, when foreign affairs made "a strong settlement of militia along our southern frontier" and the "consolidation of the Mississippi territory" important considerations. By April 1809 the Forbes company received most of what it claimed against the Choctaws' account, minus $4,304.25 disputed by agent Dinsmoor.[16]

The Treaty of Mount Dexter and other Choctaw, Creek, and Chickasaw treaties made during the first decade of the Mississippi Territory's existence reflected the entanglement of Lower Mississippi Valley Indians in a chronic cycle of trade indebtedness and land cessions, a cycle that would steadily weaken their power and eventually culminate in removal. By 1822 the Choctaw nation, for example, ceded nearly thirteen million acres of land but still owed approximately thirteen thousand dollars to the U.S. trade house. The transfer of Indian land to the United States was further accelerated, as the

Choctaw and Chickasaw treaties of 1805 explicitly illustrate, by cooperation between the federal government and merchant companies – a lesson that would not be lost on future administrators of Indian affairs.[17]

Indian inhabitants of the Mississippi Territory responded to their deteriorating economic position in a variety of ways, evincing a resourceful adaptability among American Indians too often neglected by historians. Beginning in the late eighteenth century, numerous Choctaw families and even some Creek villagers migrated across the Mississippi River and settled in the still-plentiful hunting grounds of the Ouachita, Red, and Atchafalaya river basins.[18] As government trade-house records reveal, those who remained in their homelands continued to produce, although at a diminishing rate, deerskins and other furs. Still hoping to perpetuate their exchange economy through adaptation to new circumstances, Indian men and women provided an array of other goods and services to the trade stores. On 21 September 1807 the Choctaw factor, Joseph Chambers, bought a "small Brown horse" from a Choctaw named Annuckwyer for fifty dollars. In January 1809 he "Bartered with an Indian" two yards of stroud valued at $3.50 for a "Canoe" [pirogue] that he gave to the trade house. During the five years from 1809 through 1813, the Choctaw factory received $22,877 worth of raw deerskins (44,232 skins), $4,109 worth of dressed deerskins, raccoon, lynx, and other miscellaneous pelts, $1,749 worth of beeswax (7,958 pounds), $145 worth of tallow (1,161 pounds), $249 worth of corn (443 barrels), and $24 worth of snakeroot (96 pounds). Indians occasionally sold their labor to the trade house in exchange for merchandise, working as boat hands, messengers, and day workers. In May 1817 thirteen Choctaw women spent a day and four Choctaw men three days "beating skins" for their board, valued at thirty-seven and a half cents per day for each worker. A Choctaw named Tichbayan earned $5.50 cash for carrying "sundry packets and letters" from the government agent in the Choctaw nation to Fort St. Stephens.[19]

Many Indians became seasonal laborers on farms and plantations of the Mississippi Territory, constituting the cotton economy's first migrant work force. "The pine woods . . . between the Choctaw nation and the inhabitants of the Mississippi territory," Fortescue Cuming observed in 1808, "does not prevent the Indians from bringing their squaws every fall and winter to aid in gathering in the cotton crop, for which they are paid in blankets, stroud (a blue cloth used by them for clothing), handkerchiefs, and worsted binding of various colours besides other articles of manufactured goods, which are charged to them at most exorbitant prices."[20] John A. Watkins recalled his first acquaintance with the Choctaws in 1813–14, "as they came into Jefferson Co. in the fall and winter in large numbers, the women to pick cotton, the men to hunt in the Louisiana swamps." From bark-covered huts that were always left open on the south side, hunters pursued deer and bear across the Mississippi while women worked in cotton fields east of the river. When John McKee arrived at the Choctaw agency in November 1814 to recruit warriors, he "found the towns abandoned, the people had either gone hunting or into the settlements to pick cotton."[21]

Choctaws also used the bustling towns of Mobile and Natchez as marketplaces for the produce of their own villages and camps. Throughout the eighteenth century the Gulf port of Mobile had been a very familiar place for Choctaw trade, and many families continued to market foodstuffs, pelts, horses, baskets, and firewood there well into the nineteenth century.[22] Over the territorial years of Mississippi history, however, Choctaws made their most prominent urban presence felt at the Mississippi River town of Natchez. Indian visitors were accustomed to receiving presents and provisions from Spanish officials at Natchez, but formal gift-giving declined under American dominion. "I have no Presents to make, and very seldom supply them with provisions," reported Governor Claiborne in 1802, "but they notwithstanding, will not, & cannot be persuaded to remain in their own lands." The United States's infraction of official protocol was exacerbated by frequent acts of ill treatment and violence committed against Indian travelers by territorial citizens. With as many as three hundred Choctaw men, women, and children encamped within six miles of town, Claiborne admitted to Secretary of State James Madison in April that it was "difficult to shield the Indians from much violence." Contributing to tense relations, Indians in and around Natchez frequently killed livestock, robbed households, and begged for food – partly expressions of protest against the government's penury and partly acts of desperation during famine.[23]

Illegal forms of economic exchange sometimes tested the diplomacy of native and territorial leaders alike. Laws prohibiting the sale of alcohol to Indians were less enforceable in cities than within Indian nations. Deerskins, bear oil, and venison carried into Natchez by Choctaws, as described by John Watkins, "were usually exchanged for blankets, stroud & calico supplemented by a jug of whiskey." In a letter to Ochchummey, a chief of the Upper Choctaw district, Claiborne pleaded helplessness: "Brothers! when the Choctaws come to Natchez I do everything I can to keep whiskey from them, but some of my bad men will sell liquor to the Indians." Most injuries and deaths suffered by Indians in town involved intoxication. In April 1803, for example, a drunken brawl between some Choctaws and Mississippi River boatmen at the Natchez landing resulted in several Indian men being wounded, one mortally.[24] Fear of reprisal in such cases caused territorial officials to pay merchandise to relatives of victims in compensation of their loss. The Choctaws insisted upon trying and punishing their own people when they were accused of criminal activity, but the governor often threatened to deal with them "according to the White People's Laws."[25] Acquittal by the territorial court of most persons responsible for Indian fatalities deepened resentment. In November 1812 a man named Lewis accused an Indian of stealing his gun "and by way of satisfaction tied him to a tree and gave him about thirty lashes." Lewis released him from the tree but left his hands tied, and the Indian apparently fell to his death from the Natchez bluff. When the perpetrator of this deed was acquitted of murder, Governor David Holmes anticipated "that the friends of the Indian will not be satisfied with this verdict."[26]

Occasional altercations and depredations tested the jurisdictional boundaries between Indian country and U.S. territory and therefore received notable attention in official records. But more prosaic forms of exchange between Indians and non-Indians in Natchez did not go unnoticed. Visitors described in detail a ubiquitous presence of Choctaws in the city's ethnically heterogeneous populace. They peddled goods on the streets, worked for wages at the dock, and played ball on the outskirts of town.[27] In 1808 boats were being greeted at the Natchez landing by a musical band of about forty Indian men, women, and children. Some played wind, percussive, and string instruments made from cane, while a drummer struck a two-gallon tin kettle covered with a buckskin. Their solemn march to the arriving boat, climaxed in dance and song, was reminiscent of the calumet ceremonies that greeted so many travelers in previous centuries. Only now, these Indian musicians expected "a little money, whiskey, or provisions" from passengers either stopping or disembarking at the busy Natchez docks.[28]

In and around their own villages, meanwhile, Mississippi Indians also initiated some adaptive changes in order to improve the economic base of their diminishing tribal domains. Many had been raising livestock for some time, but at the beginning of the nineteenth century that activity became a more important means of livelihood with significant impact on settlement patterns. As more grazing land was needed and as immigrants and travelers created a demand for foodstuffs, Indian villages began to spread outward from their previously more compact centers. The process was most visible among the Upper Creeks, many of whom settled on the outskirts of their towns as they became more attentive to cattle, hogs, and horses. The inhabitants of Hoithlewalli, for example, formed new settlements with fenced-in fields along the small tributaries of the Oakfuskee Creek, once reserved by the town for bear hunting and now providing "delightful range for stock."[29] Choctaw and Chickasaw farmers also homesteaded outward from their villages during the early territorial period. Traveling from Natchez to the Chickasaw nation in the summer of 1805, Dr. Rush Nutt observed some Choctaws "building log houses & cultivating the earth in corn, cotton, & other garden vegetables." Farther along the Natchez Trace – at Chukasalaya, Estockshish, and Bear Creek – he found Chickasaws establishing supply stations for travelers, raising "plenty of hogs & cattle," and farming grain crops. Chickasaw families were also settling westward in the Yazoo delta in order to use better range for their horses, cattle, and hogs.[30]

Although the expanding cotton economy ultimately threatened to displace the frontier exchange economy, Lower Mississippi Valley Indians in the early nineteenth century had good reason to expect that accommodation to new challenges would help preserve their autonomy and territory. Over the eighteenth century, after all, Indians had adopted European and African food crops, developed their own herds of livestock, and traded those and other items to colonists. In keeping with that pattern of effective adaptation, Indian villagers in the Mississippi Territory began to grow their own cotton for the export market. As early as 1802 about twelve Choctaw families reportedly "commenced the culture of cotton." Chickasaws were soon bringing cotton produced in their own fields to the federal store at Chickasaw Bluffs. George Colbert, a chief and planter of mixed descent, built a cotton gin for himself and fellow Chickasaws who raised cotton at what became the town of Cotton Gin Port on the upper Tombigbee River.[31] Deerskin traders Abram Mordecai and John and William Price established gins at "Weathersford's racetrack" and "the Boat Yard," both along the Alabama River, where they began purchasing cotton produced by Creek farmers.[32]

Indian communities in the Mississippi Territory continued to create economic niches for settlers and slaves, although their deerskin trade was rapidly declining in regional importance. Before the region became a U.S. territory, as already seen, many French and English traders had established their deerskin commerce in particular villages by marrying Indian women. Into the nineteenth century many of their offspring continued to play prominent roles in the regional economy and were joined by American newcomers licensed by the territorial government. As transportation on roads through Indian country increased, some of those traders even opened facilities that provided food and lodging to travelers. In addition to the actual traders who dealt directly with Indian villagers, Indian commerce employed black as well as white laborers at several different tasks: transporting products by packhorses or by boats, helping to preserve and to pack the deerskins, and doing construction work on the facilities. At both private trade firms and government factories, settlers worked for wages, and slaves were hired out by their owners. The experience among Indians gained by some slaves, particularly those owned by whites and Indians engaged in trade, was evident to early territorial witnesses by the presence of African Americans in settlements and villages who could interpret between the various Indian languages and English.[33]

Obstacles to landownership and uncertainties of cotton production during the territorial years challenged settlers in Mississippi to find means of livelihood that resembled the Indian mixture of hunting, farming, and herding. That adaptation by whites to the cotton market, more than the production of cotton itself, brought them face to face with local Indians. Before the United States even began to survey land in the Mississippi Territory, an estimated two thousand settlers had already squatted on unused lands. Governor Claiborne expressed hope in late 1802 "that these Citizens may be secured in their improvements, and that the Government will sell out the Vacant land in this district upon moderate terms and in small tracts to actual settlers." U.S. land policy, however, was committed to selling large rectangular tracts of land for revenues drastically needed by the treasury. Thus in March 1803 Congress extended to the Mississippi Territory the prescription that a minimum of 320 acres had to be purchased at two dollars per acre with one-fourth of the cost paid in cash at the sale or the registration. For people actually migrating into the territory, that system caused much anxiety because it encouraged speculation by land companies and required a minimum purchase unaffordable to many settlers.[34]

Several hundred Mississippi petitioners, many of them drawn to the region by the prospects of growing cotton, asked Congress in 1803 to encourage small holdings instead of large holdings, to prohibit land speculation, to reduce the national army, and to inhibit the spread of slavery. Congress responded to appeals by discontented territorial settlers both north and south of the Ohio River with new legislation in 1804 instituting the public sale of smaller tracts, 160 acres in quarter-sections, and reducing the minimum auction price to $1.25 per acre. Conditions in the Mississippi Territory, however, militated against a speedy and democratic distribution of land. The survey of lands languished for a long time, and public auctions of available tracts did not begin until August 1809. As reported by William Lattimore in 1806, the expectation by families moving into the region "of being able to purchase lands of the Government . . . has not been realized." Not enough cleared land existed for them to rent from those who already owned landed property, and the cost of purchasing land from private sellers "was beyond their resources." The only other alternatives available to settlers were to return to their home states, to acquire land "upon the easiest terms" in the Spanish colony of Florida, and to squat on vacant lands of the United States in hope of securing preemption rights to their improvements; most migrants to the Mississippi Territory chose the last, although an unknown number did resort to the other alternatives. But just when claimants were allowed to begin purchasing their preempted lands in 1809, the price of cotton began to drop sharply mainly because of the embargo imposed by the federal government in 1808. Although cotton in New Orleans had been dropping slightly from a high of twenty-five cents per pound in September 1805, after the embargo the price plummeted to twelve cents by September 1809.[35]

Farmers now faced the bleak prospect of forfeiting their newly acquired property, having counted on a promising income from cotton produced for the English market to pay off the installments due on their lands. As the territory entered the second decade of the nineteenth century, mounting hostility from the Creek Indians and impending war against Great Britain deepened uncertainty and instability, pushed down the value of cotton even more, and slowed the sale of public lands. In one petition sent to Congress by inhabitants of the Mississippi Territory, the trap that cotton already set for the South – an economy highly sensitive to the price of a single commodity – was clearly defined: "Confiding as we have done on the measures of Government which were intended to restore foreign intercourse, and which held out the probability of success, we have continued to cultivate the article of cotton, to the growth of which our soil is so propitious, and omited all or most other pursuits calculated to command money."[36]

Under these circumstances, squatting on the periphery of private landholdings and Indian villages or on federal lands and then raising livestock to sell to planters, townspeople, and newcomers became a pervasive means to economic security. Already familiar with open grazing in the backwoods of Georgia and the Carolinas, many settlers in Mississippi's promising pine forests acquired cattle, horses, and hogs from Indians. Some bought the animals; others sequestered strays. In time, a family of squatters might earn enough from its own herding to purchase title to the land, or if not, the mobility of livestock eased their relocation to another tract when threatened with eviction. Meanwhile, competition over grazing lands and ambiguity between trading and rustling heightened antagonism in their relations with Indians. Symbiotically, the success of some farmers in producing cotton and buying slaves – by creating a growing market for food – allowed those who were unable or unwilling to grow the staple a distinct avenue to economic security and social autonomy. From that process, among others, emerged the yeoman farmers of the nineteenth-century South, whose intermittent participation in the cotton economy through livestock trade buffered them from the risks of cotton agriculture and yet perpetuated their hopes of becoming slave-owning cotton farmers themselves.[37]

By the second decade of the nineteenth century, the Mississippi Territory was fast becoming a cotton export region. Within a decade the non-Indian population had surpassed the number of Indians, increasing nearly fivefold to more than twenty-three thousand settlers and seventeen thousand slaves. Although most white settlers still contended with obstacles to land acquisition and relied on multiple means of subsistence, planters who already possessed land or who could afford to purchase some in the private market committed more slaves to the production of more cotton. As one such individual described the process, "here you will ask, what do they want with so many negroes, the answer is, to make more Money – again, you will ask what do they want with so much Money, the answer is to buy more Negroes. . . . A Mans merit in this country, is estimated, according to the number of Negroes he works in the field."[38]

The influx of African-American slaves into the territory affected the economic life of Indians as deeply and equivocally as did white migration. More vulnerable to territorial laws than were Indians, African Americans also struggled to preserve some economic autonomy and resilience within the narrowing interstices of a slave-labor, cotton economy. By trading among themselves and with Indians and whites – in foodstuffs, home manufactures, and even forbidden horses – slaves tried to secure for themselves what is sometimes called an "internal economy," distinct from but tied to the larger regional system of staple agriculture.[39] But legislation and slave patrols discouraged forms of economic exchange and social interaction that had previously brought blacks and Indians together – for example, in weekend marketing on the streets of Natchez. Meanwhile, some individuals within the Indian nations – principally members of trade families with mixed ancestry – were themselves becoming owners of black slaves and planters of cotton. Although those developments eventually generated greater racial separation and stratification between American Indians and African Americans in the Lower Mississippi Valley, they were too nascent before 1820 to close all channels of interethnic communication.[40]

Throughout the colonial period slaves had perceived Indian country as a potential refuge from bondage, and the increasing presence there of blacks owned by tribal members during territorial years may have even encouraged some runaways to take advantage of the confusion accompanying the movement of slaves to and from Indian jurisdictions. Cases of slaves being arrested by U.S. Indian agents for "want of a passport" and disputes over ownership of slaves who "ran away or were stolen" suggest that the blacks involved were playing an active role in creating their uncertain status within Indian country.[41] Whether as slaves or as runaways, African Americans who interacted closely with American Indians during the early nineteenth century contributed to the formation of multiracial families and even of scattered communities across the Lower Mississippi Valley. One such community, whose members became known as "Cajuns of Alabama," grew rapidly during the territorial period along the west bank of the Mobile River; another group known as "Freejacks" took shape on the Tchefuncte River in Louisiana, along the Natchez–to–New Orleans road.[42]

Given the potential for increasing ties with blacks, Indians found their own activities and mobility being curtailed by the Mississippi territorial government's efforts to reinforce the institution of slavery. In addition to federal laws requiring licenses and prohibiting alcohol in Indian trade, which were enforced by all territorial governors, Governor Sargent issued an ordinance in May 1800 to strengthen control jointly over commerce with Indians and slaves in Mississippi.[43] "Ebriety of Indians and Negroes on Sundays," he had complained on arriving in Natchez, made it "a most Abominable place." Committed to reversing such customary trends, Sargent made the mere sight of an Indian or slave carrying into a house or store "any article which may be supposed for sale, or any bottle, jug or other thing in which liquor may be conveyed" sufficient evidence for convicting the storekeeper or housekeeper.[44] An initial law requiring slaves who participated in the Natchez marketplace to carry permits issued by their owners was extended over the entire territory in 1805 to declare that "no person whatsoever shall buy, sell, or receive of, to or from a slave, any commodity whatsoever without the leave or consent of the master, owner or overseer of such slave, expressive of the article so permitted to be bought, sold or bartered." Guilty persons would pay to receive ten lashes, and owners who allowed a slave "to go at large and trade as a freeman" had to pay a fine of fifty dollars. A statute enacted in 1810 further increased the risk of independent marketing to slaves by making it lawful for any citizen to apprehend a slave suspected of carrying goods without written consent.[45]

The exchange of two items in particular – cotton and horses – threatened the property of planters and received special attention from lawmakers. In the spring of 1800, slaves were prohibited from the "raising and Vending of Cotton" and from "holding property in horses." Although some owners apparently permitted those activities, both the need to prevent theft of those valuable products and the desire to limit avenues of financial independence activated a comprehensive prohibition against possession of cotton and horses by slaves. To reduce the chances of petty rustling by black and Indian herdsmen, an act of 4 March 1803 prescribed that "no person whosoever shall send or permit any slave or Indian to go into any of the woods or ranges in the territory, to brand or mark any horse, mare, colt, mule, ass, cattle, sheep, under any pretence whatsoever; unless the slave be in company, and under the direction of some reputable white person."[46]

Behind all of the legislative and police action directed against slaves and Indians reigned a deep anxiety over black insurrection, Indian warfare, and even combined rebellion by the two groups. News of a slave revolt that was barely averted in Virginia drove Sargent to address a circular letter of 16 November 1800 to slave owners in the Mississippi Territory, exhorting "the utmost Vigilance" toward all slaves. Recent assaults on two overseers were evidence enough that greater attention to the slave laws had to be given by "all good Citizens." Fear that the increasing in-migration of slaves would introduce experienced insurgents from other slave regions nearly produced in the territorial legislation a law that would have prohibited the importation of "Male Slaves, above the age of Sixteen."[47]

The self-conscious endeavor by white Mississippians to establish slavery safely in the midst of a large Indian population elicited from their officials an obsessive concern with well-organized and trained militias, adequate weaponry, and responsive federal army – all overtly effective means of controlling subjugated ethnic groups. Although military officials repeatedly assured the government that the army and the militia were prepared to quell any outbreak of Indian or black hostility, the very prospect of having to mobilize against rebellion in one part of the territory heightened the fear of exposing another part to concurrent attack. In January 1811 hundreds of slaves in the adjacent territory of Louisiana turned their hoes and axes against planters outside New Orleans. Their march toward the city was quickly and violently stopped by troops of the U.S. Army's Southern Division, led by the cotton planter General Wade Hampton.[48] That revolt, which resulted in the brutal and speedy killing of nearly one hundred African Americans in Louisiana, intensified apprehension in the Mississippi Territory over thinly stretched defenses against both external and internal enemies. The declaration of war against Great Britain in 1812 then brought the fear of racial war on different fronts to a climax. In a letter to General Wilkinson concerning possible withdrawal of troops from the territory for action elsewhere, Governor Holmes recited his faith in the friendship of the Choctaws but warned that "knowledge of our defenceless state . . . may tempt them to commit aggressions." Regarding blacks, Holmes continued, "Of the slaves, who compose so large a portion of our population I entertain much stronger apprehensions. Scarcely a day passes without my receiving some information relative to the designs of those people to insurrect."[49]

The Creek War of 1813–14, waged in the eastern valleys of the Mississippi Territory, has recently received skillful attention in regard to both its wide context of international and intertribal affairs and its internal dimension of tribal culture and politics.[50] But the function of the military conflict in expanding the cotton economy and in enforcing concomitant racial control is not yet fully appreciated. As already indicated, the territorialization of Mississippi imposed multiple pressures upon Indian societies. In the Creek nation, those pressures provoked increasing rebelliousness from a large segment of its population. Persistent demands by the Forbes company and the U.S. government that trade debts be paid through cessions of land severely tested the patience of Creek villagers. Indian leaders contested debts that were accounted to the nation but that actually had been incurred by individuals whose tribal status they did not recognize. When the company tried to add interest to their account, the Creeks grew angrier, insisting that "there was no word for it in their language" and accusing their old trade partner of wanting "to tear the very flesh off their backs."[51]

Further aggravating those issues, settlers were sprawling from the Tennessee and Tombigbee-Alabama Valleys, and territorial militiamen were making frequent border patrols into Creek country. The government's program of reforming, or "civilizing," Indian societies, which was aggressively implemented among the Lower Creeks by agent Hawkins, undermined the ability of the Creek nation to respond effectively to such pressures by expediting the emergence of a new class of acculturated Creek citizens who were themselves becoming cotton planters and slave owners. The tour of the rising Shawnee leader, Tecumseh, among the southern tribes during the summer and fall of 1811 injected into the already factionalized Creek nation a surge of religious nativism and political militance, which took hold most strongly among the angry young men of the Upper Creek towns. In the summer of 1812 the tribal council ordered the execution of a group of Red Sticks, as the rebels were called, who were accused of killing settlers in Tennessee on their return from the town in Indiana where Tecumseh and his brother, the "Shawnee Prophet," resided. And in November it agreed to pay some twenty-two thousand dollars in debts owed the Forbes company by turning over to the firm each year the tribe's annuities from the United States. Those two explosive developments helped bring civil war to the Creek people by 1813.[52]

U.S. intervention against the rebellious Creeks came swiftly and forcefully, making the Mississippi Territory the theater of one of the nation's bloodiest and most costly Indian wars. In July 1813 a party of Red Sticks, carrying ammunition and other supplies from Pensacola, was attacked by a joint force of territorial militiamen and Lower Creek adversaries. In retaliation Creek rebels attacked Fort Mims at the confluence of the Alabama and the Tombigbee Rivers. On 30 August 1813 approximately 250 of the men, women, and children who had sought refuge inside the fort were killed during a siege that lasted five hours. News of the "massacre," which included reports that black slaves had joined the Red Sticks, threw the Mississippi Territory and adjacent states into an alarm that speedily mobilized soldiers and citizens into action.[53]

The invasion of Upper Creek country by four separate armies of militiamen and federal troops proved to be a painful experience for Indians and non-Indians. Red Stick fighters and their families managed to evade U.S. soldiers and their Indian allies, who in turn resorted to burning abandoned villages to the ground. After suffering ten months of sickness, hunger, desertion, and severe discipline, the invading armies backed the Creek rebels into a bend of the Tallapoosa River. On 27 March 1814 approximately one thousand Red Sticks stood up against a combined force of fourteen hundred whites, five hundred Cherokees, and one hundred Lower Creeks in the Battle of Horseshoe Bend, losing by the end of the day approximately eight hundred tribesmen killed. Having led personally the western Tennessee volunteers and provided much of the strategy in the Creek War, Andrew Jackson – a merchant, planter, and land speculator long interested in the Mississippi Territory – received command of the U.S. Army's Seventh Military District and proceeded to impose a peace treaty on the Creek nation. The beleaguered Creek leaders who signed the Treaty of Fort Jackson on 9 August 1814 agreed to cede fourteen million acres of land – more than one-half of present-day Alabama – even though most of them were Lower Creeks who had not rebelled against the United States.[54]

The military subjugation of the Creek Indians greatly accelerated the transformation of ethnic relations already underway in the Mississippi Territory. Indian trade in deerskins and other forms of frontier exchange would never return to their former importance in the Lower Mississippi Valley, forcing most Indian villagers to become marginal participants in the emerging cotton economy while allowing some to accumulate their own property in cotton lands and black slaves. Although banditry and violence would continue to serve many Indians in Mississippi and Alabama as means of resistance, the Creek War demonstrated the futility and danger of military confrontation and drove surviving militants out of the territory and into Florida. The Creek land cession that resulted from their defeat drastically contracted the area of Indian country and intensified the physical isolation of Indian villages from other inhabitants. Furthermore, the sudden availability of so much land to settlers, coinciding with the post-Napoleonic expansion of the demand for cotton in Europe, set in motion the great wave of public land sales and immigration that guaranteed the dominance of cotton agriculture over the territory's political offspring – the states of Mississippi and Alabama.

The "Alabama Fever," as the postwar boom in land sales and cotton production was called, revived the conflict between immigrant settlers and land speculators. As the average price of public land in the Creek cession rose above five dollars per acre by 1818, crowds of angry squatters assembled at land auctions to push for registration of their claims at the minimum price. Hostility toward large purchasers was tempered, however, by the heady climb of cotton prices above thirty cents per pound. Eager to produce for such an export market, small farmers and wealthy planters alike borrowed more and more money in order to purchase both land and labor. In 1817, the year in which Alabama became a separate territory and Mississippi acquired statehood, cotton annually exported from the region exceeded seventeen million pounds. The fragile financial basis of the expansion, though, soon reached its breaking point. Just as Alabama was becoming a state, cotton prices plummeted in the panic of 1819 well below twenty cents per pound and stranded Alabamians with a land debt of eleven million dollars. But the cotton export economy had already taken hold of land and labor across the South. Following a short period of contraction and adjustment, white Mississippians and Alabamians proceeded to import more slaves from eastern states and to expand cotton production across more land, of course borrowing more money to finance both.[55]

Development of a cotton economy drastically altered social and economic relations of Indian peoples with citizens and slaves in the Mississippi Territory. The U.S. government, through its own trade houses and with cooperation from private companies, pressured Indian tribes into making repeated cessions of land. In the concomitant transfer of public land into the private market, the federal government allowed speculation by land companies and made ownership difficult for early-nineteenth-century migrants. Settlers coped with that obstacle and with the uncertainty of cotton production through means of livelihood similar to those of neighboring Indians. Territorial laws meanwhile restricted the economic activities of slaves and limited their interaction with free individuals, confining them more to the production of cotton for their owners. The Creek War, more than any other action, accelerated the physical confinement of Indians into ethnic enclaves. By 1820 an American Indian population of more than 30,000 persons was surrounded by 42,000 whites and 33,000 blacks in the state of Mississippi and by another 85,000 whites and 42,000 blacks in Alabama.[56]

While a new socioeconomic order originated from those processes, the strategies used to mitigate or to avert them created undercurrents of resistance that have been only slowly and inadequately uncovered by historians. The different economic adaptations selected variably by Indian inhabitants of the Mississippi Territory greatly influenced impending struggles over removal, with some committed to commercial agriculture becoming the most staunch defenders of tribal homelands.[57] Slaves in Mississippi and Alabama, meanwhile, continued to take economic initiatives in defiance of their owners' economic interests, maintaining a market in self-produced and pilfered goods reminiscent of earlier exchange with Indians and settlers. Although they had greater freedom of choice, nonslaveholding whites also struggled to secure a safe, albeit uneasy, relationship with the cotton export market. Becoming endemic to life in the nineteenth-century South, those widespread attempts to minimize dependence on the expanding cotton economy made the conquest of peoples and places by King Cotton more tenuous and complex than perhaps the participants themselves believed it to be. Old Carothers McCaslin bought the land, as portended by William Faulkner, "with white man's money from the wild men whose grandfathers without guns hunted it, and tamed and ordered or believed he had tamed and ordered it for the reason that the human beings he held in bondage and in the power of life and death had removed the forest from it and in their sweat scratched the surface of it to a depth of perhaps fourteen inches in order to grow something out of it which had not been there before and which could be translated back into the money he who believed he had bought it had had to pay to get it and hold it."[58]

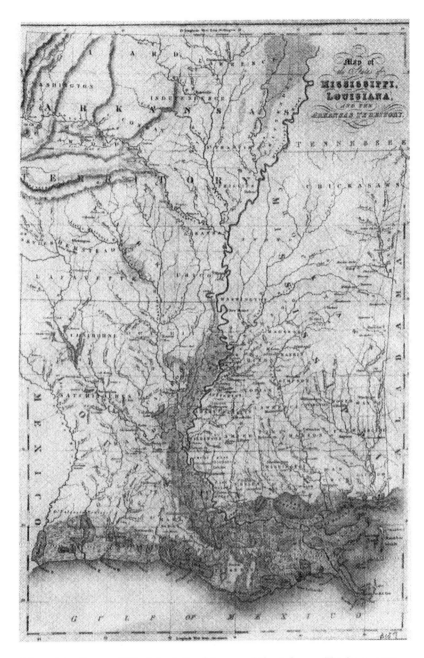

Map of the States of Mississippi, Louisiana, and the Arkansas Territory, 1831.
Special Collections Division, The University of Texas at Arlington Libraries.

SIX

Economic Strategies of American Indians in Louisiana during the Territorial and Early Statehood Era

Struggles in the realm of livelihood constitute an important borderland of American Indian adaptation and resistance to U.S. expansionism. Whether studying fur trade networks or reservation economies, historians are finally scrutinizing the initiatives taken by Indians themselves to maintain desirable forms of subsistence and exchange on their own terms. The diplomatic, military, and legal channels taken by American Indians in their struggles for independence have been well understood as strategies consciously selected by tribes. Choices made by Indian groups in the sphere of economic life, on the other hand, were less appreciated as calculated decisions about survival and identity. By focusing on economic strategies pursued by Indians in different colonial situations, historians are beginning to replace the stereotype of passive victims of dependency with a more accurate picture of resourceful participants in economic change.[1]

Many southern Indians during the early nineteenth century took up the production of cotton as a cash crop in order to reconcile their own interests with the forces of commercial encroachment. Some even became slaveowning planters.[2] Less familiar to us than this form of adaptation, however, was a more common Indian response to economic change. Many American Indians in the South resisted total subordination or relinquishment to the expanding cotton economy by marginalizing it within their own livelihood. Providing goods and services to local markets on a seasonal basis, activities that might themselves be considered marginal, actually helped Indians mitigate the immediate impact of capitalist expansion.[3]

American Indians in the Lower Mississippi Valley also used these economic strategies to redefine their cultural autonomy within a rapidly changing society. A new body of anthropological work in other regions has explored how American Indian groups shaped and reshaped their identity through economic relationships with colonial partners or patrons. As Indian communities lost control over their land and its resources to outside commercial interests, the symbolic or discursive value of subsistence practices became instrumental in the maintenance of a cultural boundary with others.[4] By representing their knowledge about local environments through an adaptive mix of foraging and farming practices and then defending their rights to this activity, Indians in Louisiana during the early nineteenth century tried to compensate somewhat for the loss of their land to the United States. Their separate identity in the midst of a skyrocketing number of American settlers and slaves came to depend more than ever on specialized production and seasonal migration on the margins of a plantation economy.

Amidst the establishment by the United States of the Mississippi Territory in 1798 and the Orleans Territory in 1804, Indians in the Lower Mississippi Valley played an active and dynamic role in adapting familiar means of subsistence and avenues of trade to new circumstances. Here we will explore how American Indians in the area that became the state of Louisiana coped with and adjusted to an encroaching plantation economy through their own production and exchange activities. Although subsistence needs and economic interests varied across the Indian population, all native communities sought some combination of pursuits that might protect their cultural and political autonomy while permitting them to participate in the wider society and economy. The dynamics of this process have been closely studied in parallel situations across Latin America but remain relatively obscure for Indians of North America.[5]

The struggles of Louisiana Indians in the political sphere of intercultural relations are somewhat more familiar than those in the socioeconomic one, and both were of course interconnected. In the Lower Mississippi Valley's uncertain international setting at the beginning of the nineteenth century, tribal delegates tried to perpetuate political ties with Spanish officials in both Florida and Louisiana. When some Choctaw chiefs visited New Orleans during the winter of 1799–1800, the Spanish government's Indian interpreter greeted them with presents and emphasized that "the Spaniards and Americans are now at peace, but are like two Traders in the same Town in their Nation, who are struggling who can get the most Skins – when they meet they Speak to each other, and behave with seeming friendship, though there is still a sourness in their hearts and in his most, who has the Smallest share of the Trade."[6] With messages like this reaching tribes from across the international boundary, Governor Winthrop Sargent of the newly formed Mississippi Territory of the United States had good reason to worry about his lack of gifts for distributing to Indian visitors and his need for an official

Choctaw interpreter at Natchez. But the secret cession of Louisiana from Spain to France in 1800 worked in favor of the United States, as Chickasaw and Choctaw emissaries grew frustrated with administrative confusion and indifference at New Orleans. A flutter of diplomatic activity broke out in 1803, when the French prefect arrived in New Orleans with abundant gifts. Only a few months after President Thomas Jefferson referred to "a light French breeze" reaching the Indians, a Creek chief in New Orleans warmly welcomed Pierre-Clément de Laussat with the words, "I have often thought that a huge cloud covered our horizon, but that a wind blowing from the other side of the great lake would arise and disperse it." The purchase of Louisiana from France, however, suddenly halted the prospect of diplomatic relief from the darkening cloud of U.S. dominion.[7]

The Louisiana Purchase gave territorial officials in Mississippi greater leeway to administer U.S. Indian policy more aggressively. For Indians inhabiting that territory, this meant that diplomacy was reduced exclusively to relations with a nation bent on their dispossession. Jefferson implored Congress to make the Louisiana Purchase itself "the means of tempting all our Indians on the east side of the Mississippi to remove to the west." In the act that divided this vast acquisition into the new territories of Orleans and Louisiana in 1804, the national legislature authorized the president "to stipulate with any Indian tribes residing thereon, for an exchange of lands, the property of the United States, on the west side of the Mississippi, in case the said tribes shall remove and settle thereon."[8] Like the Cherokees and Creeks farther east, Choctaws and Chickasaws living in villages nearest the Mississippi River were immediately targeted for negotiating such an exchange. Ephraim Kirby, land commissioner and judge in the Mississippi Territory, informed Secretary of the Treasury Albert Gallatin in 1804 that at least some of the Indian nations had to be removed before the Tombigbee River valley "can become extensively useful." He thought that the Choctaws could be easily persuaded "to exchange their country for a portion of the wilderness of Louisiana," opening for cotton agriculture "a great tract of the best part of the United States."[9] But as we know, Choctaw and Chickasaw resistance to this design on their lands was strong enough to blunt Jefferson's initially aggressive approach and thereby postpone effective removal agreements until the 1820s.

The Indian population of the Orleans Territory, subject to U.S. policy beginning in 1804, comprised a widely dispersed mélange of ancient inhabitants and new migrants, all seeking a stable economic relationship with a more rapidly growing non-Indian population. As many as five thousand Indians then lived in the area that became the present state of Louisiana. Along the Mississippi below its confluence with the Red River, Houmas, Tunicas, and some Alibamons lived in villages interspersed among the region's largest plantations. Small communities of Chitimachas occupied the Atchafalaya basin, while just west of Bayou Teche stood a village of Atakapas and another of Opelousas. Along the Red River below Natchitoches there were several different villages of Biloxis, Apalaches, Alibamons, Pascagoulas, Chahtos, and Tensaws – groups that had crossed the Mississippi during the 1760s.[10]

Farther up the Red River, one thousand people of the Caddo nation were facing new challenges and opportunities during the early nineteenth century. As the most populous single group of Louisiana Indians, the Caddos occupied the borderland between U.S. territory and Spanish Texas. They had long benefited from rich agricultural resources, access to plains buffalo, and trade ties with eastern and western Indians. In the new geopolitical setting of the early 1800s, their location enhanced their diplomatic leverage with officials in Orleans Territory. Yet Caddo society and economy suffered from mounting pressures – old and new. The Osages to the north stepped up raids against Caddo villages, as immigrant groups of both Indians and whites moved into the Red River valley. The Caddos attempted to maintain ties with both Spanish and U.S. governments, although measures taken by Louisiana and Texas authorities to stop contraband trade across the disputed international boundary weakened the Indians' trade position. Fears over American filibusters, frontier bandits, and runaway slaves to the Spanish province further destabilized the western border of the Orleans Territory.[11]

A growing number of Indian migrants were permanently settling in the Orleans Territory, as a mobile Indian populace of itinerant traders and wage laborers crossed the Mississippi River from the east. Migration itself constituted an economic strategy, allowing for flexible and even innovative responses to sudden change. Goods and services provided by Indians in Natchez and elsewhere in the Mississippi Territory, as already seen, were part of a wider Indian access to Mississippi River traffic during the early nineteenth century. Countless camps of Indian families frequented the banks of the river, being perceived oftentimes as indigent outcasts and marauders. But a growing number of eastern Indians – Shawnees, Delawares, and Cherokees among others – traveled in small groups along the Mississippi and its tributaries in order to gather food for their own subsistence and for trade.[12] Between New Madrid and New Orleans these newcomers, along with Quapaws, Chickasaws, and Choctaws, engaged in ubiquitous exchanges with settlers, slaves, and sojourners. For such items as cloth, blankets, gunpowder, and liquor, these camps commonly traded peltry, game, wild fruits, bear oil, and honey.[13]

Various groups of Upper Creeks and Choctaws were making lands west of the Mississippi their new home, just as this territory became part of the United States. Since the 1770s Choctaw hunting parties had been expanding their wintertime exploitation of deer and other game west of the Mississippi. Clashes with the Caddos and more westerly Indians caused Spanish administrators many headaches, but futile efforts to contain the Choctaws gave way to a policy of territorial retrenchment through which many of these newcomers received rights to particular locales within Louisiana.[14] The commandant of Fort Miro on the Ouachita River complained about Choctaws moving into his district in the spring of 1787, when two Choctaw men took ten horses from white settlers on Bayou Bartholomew by threatening to kill them. But during the winter of 1788–89, Jean Baptiste Filhiol expressed a better opinion of some Choctaws trading at the fort.[15]

By the Louisiana Purchase at least fifteen hundred Choctaws had settled west of the Mississippi River. Two villages were situated around a trading post on the Ouachita River, near present-day Monroe, and were joined every winter by additional Choctaws who came only seasonally into this rich hunting land. South of Red River were two more Choctaw communities, one on Bayou Chico and another on Bayou Boeuf.[16] Coushattas began migrating across the Mississippi from Creek country during the 1790s, numbering by the Louisiana Purchase about five hundred people who lived along the Sabine River near present-day Toledo Bend Dam. Approximately one hundred Pacanas, another Creek group, were situated forty miles southeast on the Calcasieu River. After 1804 some Coushattas from the Sabine joined a group of Alibamons who resettled themselves on the Red River, 120 miles above Natchitoches, at the site of an abandoned Caddo town.[17]

U.S. trade and intercourse laws were extended to all of these Indian inhabitants of Orleans Territory through the congressional act of 26 March 1804 that created two territories out of the Louisiana Purchase. The first territorial governor of Orleans was William Claiborne, formerly governor of the Mississippi Territory and therefore an official already familiar with Indians in the Lower Mississippi Valley. Among his earliest deeds in Louisiana Indian affairs, Claiborne issued licenses to Indian traders. Bartholomew Schaumberg, for example, received permission to establish posts at both

Natchitoches and Ouachitas "for the purposes of carrying on trade with such neighboring Indians as may choose to visit those posts." District commandants were authorized to stop persons without licenses from trading with Indians and to prevent the sale of alcoholic beverages to Indians. A license required the trader to submit four thousand dollars as security "with a condition that he will traffic with the Indians for Peltry alone." Officials feared that traders would purchase horses and other plunder that might be smuggled by Indians from Texas into Louisiana.[18] In 1805 Dr. John Sibley was appointed Indian agent and a federal trade house was established at Natchitoches. The governor in New Orleans, unlike predecessors of the French and Spanish periods, had minimal contact with Indian delegations, receiving the nearby Houmas only occasionally. Formal Indian relations in the entire region were now divided among agents at St. Stephens, Chickasaw Bluffs, and Natchitoches, with the respective governors of Mississippi and Orleans territories responsible for supervising policy.[19]

The economic interests of the Orleans Territory Indian populace varied somewhat from group to group, so strategies of livelihood differed according to previous experiences with production and exchange activities or to proximity to non-Indian settlements and towns. Many of the Indian migrants to Louisiana were trying to perpetuate hunting for the commercial market, whether seeking new sources of game or evading debts owed merchants in Mississippi. Trade with Indian hunters in the Ouachita and Red River drainages provided a profitable income to many white settlers in the Orleans Territory, while the government trade house established at Natchitoches provided another convenient market.[20] Charles Robin met Choctaw families descending the Black River in two pirogues loaded with bear- and deerskins, venison, tallow, and bear oil. Farther upriver he visited an encampment of about a dozen families. "The men were away hunting, scattered throughout the countryside," and the women "impatient to see what we had to trade." Each family occupied a small, palmetto-thatched hut. Among the foods prepared by the women were gruel and cakes made from the bulbs of the smilax plant. Household possessions noticed by Robin included chickens and dogs, pots made of iron, copper, wood, and clay, and racks for drying pelts and meat.[21]

When the Coushattas moved from the Opelousas district of Louisiana to the Sabine River around 1802, they intensively hunted black bears as well as white-tailed deer for the regional market. In 1806 fifteen men, women, and children from this group visited Natchitoches following a bear hunt along the Sabine and informed John Sibley that they had killed one hundred and eighteen bears. Each bear ordinarily yielded from eight to ten gallons of oil, but that year the bears were apparently less fat than usual. One Coushatta man alone killed four hundred deer along the Sabine over the summer and fall months and sold the skins at forty dollars per hundred. A gallon of bear oil never sold for less than a dollar, according to Sibley, and each bearskin brought another dollar. The Coushattas traded heavily in bear oil and skins, but consumed and sold very little of the meat. "What the hunters don't use when out," the agent reported, "they generally give to their dogs."[22]

The livelihood of most Louisiana Indian communities depended upon a mixture of activities: farming, herding, fishing, gathering, hunting, and providing goods and services to the local economy. With only a modicum of knowledge about the "many little tribes" in Orleans Territory, William Claiborne informed Thomas Jefferson in 1808 that "hunting continues a favorite pursuit; Agriculture and the raising of stock are but partially attended to; But the men are often useful, in assisting Boats in navigating the Mississippi and its waters: And the women have of late turned their attention to manufactures." Sending samples along with his letter, Claiborne told the president that "they make a variety of Baskets and mats which are exchanged with the white Citizens for provisions and clothing."[23]

Claiborne and other white observers tended to perceive these various activities as overlapping phases in a sequential evolution, assuming that all Indians had been less farmer and more hunter in their past. What they failed to discern, consequently, was a strategy of subsistence in the face of volatile economic changes. With formerly essential resources threatened by encroachment or depletion, Indians sought a new combination of production and exchange activities. "They are peaceable and friendly to everybody," agent John Sibley noted in 1805 about the inhabitants of the Atakapa village twenty miles west of St. Martinville. They "labor occasionally, for the white inhabitants; raise their own corn, have cattle and hogs." New Orleans merchant James Pitot also observed that across southern Louisiana the survivors of various Indian tribes "keep themselves busy either by farming or navigation on the waterways."[24]

The account of a journey through the Atchafalaya basin taken by James Cathcart, a U.S. navy surveyor commissioned to survey live oak and red cedar timber, vividly captures how this combination of production and exchange activities worked for some Indians in the area. For his reconnaissance of the wetland forest in 1819, Cathcart employed a Chitimacha pilot named Charles from an Indian village on Bayou Plaquemine. Traveling across Grand Lake, Cathcart's party visited a small island community known as "Postions settlement" – where families of mixed Indian, African, and European descent lived. "They seemed to live as comfortable as the lower class of whites do in general," observed Cathcart. The three huts framed with cypress timber and covered with palmetto leaves, in fact, resembled what was the typical dwelling of trappers and fishermen in south Louisiana well into the twentieth century. Their fields contained an abundance of corn, pumpkins, and turnips, with horses and cattle grazing around the village. In describing how these Indians turned down ears of corn "to preserve the grain from the birds; & weather," Cathcart delivered a narrow class and sectional judgment: "they as well as the whites in this country, are too lazy to take it in, faster than they want to use it." Postion was the chief of this community who spoke "barbarous french, & a little english besides his own tongue." He and his son had just returned from a hunting trip, apparently intoxicated, with "Bear, Deer, & Racoon skins, with Venison & wild ducks." Cathcart was informed by Charles about Postion's reputation as "a great Scoundrel," but was treated kindly by his host. Before departing the next morning, Cathcart purchased from Postion "a small Batteaux, a duck, some venison, & pompions, on reasonable terms."[25]

As in Mississippi, American Indians in the Orleans Territory also marketed food, peltry, and household manufactures in towns and settlements.[26] These visits were not all business, however, since Indians also socialized with and sometimes entertained town residents during their stay. In May 1807, for example, a group of Choctaws played the ball game called *toli* in their language, more widely known as stickball or lacrosse, against some Pascagoulas in Natchitoches. Indian men and women on both sides bet horses, guns, jewelry, and clothing. With twenty-four players on each team and twelve points needed for victory, the first game was won by the Choctaws. In a rematch two days later with some changes in team lineups, the Pascagoulas beat the Choctaws. "Their Agility & exertion is astonishing to Spectators, & very Interesting," John Sibley wrote about all players. "They Often hurt one Another by Blows & falls, Brake & Deslocate Bones & Joints, & Sometimes Kill One Another, but Never get Angry or resent Anything that is done in the game of Ball. If one ever discovers any Anger or resentment, he is turn'd Out as disqualified, & not Suffered to play in a Match Again, which is deem'd very disgracefull."[27]

New Orleans, a city of eighty-five hundred people by 1805, was an important way station for the seasonal and itinerant strategies of many Indian families. As they had done for most of the eighteenth century, groups of

Houmas, Chitimachas, and Choctaws frequently camped on the outskirts of the city.[28] Well into the nineteenth century, Indians gathered in large numbers to market their goods, participate in carnivals, and play ball games. Although the Crescent City was no longer a center of Indian diplomacy, as will be explained in the next chapter, Indian people in the Lower Mississippi Valley continued to make it a part of their social and economic life for some time to come.

In their economic resourcefulness, American Indians in Louisiana resembled those in the Mississippi Territory; they also faced similar economic problems. The in-migration of aspiring cotton and sugar planters, some bringing slave laborers with them, circumscribed Louisiana Indian communities. Small-scale farming, hunting, gathering, and herding eventually became difficult, as more and more land underwent commercial agriculture. More immediate pressure, however, came in the form of trade indebtedness. With the value of bottomlands skyrocketing, traders induced Indian villagers to pay their outstanding debts by selling land along Louisiana's waterways. In the long run, this process created a legal morass through which contemporary Indians in the state are still trudging. In the meantime these land sales helped sustain Indian communities through generally adverse conditions while contributing to rapid changes in their composition and location. Indians in the wetlands and prairies of south Louisiana were selling bits and pieces of their habitats since the 1770s. In June 1802, for example, Champana Unzaga of the Chitimachas sold to Antoine Lanclos thirty-five arpents of land at one of their two villages along Bayou Lafourche.[29]

West of the Atchafalaya basin, Atakapa and Opelousa communities sold parcels of land to settlers in order to eke out a living under increasingly precarious circumstances. The spread of livestock herds raised by some settlers threatened the hunting grounds as well as village sites of Indians in southwestern Louisiana. In transactions dating back to 1784 and 1799, an Atakapa chief named La Tortue sold land to cattle ranchers. Some Indians moved away from their villages to find unoccupied land for hunting and gathering. Others remained on land now owned by whites. As Indian families relied on credit issued by wealthier settlers, parcels of land still claimed by Indians were deeded to creditors. An Atakapa named John transferred thirty-two hundred arpents along Bayou Ouache to Louis and Pierre Richard on 5 January 1801, testifying "that he had sold the land to the claimants, and received his pay for it a long time before."[30]

During the first decade of the nineteenth century, villagers in the Red

River valley ceded much of their land to William Miller and Alexander Fulton, merchants at Rapides. In May 1802 a Choctaw village sold its land along Bayou Boeuf to this partnership in order to pay debts amounting to $3,724; $2,302 of this amount went to Miller and Fulton while the remainder went to four other creditors. Biloxis and Pascagoulas then living on Bayou Boeuf made a similar transaction with Miller and Fulton, meeting debts that totaled $6,048 and receiving $1,500 in merchandise for their village sites. These same Rapides merchants acquired title to 11,230 arpents of land along the Red River in December 1803 when they canceled $2,600 of Pascagoula and Tensaw debts and promised these Indians $5,200 in cash for their villages. Since these lands were bought for speculative purposes, the Indian residents were usually allowed to continue inhabiting them for some time.[31] "The small tribes of Indians, which reside on the Washita, and on the Red river," one army officer reported in 1818, "subsist principally on vegetables and domestic animals. Game has become so scarce in those parts of the country, that there is now but little inducement to pursue the chase."[32]

In addition to debt and land pressures, American Indians in the Orleans Territory faced mounting restrictions on their exchange activities as local and territorial authorities tried to make the region safer for slavery. As in Mississippi, interaction between Indians and blacks was increasingly viewed as dangerous to the security and property of slaveowners. Laws pertaining to alcohol usually prohibited vendors from selling liquor or wine to both slaves and Indians. Peddlers faced stronger vigilance over their visits to Indian communities and plantations as parish officials enforced strict licensing restrictions in order to reduce the marketing of stolen goods. In June 1806 a law passed by the Orleans territorial assembly grouped Indians, free people of color, and slaves together in a section prescribing the death penalty for destruction of crops or buildings, for intentionally poisoning any white, and for raping any white woman or girl. This same section also specified that if an Indian or free person of color "should maliciously steal any slave, he or she shall forfeit the value of said slave and shall be condemned to two years imprisonment at hard labor."[33]

The geographically dispersed activities of Louisiana Indians naturally brought some into sporadic clashes with U.S. citizens and territorial law. Theft and violence of both a political and personal nature, as in Mississippi, tested reciprocal obligations between Indians and the government. When a Coushatta was killed outside Natchitoches in 1807, relatives quickly demanded satisfaction and voiced faith in U.S. justice. But whites guilty of crimes against Indians usually escaped punishment, so officials sought other means of satisfying the Indian law of revenge. When the murderer of a Choctaw at Bayou Chico escaped jail that same year, Claiborne authorized the local militia officer to "propose two hundred Dollars in Goods to the family of the deceased Indian." Citing his familiarity with Choctaw law in Mississippi, Claiborne informed the colonel that "his nearest relation by the Mother's side, is the only person, with whom you need to treat."[34]

In 1808 a group of Alibamons used the occasion of a murder case, in which a white inhabitant of Opelousas had been killed by Indians, to petition for a permanent title to some land in the Opelousas district. Four Alibamon men were arrested, with cooperation from the tribe, and were sentenced to death by the territorial court. Two of the men were hanged on 3 August, but Governor Claiborne pardoned the others "in consequence of the intercession of a great proportion of the respectable Inhabitants of Opellousas, and an impression on my part that the execution of two of those unfortunate Men, would answer the purpose of an example." In support of their request for land, Claiborne reported to the secretary of war that "the Alabamas, appear perfectly satisfied and greatful for your Clemency, they however complain of great distress, in as much as they have no claim to any Land in the Country; but have resided many years on ground claimed by white Individuals, who have lately suggested to them the necessity of re-moving – they say, that they have lived here among the white people forty years; that their men are in the habit of hunting, driving Cattle, and acting as Boatmen, and their women and children of gathering Cotton. By which means, they support their families; that they are unwilling to leave the neighborhood." This group of Alibamons never received the two- or three-thousand-acre grant recommended by Claiborne, and the tenuousness of their position reflected a mounting dilemma faced by other Louisiana Indian communities.[35]

Governor Claiborne's decision to pardon two Alibamon men in the summer of 1808 murder case was also influenced by his apprehension over an earlier incident in which a Choctaw had been killed by an American named Thomas. The victim belonged to a party of Choctaws who had settled in Opelousas Parish "some years past." "Every effort to bring the offender to Justice having hitherto failed of success," Claiborne feared that execution of all four Alibamons "might awaken the vengeance of the Choctaws." Some of Claiborne's "fellow Citizens" who disapproved of his policy threatened to kill those Alibamons whom he pardoned. With a "strong escort of Militia" attending the execution, "one man only was found daring enough to endeavour to excite commotion" after the pardon was read. He was immediately taken to jail and released at the end of the day.[36]

The different systems of law clashed in an especially dramatic way in 1810, when a Choctaw in Ouachita Parish was discovered stealing from a settler's cornfield. Resisting an attempt to drive him away, he forced the owner of the field to flee. The owner assembled a posse of neighbors who, according to agent John Sibley, "Caught the Indian tied him & whiped him & let him go." The Choctaw returned the next day with an armed party of his own associates, scared the settler's family away from their farm, and "committed great Outrage at his House." Judges of the parish learned something about the background to this episode that further reveals the role of vengeance in Choctaw society. The Indians' own corn crops had suffered from drought, since as Sibley explained "where they live is on high land & of an Inferior quality of Soil." A chief apparently promised to make it rain for a certain quantity of goods. "The articles were procured & delivered to him," but it did not rain. When the Choctaws applied to another chief, he required them to kill the other rainmaker who had failed. Friends of the chief so duly killed then avenged his death by assassinating the man who ordered the execution. A revenge cycle went on until, Sibley reported, thirteen chiefs and headmen were dead.[37]

Louisiana Indians seeking trade and work opportunities often found themselves caught between the disparate interests of settlers on the one hand and the law and order concerns of officials on the other. The superintendent of the U.S. trade house at Natchitoches, William Linnaird, observed in 1813 how "vagabond Indians found always behind plantations & near fields are encouraged thereto by the employment given to them by the Planters many of whom retain constantly in their service one or more for the purposes of hunting, picking of Cotton & tending their stocks." "The intercourse between them is such," Linnaird further noted, "that there is scarcely a planter in the Parish who cannot converse in one or more Indian tongues." Federal authorities complained against private traders "who practice the most degrading and fraudulent impositions upon [Indians], without any restraint, by means of the quantity of spirituous liquors they supply them with." Indian leaders also objected to "the whites bringing whiskey among them and hunting on their Grounds," as reported by John Fowler from Natchitoches in 1817. Maintenance of a government trading post was, therefore, crucial for regulating exchange between Indians and non-Indians along the Red River. Yet local citizens petitioned against its location at Natchitoches for incongruent reasons. Some complained that Indian traffic to and from the trade house caused disorderly conduct and property damage, while others protested that the government factory unfairly diverted Indian produce away from private commerce.[38]

By minimizing confrontation with white police and judicial forces, Indians in territorial and early-statehood Louisiana effectively maintained their own internal systems of revenge law. Autonomous penal practices could be tolerated by employers and patrons of scattered Indian families, as long as non-Indians were not involved. An interesting case of Indians freely enforcing their own law in Louisiana began around 1816 when Hocktanlubbee, about twenty-five years old and known by whites as Tom, killed an elderly Choctaw. Some fourteen years earlier his parents had fled across the Mississippi River to Louisiana with young Tom and three or four siblings because his father had murdered a fellow Choctaw. Tom's father was pursued and executed under Choctaw law. So his mother, Totapia, raised her children alone near St. Francisville, where she was called Jenny and befriended by a wealthy widow.

For his killing of another Choctaw on Louisiana soil, Tom was to be executed by relatives of his victim. Choctaws who killed one of their own people usually accepted the sentence and appeared voluntarily on a fixed date for their execution. On the day set for Tom's execution, Jenny pleaded that she be killed instead of her son. He was a young man with a wife, children, and siblings to look after, while she was old like the murdered man. Her request was honored, and within a few hours Jenny was shot to death. Over ensuing years, however, Tom was treated with contempt by the murdered man's relatives who called him a coward for letting his mother die for him. In 1821 Tom met one of the old man's sons on the bank of the Mississippi and, tormented with ridicule once again, killed him with a knife. With the bloody knife still in his hand, he declared that this time he would die "like a man."

At noon on the next day Tom shot himself in a solemn ceremony attended by about twenty Indians and a few white witnesses. A special shirt was made for his burial. He tied black handkerchiefs around his arms and head and a blue ribbon in his long hair. A pipe was passed around three times. The old chief's wife sang the death song in the bushes. Tom shook hands with everyone three times, rejecting pleas that a ransom be offered the young man's friends. He even laid himself in the grave to make sure it was long and wide enough. Tom presented the bloody knife to his wife, "a young woman of eighteen, with an infant in her arms, and another little child two or three years old, standing by her side. "She averted her face to conceal a falling tear," as described by one white witness, "but recovering herself, turned, and with a faint, forced smile, took it." He then gave his pipe to a young brother, "who struggled hard to conceal his emotions." After drinking a little whiskey and water and dashing the bottle on the ground, Tom hurried to his grave "with a jumping, dancing step." With a sapling fixed to the gun to enable suicide, Tom shot himself in the heart. The women rushed to his body, some holding his hands and feet. "He had charged them to show no signs of grief while he lived, lest it should shake his resolution. As far as possible, they had obeyed." Restraining their grief until he died, "it then burst forth in a torrent, and their shrieks and lamentations were loud and undissembled." Although the anonymous female author of this romanticized account wrote it to demonstrate a need for sending the "blessed gospel" to "these children of the forest," it vividly describes the perseverance of honor and ritual in Choctaw law even among widely dispersed groups living on the margins of plantation society.[39]

By the second decade of the nineteenth century, many Indians were migrating out of Louisiana and into Texas. As early as 1800, Captain Chuichuchabe received a license from the Spanish commandant of Nacogdoches permitting his group of Choctaws to hunt in the province of Texas. Six years later a Pascagoula chief named Cons Conche Blonkim sought and acquired permission from Texas officials to move his people to the Sabine River.[40] The non-Indian population in Louisiana exploded from 55,000 in 1806 to over 150,000 in 1820. The revolution in Mexico intensified dispute over a Louisiana-Texas border and drew Indians as well as U.S. citizens into military forays on the Mexican frontier. The war with Great Britain further heightened tension in the area. In 1813 emissaries from the rebellious Creeks in Alabama traveled among Louisiana Indians with "talk and Tobacco," causing agent Sibley to hold an emergency council with Red River villagers. Continuous efforts by officials in Texas to encourage Louisiana Indians to move west of the Sabine gradually paid off. Groups of Coushattas, Alibamons, Pascagoulas, and Choctaws decided to leave their struggles with the United States over land and law behind them by moving to the Sabine and Trinity Rivers, although many of these people continued to trade at Natchitoches. With no guarantee of land rights within the state forthcoming by the 1820s, even the Caddos took initiatives toward relocating themselves in Mexican territory.[41]

In 1825 Thomas McKenney issued a census numbering 1,313 Indians in the state of Louisiana. Secretary of War John C. Calhoun classified these people as "remnants of tribes" so small in population that "very little expense or difficulty will be found in their removal." But most of them, despite Calhoun's wishful thinking, remained in Louisiana, and no official record could have accurately counted the Choctaws who still inhabited the state in scattered bands.[42] Use of land in Louisiana by these groups, meanwhile, became increasingly important in the struggle of nearly twenty-five thousand Choctaws and Chickasaws to remain in Mississippi. Before 1820 officials in Mississippi worried that seasonal migration across the river would thwart efforts to convince the entire Choctaw nation to remove, since successful hunting and trading in Louisiana helped sustain the traditional economy without ceding more territory.[43] Negotiating the Treaty of Doak's Stand in 1819–20, U.S. officials now pointed to the dispersed Choctaws as a reason why the nation should exchange all its Mississippi lands for lands above the Red River. Andrew Jackson attributed their supposed wandering to a "distressed condition" within the Choctaw homeland. In response to this political manipulation of the facts, Pushmataha disavowed the Louisiana Choctaws: "Those of our people who are over the Mississippi did not go there with the consent of the nation; they are considered as strangers; they have no houses or places of residence; they are like wolves; it is the wish of the council that the President would direct his agents to the west to order these stragglers home, and if they will not come, to direct them where he pleases."[44]

The politicization of economic strategies being pursued west of the Mississippi, as a rationale for systematic removal, marked the beginning of a new phase in Indian-U.S. relations in the southeast. At the Treaty of Doak's Stand, Indians for the first time exchanged land in Mississippi (thirteen million acres) for a tract in the Louisiana Purchase territory. Although the Choctaw and Chickasaw nations did not leave their homeland until the 1830s, a wedge was now cut into their resistance to removal. In Louisiana, Indian sales of land to creditors constituted micro-removals in themselves, since many villages eventually abandoned an area to which they were losing rights. For the Caddos, the start of relocating eastern tribes up the Arkansas and Red Rivers carved deeply into their already endangered homeland.

But before the political assault on these Indian groups caught momentum in the 1820s, the economic transformation of the Lower Mississippi Valley into what historians call the cotton kingdom had evoked significant strategies of survival. More extensive hunting and trading, like the diversification of production in their villages, helped buffer many Indians from new economic pressures. In what was more than a clinging to old ways, they widened their use of the countryside – seeking resources for subsistence and avenues for exchange farther away from their own towns and amidst newly forming American settlements. This intentional interspersion with other inhabitants of the area made the waterways of Louisiana a special catchment for seasonal and permanent Indian pioneers. American Indians thereby appropriated for themselves geographical and occupational niches on the cotton frontier in the face of a tidal wave of immigrant settlers and slaves. Some of these enclaves persisted as distinct Indian groups to the present, while new peoples of mixed ancestry emerged around them. Economic strategies devised during the early nineteenth century helped guarantee the survival of American Indians in both Mississippi and Louisiana.

SEVEN

American Indians in Nineteenth-Century New Orleans

Scattered but recurrent depictions of Indians in New Orleans – in both written and pictorial form – invite an examination of the changing roles and images of American Indians in this old North American city. While the literature on Indians in modern cities has grown rapidly, the earlier presence of Native Americans in colonial and nineteenth-century towns still remains neglected.[1] Evidence from such an array of places as seventeenth-century New York City, eighteenth-century Charleston, and nineteenth-century Los Angeles suggests that Indians actively participated in the formative development of American towns. In many cases, American Indians integrated towns and cities into their own networks of migration and exchange.[2] During the eighteenth century many Lower Mississippi Valley Indians frequented New Orleans in various capacities. The capital of colonial Louisiana was home to Indian slaves captured in warfare and host to Indian diplomats from neighboring tribes. Many local villages also produced valuable trade items, especially food, for the New Orleans market and thereby established enduring ties to the colonial town.[3] Although the Indian presence diminished after the Louisiana Purchase, marketing by Choctaw, Chitimacha, and Houma Indians represented a notable Indian persistence in New Orleans street life for the entire nineteenth century.

The experience of Indians in New Orleans during the nineteenth century indicates that towns played an important part in the survival of the many small Indian communities not removed from the eastern United States in the antebellum period. Because obvious signs of alienation and crisis have accompanied recent Indian migration to metropolitan areas, a great proportion of the scholarship concentrates on pathological behavior evinced by urban Indians. There is a temptation to transfer this emphasis to earlier urban experiences, especially if the commentary left by white observers is accepted uncritically. The image projected by American Indians in such early cities as New Orleans should not be dismissed, yet the historian must penetrate the biased perceptions of others in order to reconstruct a more complete picture of the Indian presence in town.[4] Although New Orleans became a stranger and stranger place to Indians in the area – Choctaws called it Balbancha, "a place of foreign languages" – they managed to use its opportunities to adjust their livelihood to changing conditions. In the eighteenth century local villages had secured their leverage in Louisiana by providing vital political and economic services to New Orleans through defense and trade. By the next century Indians became increasingly marginal people on the rapidly changing urban scene, but they continued to integrate the New Orleans marketplace into their own annual cycle of social and economic activities.[5] Through this evolving relationship with the city, American Indians distinctively influenced the culture and landscape of New Orleans.

From 1783 to 1803 Indian diplomacy flourished in New Orleans for the last time, as Spain contended against the United States for Indian allies and the Creek, Chickasaw, and Choctaw nations maneuvered to preserve their sovereignty. Indian missions to New Orleans, including delegations of Cherokees, came frequently and in large numbers during the 1790s, but the tribes avoided symbols of exclusive allegiance and therefore refused to make visits to the Spanish governor a routine. Chiefs often excused themselves from traveling to the city because of bad weather or poor health and, whenever they did complete a junket, complained about inadequate provisions and insulting treatment. "They don't say anything in the City," reported Juan de la Villebeuvre from the Choctaw village of Boukfouka, "but in the Nation they murmur very much."[6] At the time Spain ceded Louisiana to the French Republic in 1800, the intensity of intrigue and diplomacy in the city led Pierre-Clément de Laussat, prefect charged with overseeing the transfer, to "count on there descending, after the expression of the country, 2 to 3,000 Indians per year to New Orleans: others say 3 to 400 chiefs."[7]

Purchase of Louisiana by the United States in 1803 suddenly dissolved Indian political activity in New Orleans. Agencies established near the large interior nations – at Fort St. Stephens, Chickasaw Bluffs, and Natchitoches – virtually ended their diplomatic ties to the Crescent City. For another decade small nations in the area continued making formal visits to territorial officials. In 1806 Governor Claiborne of the Orleans Territory presented uniform coats to two representatives from the Houma tribe in Ascension Parish, and in 1811 he distributed one hundred dollars worth of articles to Chief Chac-Chouma of the Houmas and to his attendants. "From the different Governors of Louisiana," Claiborne wrote to the secretary of war, "they were accustomed to receive marks of friendly attention. At the present day, the number of this Tribe is greatly diminished; it does not exceed 80 souls, but their conduct is exemplary and the late visit of the Chief being the first he paid me, I thought it a matter of policy to make him a small present." This meeting marked the beginning of the Houma Indians' struggle for official recognition by the U.S. government. But they and other *petites nations* along the lower Mississippi and Red Rivers were denied the political protection needed to secure their small land bases. After a century of alliance with colonial governments in New Orleans, the Chitimachas, Houmas, Tunicas, and others were finally pressured into the backcountry of Louisiana. The federal government indifferently lost sight of them – for the time being.[8]

As the New Orleans population rapidly grew and the United States managed Indian affairs from other places, formal visits by Indian people seldom occurred during the nineteenth century. Whenever the city did host a group of touring Indian celebrities, residents perceived them with increasing amusement and fascination; memory of the city's imperative relations with local Indian nations receded with each newspaper report of exotic visitors.[9] The Seminole War in Florida in 1836–43 temporarily animated interest in Indians throughout the South. Not only did many New Orleans men volunteer to fight in the Florida swamplands, but hundreds of beleaguered and dying Seminole captives passed through the city for passage up the Mississippi River. On 16 October 1836, 160 Delawares and Shawnees arrived from the West on their way to assist the U.S. Army in its war against the Seminoles. "Said to be fine warriors," the *New Orleans Picayune* announced, they "may be seen at the New Barracks below the city." That same day a Creek chief named Jim Boy began a short visit to New Orleans. He attended the St. Charles Theatre two nights in a row and drank with "some good natured fellows" whom the *Picayune* editor reproached for "making this big child of the forest royally tipsy."[10]

Jim Boy and thousands of his people had been encamped for three months at Pass Christian, waiting to be transported by rail and steamboat to the Creek Nation already removed from Alabama to the Arkansas country. New Orleanians who could afford a boat ride over Lakes Pontchartrain and Borgne were entertained at ball games played by these refugees. Nevertheless, a city newspaper could not avoid articulating what was becoming the predominant bourgeois image of the nineteenth-century Indian: "We do not see the North American Indian now, as he once was. The white man has invaded his wigwam and ruined his peace and pride. But a few years more, and the remote shores of the Pacific will receive the miserable remnant of countless tribes, that once in their native majesty ruled the fairest and richest continent under the sun. Is there no feeling for glory and shame?" A week later the *Picayune* reported that the steamer *Monmouth* carrying 611 Creek Indians upriver struck the *Tremont* on the evening of 31 October. "It sank immediately and only about 300 Indians were saved." This and subsequent costly passages of removed southern Indians marked a tragic final chapter in New Orleans' long history of official Indian affairs.[11]

Although the political presence of American Indians in New Orleans waned during the early nineteenth century, Indian people from communities still in the vicinity continued to market food, peltry, and household manufactures in the city. Numbering eighty-five hundred residents by 1805, New Orleans actually became more important than ever before to Indians who were now devising new means of coping with the loss of political autonomy and with the socioeconomic displacement suffered during the early nineteenth century. Peddling and casual labor by Indians in the burgeoning commercial center became part of a wider seasonal round of itinerant economic activities performed in the surrounding countryside. Faced with declining opportunity in the deerskin trade, with growing numbers of Anglo-American settlers, and with mounting pressure to relinquish land, Indian people in the Lower Mississippi Valley mitigated disruption and eased transition in ways that were widely employed by American Indians under similar circumstances.

Camps of extended families – formerly the units that spent only winter hunting seasons away from their villages – sojourned more frequently along waterways and roads across the region and traded small quantities of goods with other travelers, farmers, and slaves. While the men hunted for local meat markets, women vended leaves and roots, baskets and mats, and even picked cotton during the harvest season.[12] Groups of Indians camping around towns or behind plantations developed special ties with particular families by provisioning their kitchens with game and seasonings. During his stay at James Pirrie's house near St. Francisville, John Audubon recorded, "yesterday the 25th of July 1821 an Indian of the Choctaw Nation, who habitually hunts for Mr. Perrie – brought me a femelle of the Chuck Will's Widow in full and handsome plumage."[13] Nearly two decades later Victor Tixier observed a group of Choctaws camped behind the plantation of Pierre Sauvé, some twenty miles above New Orleans. They hunted in the area during the winter months, killing "every year a large number of rabbits and stags which are sold in the settlements or in New Orleans." The leader of this camp, a Choctaw named Baptiste, spoke to Tixier in a French-Creole dialect "which resembled the one spoken by the Negroes of Louisiana."[14]

At the beginning of the nineteenth century, Pierre-Louis Berquin-Duvallon reported that many Indians gathered at New Orleans every winter. "Each band has its encampment in the vicinity of town, composed of huts covered with the skins of bears and other beasts." Paul Alliot, another traveler at the time, thought that "hundreds of savages with their wives and children live on the outskirts of New Orleans, and live apart in the huts which they have constructed on the vacant lands." Both observers noted that these Indians received annual gifts from the government and participated in carnival. As governor of the Orleans Territory, William Claiborne wanted "to relieve the Inhabitants of the Sixth District of this City, from those vexatious Indian visits of which they complain." He notified Mayor James Pitot in May 1805 that "I am however at present without an Indian Interpretor, nor do I know of one whose services I could command."[15] On a more continuous basis American Indians used the city as a periodic marketplace. Traveling in pirogues along Lake Pontchartrain and up Bayou St. John, many local Indians reached New Orleans by the ancient Indian portage connecting bayou and town, or by the Carondelet Canal after its completion in 1817.[16] Once in the city, Indian women peddled baskets, mats, sifters, plants, herbs, and firewood, while their men sold venison, wild fowl, and cane blowguns and occasionally earned wages as day laborers and dock workers. On his way to a Choctaw camp behind the city gates, Fortescue Cuming met on a March afternoon in 1799 "numbers of Indian women with large bundles of wood on their backs, first tied together and then held by a strap carried over their foreheads." A few years later Paul Alliot observed that the Indian men "kill game with great dexterity, and sell it for excellent prices" and that the women "busy themselves in making reed baskets which they sell at good prices."[17]

Indian participation in the city's first public food market, instituted in 1784, had evolved naturally over the eighteenth century. Now known as the "French Market," the terminus of the old portage road at the Mississippi River served as an enduring nexus of Indian, African-American, and Euro-American exchange in New Orleans. Indians did not hesitate, however, to take advantage of new markets as they opened in different neighborhoods during the nineteenth century. The Lebreton Market, started by the city in 1867 along Bayou Road, was previously known as the Indian market. New Orleanian Henry Castellanos remembered it as "once the bivouac of the vagrant Indians that abounded in that vicinity."[18] Recalling St. Mary's Market

(between Tchoupitoulas Street and the Mississippi River) for an inter-
viewer as recently as 1976, one New Orleans woman remembered that when
she was very young "Indians would come . . . and spread their wares out on
the grass."[19]

Removal of the Choctaw nation from Mississippi following the 1830
Treaty of Dancing Rabbit Creek drastically reduced the Indian population
in the area but did not eliminate Indian people from New Orleans. Many Indian migrants to the Arkansas country continued to make periodic trips
through Louisiana. "We come to spend the snow season on the grounds of
this country," the leader of a Choctaw band told Victor Tixier.[20] Other
Choctaws never left the Lower Mississippi Valley at all, with several communities remaining scattered in Louisiana, Mississippi, and Alabama. Although the Houma Indians withdrew from the banks of the Mississippi and
settled farther down Bayou Teche, they also never completely severed their
ties to the Crescent City.[21] All of these Indians integrated New Orleans into
a pattern of livelihood vividly described by Dominique Rouquette, a native
New Orleanian who grew up along Bayou St. John and across Lake Pontchartrain:

It is also by hunting that the Choctaws, who did not want to emigrate west of the
Mississippi, live; they obstinately refuse to abandon the different parishes of Louisiana, where they are grouped in small family tribes, and live in rough huts in the vicinity of plantations, and hunt for the planters, who trade for the game they kill all
that they need: powder, lead, corn, woolen covers, etc. Their huts are generally by a
fence. In this enclosure their families plant corn, pumpkins and potatoes, and raise
chickens. The women use a kind of cane, which they knew how to dye different colors, to make baskets, *lottes* [baskets carried on the back], and sieves, from which they
derived a good profit. They also sold medicinal plants, which they gathered from the
neighboring forests: Virginia snake-root, sage, plantain, tarragon, wild fruit, *pom-
metes* [medlar tree], blue bottle, persimmons, and Scuppernongs, also, roots of
seguiena, sarsparilla, and sassafras. They also do a little trading in ground turtles,
which they find on the prairies. They dispose of these wares at the plantations, in
country towns, and at New Orleans. Nothing is more interesting to the tourists than
to see them wandering along the streets of The Queen of the South, The Crescent
City, with their *pauvres pacotilles* [cheap small wares], in their picturesque costumes,
half savage and half civilized, followed by a number of children of all ages, half na-
ked, and carrying on their backs a papoose snugly wrapped in the blanket, with
which they envelope themselves, like a squirrel in moss. Sometimes, they squat in a
circle, at the big market place, on the banks of the old river, patiently waiting with

chaste downcast eyes, for the customers who buy what they offer, more for the sake of charity than from necessity.[22]

While contributing to their livelihood, the exchange of a particular combination of foods and wares in and around New Orleans also provided American Indians with a means of expressing their distinct identity. In the midst of a rapidly growing non-Indian population, scattered groups of Indians were likely to become absorbed into any one of the region's larger racial categories – Negroes, free people of color, or whites. By finding a social niche compatible with their own customs and needs, Louisiana Indians participated in the larger nineteenth-century society without losing their separateness. In their temporary dwellings in the backwoods of plantations and towns, in the array of game, baskets, and plants sold, in their style of clothing and adornment, and in the evasive demeanor exhibited at the market, Indian people marked a symbolic boundary between themselves and others.[23]

Residents and tourists in New Orleans came to expect certain peculiarities in Indian behavior. Walking back into town from Bayou St. John in 1835, Tyrone Power stopped briefly at a Choctaw camp of a dozen huts, "about which crawled or ran as many children of all ages, looking remarkably healthy and well-formed." Inside one of the huts "sat the chief and his squaw, upon whose lap lay numberless strings of blue and white beads, which she was admiring and arranging with as much delight as a London girl would her first suite of pearl." Amusement over hair grooming and face painting among Indians gathered around the Place d'Armes did not prevent the English actor from flirting with "a little Choctaw belle" for several days. "The costume of these people," Power observed about the women's brightly colored and feathered clothing, "is showy, and at times even becoming, and pleasing."[24] One of Walt Whitman's "choice amusements" during his several months of working for the new daily paper, *The Crescent*, in 1848 was to stroll through the French Market on Sunday mornings. As he later recalled, "the show was a varied and curious one; among the rest, the Indian and negro hucksters with their wares. For there were always fine specimens of Indians, both men and women, young and old."[25]

The public presence of Indians in antebellum New Orleans more commonly tended to evoke disparaging impressions among white observers who saw them as abject outcasts or shiftless paupers. Before the nineteenth century the range of different roles and the political power still possessed by tribes had generated a complex image of Indian people; close personal interaction and reciprocal diplomatic relations undercut feelings of superiority in the colonial populace. But as the number of Indians declined in places like nineteenth-century Louisiana, one-dimensional perceptions of Indian behavior colored the vision of nineteenth-century urban Americans — especially in cities or towns where Indian people assumed a visibly marginal presence.[26]

To some degree the pervasive characterizations of New Orleans Indians during the nineteenth century resembled those applied to Irish-Catholic and other European immigrants as well as to African-American slaves in the city. Relegated to a subordinate socioeconomic status, their conspicuous appearance on streets and levees reinforced hostile attitudes toward them.[27] The more Indians tried to evade the disapproving eyes of whites by finding privacy in the outskirts or alleys of the city, the more they confirmed critical judgment.[28] Observers who saw Indians in no other context were struck mostly by the drunkenness, idleness, and disorderly conduct that was noticeable in New Orleans. Outside the city gate in 1799, Cuming "saw a large circular shade for drying and manufacturing bricks, under which were upwards of fifty Indians of both sexes, chiefly intoxicated, singing, drinking, rolling in the dirt, and upon the whole exhibiting a scene very disgustful." In 1819 Benjamin Latrobe noticed "Towards noon men & women have sold their game or skins, have bought whiskey, & are *hocksy*, that is, half drunk." "A party of Choctaws are pow-wowing, hooting and dancing about our streets," a city newspaper reported on 2 April 1839, "entering every man's house, and by their noise and dancing levying a direct contribution from all whose premises they encroach upon. Their system of begging is decidedly independent: they ask for nothing, but make such a confounded fuss and racket that any one will pay them in order to get rid of their outrageous noise." Alcoholism and a language barrier made Indians vulnerable to physical as well as literary abuse. Dominique Rouquette recalled from his youth seeing sailors tie together the long hair of inebriated Indian men and women lying on the levee.[29]

Most descriptions of Indian behavior in New Orleans did not stop at mere condemnation. A resemblance in Indian people's appearance and status to other impoverished urban occupants was unacceptable. Indians looking or acting like members of an underclass could only be interpreted as byproducts of de-Indianization. Henry Castellanos called Indians in New Orleans "fragments of this erratic race."[30] Such impressions of Indians still scattered around eastern towns and cities were often deployed by proponents of Indian removal to justify a policy that eventually relocated tens of thousands of people west of the Mississippi River.[31] Disappointed in not finding "noble savages," observers tended to forecast imminent extinction. "One sees many Indians in New-Orleans," a French visitor in 1817 wrote, "but these have in general lost their spirit of national unity and distinctive character through their proximity to the city." Observation of Indians in New Orleans drove architect Benjamin Latrobe to wax philosophical in his journal about "the march of white Society, which tends inevitably to their extirpation." To him the Choctaws in the city were "a sort of outcasts, the fag end of the tribe, the selvage, the intermediate existence between annihilation & savage vigor."[32] The gloomiest characterizations were written by individuals bringing the most romantic expectations to an Indian setting, as exemplified in one German visitor's account from the 1870s:

These Indians are pitiful remnants of Atala's tribe, who lead their gypsy-like existence out on the prairie, but clearly their blood is strongly mixed. They have yellow-brown facial coloring, broad faces with flat noses and thick lips. Their sad, shy manner contrasts sharply with the lively cheerfulness of the Negroes, mulattoes, and Creoles. They all have a cloth thrown over head and shoulders that they hold together in front of their mouths so that you see little of their faces. Their pitch-black hair, which often has a pronounced auburn sheen, is tied in a knot on the top of their heads and hangs straight down in the back. But they do not feel at home even in this very diverse crowd in which the darkest Negro moves comfortably, and even without any thought of their poetically celebrated past, their presence is for everyone a sight that arouses sympathy.[33]

Ideological commentaries about their degraded condition aside, Indians never really posed a law and order problem for New Orleans officials during the nineteenth century. Noticing consistent displays of honesty, chastity, and conviviality among Choctaws in the city, even an observer as callous as Latrobe had to concede that they "are not without negative, if not positive virtues."[34] Minor offenses and major crimes committed by Indians seem to have been handled under their own customs, indicating that well into the nineteenth century Indians managed to preserve jurisdiction and responsibility over injuries inflicted on each other – even in a city as large as New Orleans.

A customary understanding existed in New Orleans, consistent with circumstances in the countryside, that crimes committed by Indian against Indian would be handled by the tribe and not by city police. Several stories about a guilty individual or relative fearlessly facing execution for killing another tribesman exist in travel accounts, reminiscences, and newspaper reports. On at least a few occasions public attention mobilized city residents to collect enough money to commute a Choctaw's sentence through a monetary payment to the tribe. Cynics may marvel over possible scams played by shrewd Indians upon gullible yet compassionate citizens, so one case is worth recounting. In April 1837 the *Picayune* reported that "A few weeks since, one of our Indians accidentally, in a drunken frolic, killed one of his tribe, in the vicinity of this city, by striking him upon the head with a bottle." The Choctaws assembled in council to try the murderer and sentenced him "to be shot this day, or raise the sum of three hundred dollars." One day before the scheduled execution, "notwithstanding the pressure in the money market" the newspaper reporter was quick to note, "the prisoner with two of his brothers who had him under guard, succeeded in collecting this amount from the liberal citizens of New Orleans, the last of which was obtained in Hewlett's Arcade, when one of the brothers of the prisoner mounted a table, and returned thanks to the crowd around him; but as the speech was in the Choctaw language we could not tell whether it was good or otherwise. The prisoner wept, and joy was plainly depicted in the countenances of the three brothers."[35]

Far more important at the time to Indian vendors and visitors than moral judgments made by commentators were their relations with other people who worked and played on the streets of New Orleans. We must settle for passing glimpses of Indian participation in such social gatherings as dances in Congo Square and Mardi Gras, which brought slaves, white laborers, and other underclass New Orleanians together. Castellanos recalled that after city officials stopped granting them annual gifts, "the Indians would resort to *padegaud* shooting," their version of the charivari familiar to Creole residents. Dancing around "a wooden rooster decked with ribbons for target practice," they begged from house to house in the suburbs for "powder and shot" coins – which meant to Castellanos "whiskey and ration" money. Lasting several days, this carousal also accompanied weddings and other ceremonies "from which they reaped rich harvest, as their exhibitions naturally attracted throngs of sojourners and sightseers."[36]

The most fascinating Indian contribution to social life in nineteenth-century New Orleans was raquettes, a ball game called *toli* by the Choctaws that became the Crescent City's first popular, spectator sport. Raquette contests between Negro, white, and Indian teams, played then behind the city gates, were regular Sunday afternoon events by the time the United States acquired Louisiana. Early in the nineteenth century spectators assembled on the "Communes de la Ville," also known as Congo Plains, where players carrying short sticks in both hands tossed the small buckskin ball between two goal posts sometimes placed a half-mile apart. "There was wide room for much field sport," reported George Washington Cable, "and the Indian villagers of the town's outskirts and the lower class of white Creoles made it the ground of their wild ball game of *raquette*." Two prominent black teams were the "Bayous," players from the Bayou St. John area, and the "La Villes," those from the city proper. They competed against white Creole teams as well as against each other, and some Indians reportedly played on the "Bayous" team. The main field eventually shifted eastward to "La Plaine Raquette" (bounded today by Galvez Street and St. Bernard, North Claiborne, and Elysian Fields Avenues), but African-American teams also played in Algiers and other suburban grounds available to them.[37]

New Orleans raquettes closely resembled Choctaw *toli* in style of play and public ritual, illuminating some cultural influence made by Indians upon city life. While studying Indian games for the Smithsonian Institution's Bureau of American Ethnology, Steward Culin witnessed, during the summer of 1901, a game of raquettes played in New Orleans one Sunday afternoon:

The players, some hundreds of French-speaking negroes, had assembled in a level, uninclosed field. The majority were armed with rackets, each consisting of a piece of hickory bent over at one end to form a spoon, which was netted with a thong, precisely like those used by the Choctaw. A racket was carried in each hand, and the ball was picked up and thrown with them in the same way as in the Indian game. The players appeared to own their own rackets, and I purchased a pair without difficulty. . . .

The goals or bases were two tall poles about 600 feet apart, having a strip of tin, about a foot wide and 10 feet long, fastened on the inner side some distance above the ground. These goals, called plats, were painted, one red with a small double ring of white near the top, the other blue with a black ring. Midway in a straight line between was a small peg to mark the center of the field, where the ball was first thrown. . . . The game appeared to be open, free for all, without reference to number; but in more formal matches the sides are equalized and regulated. The ball was put in play at the center flag, being tossed high in the air, and caught on the uplifted ball sticks. Then there was a wild rush across the field, the object being to secure and carry the ball and toss it against the tin plate, making a plat. The game was played with much vigor and no little violence. A blow across the shins with a racket is permissible, and broken heads are not uncommon. Play usually continues until dark, and, at the close, the winners sing Creole songs, reminding one of the custom at the close of the Choctaw game.[38]

Henry Castellanos vividly described the excitement that surrounded raquette games in the late nineteenth century. "The running, wrestling and
dexterity of the players were not only very exciting spectacles," he noted,
"but the eager crowd of spectators and acquaintances, running into the
thousands . . . made such occasions a source of social entertainment."
Around the field stood "improvised places of refreshment, small booths for
all sorts of cakes, fruits, sweet beer, ice cream, etc." In addition to drinking
and eating throughout the match, New Orleanians also enjoyed gambling
on the hard-fighting teams – a practice that the Choctaws always attached to
the contest. Competitors and spectators paraded into town after the game,
"singing in mockery of the losing party" and waving the prize "of a pretty
silk flag, of fanciful design."[39] An exact cause of raquettes' disappearance
from the New Orleans scene is not evident, although the rise of baseball
must have helped push the older ball game aside. Black residents perpetuated the game into the twentieth century, but by the 1930s writers for the
WPA's *Guide to New Orleans* were able to presume that "even they have long
since become too 'soft' for it."[40]

During the second half of the nineteenth century, Choctaws living on the
north shore of Lake Pontchartrain were mostly responsible for the continuing Indian presence in New Orleans. By the 1850s several groups of Choctaws were situated between Biloxi Bay on the Mississippi Gulf Coast and the
northern shore of Lake Maurepas. They clung tenaciously to the Choctaw
language through years of interaction with French- and English-speaking
neighbors and supported themselves in a seasonal round of farming, hunting, gathering, peddling, and earning day wages. The largest Choctaw village, Buchuwa, occupied the head springs of Bayou Lacombe. Villagers
planted a variety of food crops around their log cabins and raised cattle and
hogs on the open range. In October of each year, they camped in palmetto
lodges along the Pearl River and Bogue Chitto in order to gather sassafras,
river cane, and other plants.[41]

Into this world entered Father Adrien Rouquette – younger brother to
Dominique, romantic poet and recluse, and missionary to the Choctaws at
Bayou Lacombe until his death in 1887. Rouquette had known the Choctaws from the north shore of Lake Pontchartrain since his birth at New Orleans in 1813. Later describing how "Bayou St. John was lined with their en-
campments," he remembered with some exaggeration that in 1820 "there
were more Indians in the city than there were whites or negroes."[42] Rouquette's mother bought game and seafood from Indians at her house on the

bayou, and he spent much of his youth at an uncle's estate on Bayou La-combe. After Rouquette was ordained into the Dominican Order in 1845, his desire to write and preach away from the worldly distractions of city life naturally drove him to the Choctaws across the lake. In 1859 Rouquette built his first chapel at Buchuwa. He initially intended to apprentice and then persuade converts there to accompany him to Indian Territory, where thousands of Choctaw souls might be converted. The Buchuwa Choctaws first suspected the priest of being a government agent but soon accepted him warmly. Rouquette then devoted his life to teaching Catholicism, in the Choctaw language, to the Indians of St. Tammany Parish. "To be respected by them," Rouquette learned, "you must stand apart, be serious, and speak little."[43]

The American Civil War wreaked havoc on the Buchuwa Choctaws in 1862, when their homes, fields, and chapel were destroyed by jayhawkers and deserters. Some were killed and others died with fever, according to Rouquette, and the eighty or so survivors scattered into smaller camps. By the early 1880s Rouquette, "Chahta-Ima" or "Like a Choctaw" to his Indian flock, built four small "cabin chapels" among these refugees. The Nook at Lacombe served as both his home and the largest chapel. Ravine aux Cannes stood mid-way between Lacombe and Mandeville, Chuka-Chaha one mile east of Mandeville, and Kildara at Chinchuba two miles west of Mande-ville.[44] Rouquette remained reticent about the success of his proselytization efforts. But a conversation between Rouquette's uncle Talence and a Choc-taw named Vincent, as reported by the priest, perhaps discloses the kind of resistance that he daily met. Talence asked Vincent if he would like to go to heaven "where there is so much happiness." The Choctaw thought for a mo-ment and asked whether there are "Americans up there." When Talence an-swered, "Doubtless," Vincent decided, "Well, I do not want to go there." Adrien Rouquette nonetheless accepted responsibility for abolishing the Choctaws' "blood law," reducing their drunkenness, and baptizing James Mehataby – who in 1882 was thirty years old and hereditary chief of the group around Bayou Lacombe.[45]

Burial customs had long been prominent features of Choctaw ritual, and throughout the nineteenth century the communities near New Orleans bound themselves together through a death feast held at least once a year. Their version of the ceremony, as described by Rouquette, brought Choc-taws from Biloxi, Pearl River, and Amite River to Ravine aux Cannes to mourn those who died during the preceding months. "They are adopting the dress of the whites," Rouquette explained, but during this feast Choctaw men and women "dress in a peculiar costume made up of calico of the most showy colors, such as red, blue, and yellow, these being the favorite tints." The ceremony began with all-night dancing. Then participants wept dolefully while facing the rising sun and completed the ritual with a bountiful feast. When they were gathered "in great number at these festivals," Father Rouquette used the occasion to address the Choctaws "in instructive and touching words."[46]

Commuting by steamboat from Mandeville as many as three times a week, women from these Choctaw communities sold sassafras and laurel leaves, gumbo filé, and baskets at the French Market and other neighborhood markets in the city. The men found less time to hunt and fish as they became woodchoppers for railroads and other construction projects, so their presence in town diminished over the last decades of the nineteenth century.[47] Seated in open spaces between the stalls of the French Market and displaying their baskets and food items, Indian women were picturesque subjects for curious visitors and residents alike. In 1866 Alfred R. Waud of *Harper's Weekly*, one of several artists who illustrated these Indian vendors, most vividly captured the women "grouped around in stolid indifference to the heat, with heavy folded wraps resting on their heads" who "patiently await customers for their okra, and other herbs and roots."[48] Martin Behrman never forgot from his youthful days at his mother's dry goods stand "the Indians who sold herbs, beads and leaves of plants used to flavor food. I remember standing there and watching the Indians by the hour." Behrman was elected mayor of New Orleans in 1904 as head of a political machine named the Choctaw Club.[49]

The World's Industrial and Cotton Centennial Exhibition held in New Orleans during 1884–85 created a temporary environment for residents and visitors to observe starkly contrasting Indian scenes. On the one hand, exhibition tourists were informed by a travel guide that "of the many thousands of aborigines who once held . . . the vast territory that composed old Louisiana, the fifteen or twenty Choctaw women whom one sees at the French Market, sitting patiently, silent and motionless, waiting (with some contempt, if the truth were known) for the paleface purchaser . . . are, with the males of their families, almost the sole survivors of the race which inherited the land from their fathers." "That triumph of Louisiana cookery, the gumbo filé," its authors did not fail to mention, derived from the "pounded laurel and sassafras leaves" still being sold by local Choctaws.[50] On the other hand, the appearance of Buffalo Bill Cody's Wild West Show in New Orleans during the exposition months exposed curiosity-seekers to what was fast becoming the popular, and exclusive, depiction of American Indians. To the delight of New Orleanians from late December to early April, Plains Indian performers attacked a stagecoach, high-stepped to a war dance, and hunted a buffalo. Thousands of spectators crowded into the show at Oakland Park on 4 January 1885 to catch a glimpse of famed Chief Gall of the Teton Sioux.[51]

Some African Americans in New Orleans responded to the "Wild West" stereotype of American Indians in a unique way, creating one of the city's most fascinating and durable traditions. The Creole Wild West Tribe was organized by Becate Batiste in the 1880s and was joined by several other black groups that began to dress in fancy Indian costumes every Mardi Gras. While some members of these Mardi Gras Indian tribes had local Indian ancestry, the main inspiration for their formation came from the Wild West shows that frequented American cities during the late nineteenth century. Black New Orleanians appropriated the popular image of dangerous yet free-spirited Plains Indian warriors to disguise their own defiance and prowess behind an acceptable mask of wild Indian behavior. In her short story entitled "A Carnival Jangle," Alice Dunbar-Nelson depicts a Mardi Gras gathering in Washington Square where blacks were performing "a perfect Indian dance." Spectators filled the square "to watch these mimic Redmen, they seemed so fierce and earnest."[52]

By mimicking aggressive Indian behavior, obviously not threatening to non-Indians in late-nineteenth-century New Orleans, these black revelers in showy Indian headdresses safely protested the city's white-dominated racial order in a symbolic, even amusing, form. During slavery, flight to Indian nations had served as a means of resistance and liberation. Now, pretending to be Indians represented some common tradition of protest. Also through ritualistic competition with each other, Mardi Gras Indian tribes creatively channeled African-American song and dance into a new ceremonial pattern. "It all started when young men ran away from their masters and lived with the Indians," according to one Mardi Gras Indian who began marching in 1929. "After slavery they never forgot the tribes they lived with. . . . At first the Native Americans thought we were making fun of them. But they found out better."[53]

New Orleans poet and historian Marcus Christian, while gathering material during the 1930s for a history of African Americans in Louisiana, captured some important ambiguity in how these Mardi Gras Indians understood their own relationship to American Indian history. Noting how several writers had commented upon the "great amount of blood from 'some mythical Indian tribe' claimed by New Orleans Negroes," Christian observed that "even the scoffers have held their tongues in amazement as they gazed upon Negro Carnival clubs." He identified six major clubs and located them by neighborhood: "Yellow Pocahontas" near St. Bernard and North Claiborne Avenues, "Wild Squatulas" from South Tonti and Tahlia Streets, "Red, White and Blue Eagles" from Cherokee and Ann Streets in Carrollton, "Eight Red Men" from Algiers, "101 Ranch" from St. Phillip and Burgundy Streets, and "Creoles of the Wild West" from the outskirts of Carrollton. "Very much like their Indian prototypes," Christian asserted, these clubs were "very loosely organized." But he also detected an "un-Indian" turn of mind among Mardi Gras Indians by playing up a familiar Indian stereotype. "Unlike their great ancestors that gave the White Brother millions of acres of the best land on earth in return for a few gaudy beads and trinkets, these spurious editions of Redskins preferred greenbacks to beads, and accordingly, sold the latter at fantastic prices." One Mardi Gras Indian swore to Christian that "he once sold one bead for as much as $15" and on another occasion "he stationed himself in front of the Athenium where the Rex Carnival Ball was being held, and there sold $80 worth of trinkets from the many that he had sewed upon his costume."[54]

While New Orleans blacks turned popular stereotypes of western Indians to their own use, other groups were taking a new interest in the real Indians still living around New Orleans. James Dorsey, Oliver LaFarge, David Bushnell, and other anthropologists were beginning their ethnographic reconnaissance of Louisiana Indians by the end of the nineteenth century.[55] Local curiosity was sparked, meanwhile, by a proposed exhibit for the 1893 Chicago World's Fair that would display Choctaws in their "peculiar industries" of basketmaking and pounding gumbo filé. An inquiry by the *Daily Picayune* at the Catholic Archbishopric disclosed that 150 Choctaws still lived in St. Tammany Parish, not counting about another one hundred in Tangipahoa Parish just to the west and Hancock County, Mississippi, to the adjacent east. The exhibit never materialized, but women in the New Orleans chapter of the National Indian Association did begin efforts to promote public education for Indian children in Louisiana and Mississippi.[56] This interest among anthropologists and philanthropists, however, came too late for many of the Choctaw people in the New Orleans area. For years the U.S. Bureau of Indian Affairs had been trying to remove all Indian families still living in both Mississippi and Louisiana to the Choctaw Nation in Indian Territory. During the first decade of the twentieth century, it succeeded in transporting nearly fifteen hundred men, women, and children to Oklahoma. Drastically reduced in number to about one thousand people in Mississippi and a few hundred in Louisiana, the Choctaws who evaded this latest removal entered a new phase of rebuilding their communities in the South.[57]

Historians are finally devoting attention to the various ways that scattered communities of American Indians survived the U.S. government's removal policy of the antebellum era.[58] The Choctaws and other Indians who frequented New Orleans during the nineteenth century illustrate that city streets were as useful as backcountry forests or remote swamplands in the day-to-day struggle for survival. Peddling baskets and seasonings and performing casual labor in town allowed some Indians the kind of marginal economic role that insulated them from coercive threats to their language and values. The presence of Choctaw women in the marketplaces of New Orleans became a symbolic and remunerative form of asserting an Indian identity, which city boosters found quaint enough to publicize as a tourist attraction.[59]

But even within the most heterogeneous metropolis of the South, Indians could not escape the severe judgment of racial ideologues. As Indian diplomacy became less important to the city of New Orleans, formal visits by Indian delegations waned over the antebellum period. Defeated Indian leaders occasionally passed through town like celebrities, attracting attention from curious urban onlookers. The marginal presence and subordinate status of those Indian families who visited the city for trade, work, or amusement disappointed many observers who idealized "noble savages" from the obscure past or the distant West. Some even framed their critical commentary about lesser Indians in terms of the inevitability of extinction or the necessity for removal. But in the shadow of a predominant image that increasingly relegated American Indians to museums, exhibitions, and Wild West shows, real Indian people in the Lower Mississippi Valley continued their barely visible presence in New Orleans. Efforts at making the city a useful place for their own survival carried on into the twentieth century.

EIGHT

Images of Lower Mississippi Valley Indians in the Nineteenth Century

Depictions of American Indians on the Lower Mississippi Valley landscape during the nineteenth century reflected common attitudes toward American Indians in the United States. Painters and writers shared an ideology that divided the Indian population into two, almost antithetical, categories. Tribes in the trans-Mississippi West were considered noble savages, still living freely in a primitive state. Indian communities and individuals in the East were viewed with pity and scorn because they represented the tragic, albeit inevitable, consequence of the noble savage's encounter with civilization. This self-serving bifurcation of the native world, a version of what anthropologist Renato Rosaldo called "imperialist nostalgia," pervaded American arts and letters by the mid–nineteenth century.[1]

As viewed in previous chapters, most written descriptions dismissed Lower Mississippi Valley Indians occupying the margins of white society as pathetic remnants of once nobler tribes. The overall effect of such accounts is virtually to erase a sizable number of Indian people from history as they are contrasted with romanticized images of Indians once living, or still living elsewhere, in temporary isolation from "civilization." This attitude no doubt influenced observers who produced pictorial images: sketches, drawings, paintings, and photographs.

Individuals and groups depicted in these images were pursuing an improvisational pattern of livelihood shared by many North American Indians at one time or another, as they pieced together traditional and new means of subsistence in order to cope with economic adversity. Perceptions of southern Indians who traveled and lived on the margins of non-Indian society, however, tended to be demeaning and debasing. Observers either pitied or loathed Indians living in small and scattered communities in close proximity to towns and plantations, so both pictorial and literary representations of them are loaded with biases – biases based on popular assumptions about the fate of American Indians.

Yet these images can still enhance our understanding of much maligned Indian groups. In various kinds of texts – official records, travel accounts, pictures, and fiction – descriptive information about Indian communities must be carefully filtered and analyzed apart from the observers' judgments that often frame them. A critical reading of literary and visual representations of Indians commonly seen across the nineteenth-century Lower Mississippi Valley – along roads and rivers, at marketplaces and social gatherings – can therefore garner valuable insight into the social and economic history of the Choctaws and other southern Indians.

Well-known painter George Catlin found Indians at Sault Ste. Marie and Mackinac Island too acculturated and, therefore, of little pictorial interest. He saw wretchedness and drunkenness among Great Lakes Indian communities and blamed fur traders and other whites for luring them into debauchery. Eager to travel farther west in order to portray Indians still untouched by civilization, Catlin paused to paint scenes of Chippewas netting fish and playing ball. "Of the two millions remaining alive at this time," he wrote in 1840, "about 1,400,000 are already the miserable living victims and dupes of white man's cupidity, degraded, discouraged and lost in the bewildering maze that is produced by the use of whiskey and its concomitant vices; and the remaining number are yet unroused and unenticed from their wild haunts or their primitive modes, by the dread or love of white man and his allurements." Catlin devoted his career to producing and selling an image of the latter group, against which he and his audience measured all other Indians.[2]

Some painters proved to be more interested than Catlin in the prosaic activities of various Indian groups. Among all of the familiar artists of nineteenth-century frontier regions, Seth Eastman was exceptional for his casual approach to American Indian scenes. As a captain stationed at Fort Snelling in the upper Mississippi Valley during the 1840s, Eastman produced scores of miniature watercolors of the surrounding landscape. Rather than idealize Indian life as it might have been in the past, this realist painter was interested in the customs and activities of local Indians living in the present. So Eastman depicted Chippewas, Winnebagos, and Sioux in everyday life – fishing, camping, hunting, fighting, mourning, dancing, and traveling – without delivering a social commentary or romantic vision.[3] Trade with non-Indians also constituted an important feature of everyday life in many Indian communities, and a few artists managed to capture places and situations where exchange ordinarily occurred. Not as dramatic or romantic as scenes of remote Indian life, episodes of exchange were depicted by such well-known painters as Alfred Jacob Miller and Karl Bodmer. Artists who illustrated eastern Indians engaged in everyday interaction with non-Indians during the nineteenth century might be less familiar but are no less interesting as sources of pictorial information.[4]

Derogatory perceptions of Indian communities located close to non-Indian towns and cities also shaped historical works written about American Indians in earlier times. Writing about Indians in seventeenth- and eighteenth-century North America, Francis Parkman scorned those Indian communities that were still situated along the St. Lawrence River during his own lifetime. As he described the Huron mission town of New Lorette, in closing a chapter on refugees of the Iroquois War, "here, to this day, the tourist finds the remnant of a lost people, harmless weavers of baskets and sewers of moccasins, the Huron blood fast bleaching out of them."[5] Growing up in Portage, Wisconsin, young Frederick Jackson Turner visited Winnebago and Menominee villages on frequent fishing trips and saw Indian people when they visited his town. As owner and publisher of the *Wisconsin State Register*, Turner's father often condemned these "worthless savages," demanding in at least one issue of his newspaper that the government remove them from "a community where they are utterly despised, disgusting everyone with their filthiness and alarming timid women by their frightful appearance as they go begging from door to door." Writing about a westward-moving line of civilization, with these childhood memories of Indian acquaintances, Turner the historian must have felt some ambivalence toward the fate of American Indians left behind the frontier.[6]

As in northern states, the sight of Indian groups traveling and camping in pursuit of resources and income was not uncommon in the southeastern United States. Artists, like other travelers, often approached American Indians who occupied the margins of plantation and urban society with great interest. Pictorial impressions of Lower Mississippi Valley Indians over the nineteenth century are available in a variety of sketches, drawings, and paintings.

Charles A. Lesueur, French naturalist and artist, traveled down the Mississippi River to New Orleans at least six times during the 1820s and 1830s. Among several sketches of American Indians in the Lower Mississippi Valley, Lesueur drew a makeshift cabin built by Indian campers outside Memphis (plate 1). Back in 1808 Fortescue Cuming noticed a recently abandoned

Indian camp along the Mississippi River just above Memphis. The temporary huts were formed "with two forked stakes, stuck in the ground, at from six to twelve feet apart, and from four to six feet high. A ridge pole is laid from fork to fork, and long pieces of bark stripped from the neighboring trees, are placed on their ends at a sufficient distance below, while the other ends overlap each other where they meet at the ridge pole."[7] Lesueur also drew a portrait of a Choctaw named James at Petit Gulf (plate 2), two Indians at Baton Rouge (plate 3), and a ball game being played by Indians at New Orleans (plate 4).[8] Felix Achelle Beaupoil de Saint Aulaire's drawings done around 1821 depict Indian families in the New Orleans area, one crossing a street (plate 5) and the other standing on the bank of the Mississippi (plate 6).

Swiss painter Karl Bodmer also captured the ordinary presence of American Indians in New Orleans and other Mississippi River towns in the early nineteenth century as they traveled across the countryside to hunt and trade. Based at the utopian colony of New Harmony, Indiana, with Prince Maximilian, Bodmer traveled alone to New Orleans in January 1833. He stayed for a week with Joseph Barralino, an Italian druggist, who arranged for him to paint American Indians depicted in plates 7–9. Maximilian later recorded in his own diary Bodmer's impressions of the Indians who frequented New Orleans. "Some of them make their fires on the streets," he wrote, "and, like the Negro women, also cook their coffee as well as their *somsé*, and overboiled meat dish." On his return trip to New Harmony, Bodmer spent three days in Baton Rouge and a week in Natchez, painting additional images of Indians in those places (plates 10 and 11).[9]

Bodmer's *Choctaws at Natchez* might be matched with a description written by Joseph Ingraham in the early 1830s. Ingraham had recently moved to Mississippi from Portland, Maine, to teach languages at Jefferson College and later became an Episcopal clergyman and novelist. The New Englander expressed disdain toward quite a few characteristics on the cultural landscape of the Lower Mississippi Valley but aimed some of his most robust prejudice at a group of Choctaw Indians in Natchez:

As I was crossing from the bluff to the entrance of one of the principal streets – a beautiful avenue bordered with the luxuriant China tree, whose dark rich foliage, nearly meeting above, formed a continued arcade as far as the eye could penetrate – my attention was arrested by an extraordinary group, reclining in various attitudes under the grateful shade of the ornamental trees which line the way. With his back firmly planted against a tree, as though there existed a sympathetic affinity between the two, sat an athletic Indian with the neck of a black bottle thrust down his throat, while the opposite extremity pointed to the heavens. Between his left forefinger and thumb he held a corn-cob, as a substitute for a stopper. By his side, his blanket hanging in easy folds from his shoulders, stood a tall, fine-looking youth, probably his son, his raven hair falling masses over his back, with his black eyes fixed upon the elder Indians, as a faithful dog will watch each movement of his intemperate master. One hand supported a rifle, while another was carelessly suspended over his shoulder. There was no change in this group while I remained in sight; they were as immoveable as statues. A little in the rear, lay several "warriors" fast locked in the arms of Bacchus or Somnus, (probably both,) their rifles lying beside them. Near them a knot of embryo chiefs were gamboling in all the glorious freedom of *"sans culottes."* At a little distance, half concealed by huge baskets apparently just unstrapped from their backs, filled with the motley paraphernalia of an Indian lady's wardrobe, sat, cross-legged, a score of dark-eyed, brown-skinned girls and women, laughing and talking in their soft, childish language, as merrily as any ladies would have done, whose "lords" lay thus supine at their feet. Half a score of miserable, starved wretches, "mongrel, whelp and hound," which it were an insult to the noble species to term dogs, wandering about like unburied ghosts "seeking what they might devour," completed the novel and picturesque *ensemble* of the scene.[10]

The disheveled and indigent appearance of Indians in some of Bodmer's pictures seems to represent a derisive attitude profusely expressed in Ingraham's words. The Indian's son resembles a "faithful dog," a rifle is "carelessly" hanging over his shoulder, playful boys are "embryo chiefs," Indian women and girls show "dark eyes and brown skin," their baskets contain "motley" possessions, the language is "childish," and – in what the author perhaps considered his most stinging insult – their dogs are "mongrels."

Many observers believed that only women toiled in Indian society. This reflected a deepening sentiment in middle-class urban culture that men should be the principal breadwinners, whether by farming or by some other means of livelihood.[11] Alfred Boisseau's *Louisiana Indians Walking along a Bayou* (plate 12), painted in 1847, depicted a man with a rifle on his shoulder followed in line by a boy with a blowcane, a woman carrying a basket on her back, and another woman with a baby. This Paris-born painter captured the movement of an Indian family in a way that reflected bourgeois attitudes toward gender. "In a march of these savages," Berquin-Duvallon recorded during his travels through Louisiana in 1802, "I have seen the squaws bend-ing beneath their burdens, while the men walked gravely before, painted with vermilion, and carrying on their shoulders only a light fusee."[12] Harriet Martineau's description of Indians around Columbus, Georgia, in April 1835, also bears an uncanny resemblance to Boisseau's painting:

Groups of Indians were crouching about the entries of the stores, or looking in at the windows. The squaws went by, walking one behind another, with their hair, growing low on the forehead, loose, or tied at the back of the head. . . . These squaws carried large Indian baskets on their backs, and shuffled along, barefooted, while their lords paced before them, well mounted; or if walking, gay with blue and red clothing and embroidered leggings, with tufts of hair at the knees, while pouches and white fringes dangled about them. They looked like grave merry-andrews; or, more still, like solemn fanatical harvest men going out for largess. By eight o'clock they had all disappeared; but the streets were full of them again the next morning.[13]

In accounts of Indian activity around Lower Mississippi Valley towns, the women were usually described as busily making baskets or gathering plants and firewood for sale while the men were portrayed as idle or lazy. "The men kill wild fowl, drink rum, or sit on the ground in a pensive posture doing nothing," wrote Berquin-Duvallon. "The men, when not hunting," according to Fortescue Cuming, "lounge at full length wrapped in their blankets, or sit cross legged, while the women do the domestick drudgery, or make baskets of various shapes with split cane, which they do with great neatness, and a certain degree of ingenuity." Unable to view hunting as a form of work, many observers were nonetheless impressed by the men's skill at the chase. "Those among them who have no guns," Paul Alliot observed about Indian men in the New Orleans area, "make use of a reed in which they place small pebbles or round peas, and by blowing through the reed, they strike rabbits so well that they kill them with as great skill as if they were using guns."[14]

Two paintings by François Bernard are perhaps the most vivid representations of Indian family life in the New Orleans area during the mid–nineteenth century. Born in France, Bernard painted in and around New Orleans from 1856 to 1860 and returned for a short visit in 1867. *Choctaw Village near the Chefuncte* (plate 13) depicts one of the permanent Choctaw communities that formed across Lake Pontchartrain from the city. As discussed in chapter 7, these Indians were becoming the parishioners of Father Adrien Rouquette at about the time this painting was done. In *Louisiana Indian Encampment* (plate 14) Bernard painted a temporary camp that Choctaws and others periodically set up on the outskirts of New Orleans, either on the north or south shore of Lake Pontchartrain. Both paintings capture a leisurely mixture of preparations for both household needs and market sales during the families' more relaxed time together.[15]

Camps of Mississippi and Louisiana Indians scattered across the Lower Mississippi Valley provided subjects for various kinds of literary creativity and social commentary. In 1841 William Gilmore Simms published a short story called "Oakatibbe, or the Choctaw Sampson," which centered on a group of Indians seasonally employed by a planter near Natchez to help pick cotton. Simms had traveled across Mississippi with his father and uncle in 1824, when he was eighteen years old, so he was familiar with this form of Indian-white interaction. In Simms's story, Oakatibbe kills Loblolly Jack in a drunken fight and is sentenced to death by his chief for murdering another Choctaw. The planter views his employment of Indian workers as an experiment in "civilization." The author is skeptical of this plan, however, and depicts Loblolly Jack trying to cheat the planter by pressing down on the scales that weighed his wife's basket of cotton. The courage of Oakatibbe, who accepts responsibility for his actions and refuses to take the planter's advice to flee, represents what Simms saw as the high principles of Indian culture in face of white interference and encroachment. The Indian hero faces execution with nobility.[16]

In *L'Habitation Saint-Ybars*, New Orleans novelist Alfred Mercier tells the story of Titia, a light-skinned young slave who is pregnant with a child conceived in a love relationship with her owner's son. When Titia and her grandmother, Old Lagniappe, are sold in New Orleans to an upriver planter, Old Lagniappe conspires to conceal all traces of African ancestry in Titia's expected child. "She dickers with a wandering band of Choctaws until they agree to let the granddaughter run away with them and bear her child in their midst." Here the marginal and transient presence of Indian families provides a safe space for crossing society's racial lines.[17]

In the 1830s the family of Louis Moreau Gottschalk, New Orleans–born composer and pianist, spent time at a cottage in Pass Christian on the Mississippi Gulf Coast. Choctaws regularly passed through the resort town to sell game and wares, stopping at the Gottschalk residence on occasion. Recalling one such visit during his early childhood, the virtuoso musician deployed a stereotype of American Indians to comment on a lack of refinement among critics and audiences in the United States:

One evening when I was playing "Hail Columbia" a large Indian stopped at the door and inquisitively watched my hands running over the keyboard. My father (although a man of great intelligence, he was not without that weakness in which all fathers participate, who think their children phoenixes) said to the Indian, "You see what this little paleface can do." The vanity of the savage was so much the more wounded as he could not deny that the child did what neither he nor his had ever done. He came in and attentively examined the box where the strange sounds had come from. Tea was ready. We passed into the next room without thinking of the Indian. I alone secretly observed him. His great size and hoarse voice inspired me with childish fear. I saw him, after satisfying himself that he was not observed, slowly approach the piano; he looked attentively at the keyboard, then carelessly, and if by accident, he let his hand fall upon a key, which returned a sound. Scarcely had he heard it when his countenance, which had remained morose, brightened, he sat down at the piano, and with all the force of his arms he began to beat the keys, calling out triumphantly to my father, "You see, I never tried before, and I make more noise than he."

Do you understand my comparison? "No!" Very well, then. Go to B——, and when you are told what someone told me – "Mrs. —— is the best singer here, because you can hear her a mile off" – recall to yourself the Indian of Pass Christian. "This gallery of paintings is the largest we have in America." The Indian of Pass Christian. "Mr. So-and-so is an excellent judge of music; he has spent six months in Europe." Again, my Indian. "Our hotel is as good as the Fifth Avenue or the Continental; look at the number of dishes on the bill of fare." The Indian, always the Indian.[18]

Drawings, photographs, and fiction captured the presence of American Indians in the New Orleans market over the second half of the nineteenth century. Alfred R. Waud's *Sunday in New Orleans – The French Market* (plate 15), from *Harper's Weekly* in 1866, is one of the most detailed illustrations of Indians and their wares in the market. Other drawings offer a closer view of Indian women. *Indian Gumbo Sellers* (plate 16), a sketch by Waud, depicts three women seated before baskets filled with powdered sassafras leaves. *In the French Market* (plate 17) portrays a back view of perhaps a mother and her daughter sitting between a pile of leaves and a large cane basket. The pack basket or *kish'e* made and carried by Choctaw women had long been a distinctive feature of their presence across the Lower Mississippi Valley landscape. Plates 18–20 are photographs of Indian women at the New Orleans market taken during the last decade of the nineteenth century. American Indian women peddling foraged and handcrafted products represented, in the imagination of non-Indian observers, the emasculated condition of a formerly virile people. As Grace King wrote in a history of Louisiana for school-age readers, "the Indian women who to-day sell sassafras and herbs in the French market are descended from the once dreaded tribe of Choctaws."[19]

Choctaw women in the French Market also appear in passing scenes of local literature. In Kate Chopin's 1897 short story, "Nég Créol," the itinerant laborer named Chicot works around the fish market for wages in kind. Depicting this old African American's barter activity, Chopin writes, "He was glad to get a handkerchief from the Hebrew, and grateful if the Choctaws would trade him a bottle of *filé* for it." With a soup bone from the butcher and a few crabs or shrimp from the fishmonger, Chicot was ready to make himself some gumbo.[20] The popular image of Indian women always present at New Orleans markets provided George Washington Cable with an effective simile in his short story "Café des Exilés." To create an opening portrait of the café on Burgundy Street, Cable describes "an antiquated story-and-a-half Creole cottage sitting right down on the banquette, as do the Choctaw squaws who sell bay and sassafras and life everlasting."[21]

J. Dallas's illustration (plate 21) appeared in *Emerson's Magazine* in 1857. It accompanied an article written by Richardson Cox, who wrote that "picturesque groups are often seen under the shadows of the markets, which the artist's eye will seize; not unlikely a party of Indian girls, ready to sell their small wares and willing to be gazed upon."[22] The New Orleans French Market was indeed picturesque, eliciting from visitors countless descriptions of how diverse and lively its vendors were. The gaze directed at scattered groups of Indian vendors is especially interesting, as observers tried to set them peculiarly apart from the rest of the crowd. The disheveled and forlorn look of Dallas's subjects caters to a prevailing opinion among observers about the impaired character of Indians who frequented town. Englishman Charles Latrobe, visiting New Orleans back in 1834, voiced in words a sentiment that the later illustrator perhaps wanted to express:

In the midst of this crowd there was one little cluster of human beings, posted a little apart from the main thoroughfare, which for several days drew my attention and caught my sympathies more than any other. It was a solitary Indian family of the Chocktaw tribe, consisting of a mother and several female children, together with a youth on the verge of manhood. They had come down the river in a small canoe which lay moored in among the shipping, with a petty cargo of coarse basket-work which they were attempting to dispose of. The mother sat on a mat surrounded by her store and occupied with the cares of her restless progeny; while her son, clad in blanket and bright scarlet leggings, lounged against a neighboring pillar with the graceful posture but vacant eye of his race. Every thing about all their little contrivances spoke to my memory of the Forest and Prairie . . . and more than all, of the desolate fortunes of their race — now strangers in their own land — and craving food from the hands of the alien![23]

Racialized images of American Indian groups living in the shadow of the Cotton South mixed pity for their lost past with contempt for their lingering presence. In words and pictures produced by many white observers during the nineteenth century, Indian people still inhabiting their homeland were represented mainly as a sad reminder of civilization's inevitable impact upon the noble savage. This prevailing view not only sentenced them to a hopeless future but also confined them to a predictable past. The history and culture of southern Indians were consequently denied their importance for a long time. But now, the many clues of Indian resilience and survival – even those framed within a language of decline and extinction – are fortunately being investigated with vigor. Once portrayed in American arts and letters as outcasts in the land of their ancestors, American Indians who have struggled through time both to make a decent living and to preserve their cultural identity in the Lower Mississippi Valley play a significant role in the American story.

Notes

1. AMERICAN INDIANS IN THE EARLY SOUTH

1. Neil M. Judd, *The Bureau of American Ethnology: A Partial History* (Norman OK, 1967), 42–43. Also see George E. Lankford's introduction in the University of Oklahoma Press edition of Swanton's *Myths and Tales of the Southeastern Indians* (Norman OK, 1995), xi–xix.

2. A. L. Kroeber, "The Work of John R. Swanton," in *Essays in Historical Anthropology of North America*, Smithsonian Miscellaneous Collections (Washington DC, 1940), 100:2–3. This volume of the Smithsonian Miscellaneous Collections was published in honor of Swanton to celebrate his fortieth year with the Smithsonian. It contains a useful bibliography of Swanton's works through 1939.

3. Kroeber, "The Work of John R. Swanton," 3.

4. See, for example, James Mooney, *Myths of the Cherokee*, Smithsonian Institution, Nineteenth Annual Report of the Bureau of American Ethnology (Washington DC, 1900); Frank G. Speck, "The Creek Indians of Taskigi Town," *American Anthropological Association Memoirs*, no. 2, pt. 11 (1907): 99–164; and David I. Bushnell Jr., *Native Villages and Village Sites East of the Mississippi*, Smithsonian Institution, Bureau of American Ethnology Bulletin 69 (Washington DC, 1919).

5. For a splendid historiographical assessment of American Indian History in general, see R. David Edmunds, "Native Americans, New Voices: American Indian History, 1895–1995," *American Historical Review* 100 (June 1995): 717–40.

6. Herbert Eugene Bolton, ed. and trans., *Athanase de Mézières and the Louisiana-Texas Frontier, 1768–1780* (Cleveland, 1914), two volumes of documents published from original Spanish and French manuscripts chiefly in the archives of Mexico and Spain; Bolton, *Texas in the Middle Eighteenth Century: Studies in Spanish Colonial History and Administration* (Berkeley CA, 1915); Bolton and Mary Ross, *The Debatable Land: A Sketch of the Anglo-Spanish Contest for the Georgia Country* (New York, 1925); John Walton Caughey, *McGillivray of the Creeks* (Norman OK, 1938).

7. John Tate Lanning, *The Spanish Missions of Georgia* (Chapel Hill NC, 1935) and

The Diplomatic History of Georgia: A Study of the Epoch of Jenkins' Ear (Chapel Hill NC, 1936).

8. Anna Lewis, *Along the Arkansas* (Dallas TX, 1932) and *Chief Pushmataha, American Patriot: The Story of the Choctaws' Struggle for Survival* (New York, 1959); Winnie Lewis Gravitt, "Anna Lewis: A Great Woman of Oklahoma," *Chronicles of Oklahoma* 40 (winter 1962–63): 326–29.

9. Verner W. Crane, *The Southern Frontier, 1670–1732*, with a new preface by Peter H. Wood (1928; New York: W. W. Norton, 1981), ix–xiv.

10. Helen Louisie Shaw, *British Administration of the Southern Indians, 1756–1783* (Lancaster PA, 1931); Chapman J. Milling, *Red Carolinians* (Chapel Hill NC, 1940); John R. Alden, *John Stuart and the Southern Colonial Frontier* (Ann Arbor MI, 1944).

11. David H. Corkran, *The Cherokee Frontier: Conflict and Survival, 1740–62* (Norman OK, 1962); Corkran, *The Creek Frontier, 1540–1783* (Norman OK, 1967); Louis De Vorsey Jr., *The Indian Boundary in the Southern Colonies, 1763–1775* (Chapel Hill NC, 1966); J. Leitch Wright Jr., *William Augustus Bowles: Director General of the Creek Nation* (Athens GA, 1967); James H. O'Donnell III, *Southern Indians in the American Revolution* (Knoxville TN, 1973).

12. Douglas L. Rights, *The American Indian in North Carolina* (Durham NC, 1947); Henry Thompson Malone, *Cherokees of the Old South: A People in Transition* (Athens GA, 1956); Douglas Summers Brown, *The Catawba Indians: The People of the River* (Columbia SC, 1966).

13. R. S. Cotterill, *The Southern Indians: The Story of the Civilized Tribes before Removal* (Norman OK, 1954), ix.

14. Steven C. Schulte, "Robert S. Cotterill," in *Historians of the American Frontier: A Bio-Bibliographical Sourcebook*, ed. John R. Wunder (Westport CT, 1988), 199–213.

15. Grant Foreman, *Indian Removal: The Emigration of the Five Civilized Tribes of Indians* (Norman OK, 1932). Foreman wrote about southern Indians' postremoval experiences in *Advancing the Frontier, 1830–1860* (Norman OK, 1933) and *The Five Civilized Tribes: Cherokee, Chickasaw, Choctaw, Creek, Seminole* (Norman OK, 1934). For a discerning analysis of Foreman's work, see Michael D. Green, "Grant Foreman," in *Historians of the American Frontier*, 262–78.

16. Angie Debo, *The Rise and Fall of the Choctaw Republic* (Norman OK, 1934); Debo, *The Road to Disappearance: A History of the Creek Confederacy* (Norman OK, 1941).

17. Perhaps the best book on southern Indians published in the Civilization of the American Indian series that followed this format to some extent but devoted more than usual attention to the colonial period is Arrell M. Gibson, *The Chickasaws* (Norman OK, 1971).

18. Charles M. Hudson, *The Catawba Nation* (Athens GA, 1970); Hudson, ed.,

Red, White, and Black: Symposium on Indians in the Old South (Athens GA, 1971); Hudson, ed., *Four Centuries of Southern Indians* (Athens GA, 1975), quote from p. 1; Hudson, ed., *Black Drink: A Native American Tea* (Athens GA, 1979).

19. Charles Hudson, *The Southeastern Indians* (Knoxville TN, 1976). Hudson's book-length studies of the sixteenth century include *The Juan Pardo Expeditions: Exploration of the Carolinas and Tennessee, 1566–1568* (Washington DC, 1990); *Hernando de Soto and the Indians of Florida* [co-authored with Jerald T. Milanich] (Gainesville FL, 1993); and *Knights of Spain: Warriors of the Sun: Hernando de Soto and the South's Ancient Chiefdoms* (Athens GA, 1997).

20. Wilcomb E. Washburn, *The Governor and the Rebel: A History of Bacon's Rebellion in Virginia* (Chapel Hill NC, 1957); Mary Elizabeth Young, *Redskins, Ruffleshirts, and Rednecks: Indian Land Allotments in Alabama and Mississippi, 1830–1860* (Norman K, 1961). For examples of Mary Young's recent work on the Cherokees, see "The Cherokee Nation: Mirror of the Republic," *American Quarterly* 33 (winter 1981): 502–24, and "The Exercise of Sovereignty in Cherokee Georgia," *Journal of the Early Republic* 10 (spring 1990): 43–63.

21. Frederick O. Gearing, *Priests and Warriors: Social Structures for Cherokee Politics in the 18th Century* (Menasha WI, 1962); John P. Reid, *A Law of Blood: Primitive Law of the Cherokee Nation* (New York, 1970); Reid, *A Better Kind of Hatchet: Law, Trade and Diplomacy in the Cherokee Nation during the Early Years of European Contact* (University Park PA, 1976); Rennard Strickland, *Fire and the Spirits: Cherokee Law from Clan to Court* (Norman OK, 1975); Gary C. Goodwin, *Cherokees in Transition: A Study of Changing Culture and Environment Prior to 1775* (Chicago, 1977).

22. Daniel F. Littlefield Jr., *Africans and Seminoles: From Removal to Emancipation* (Westport CT, 1977); Littlefield, *Africans and Creeks: From the Colonial Period to the Civil War* (Westport CT, 1979); Theda Perdue, *Slavery and the Evolution of Cherokee Society, 1540–1866* (Knoxville TN 1979); Michael D. Green, *The Politics of Indian Removal: Creek Government and Society in Crisis* (Lincoln NE, 1982).

23. William G. McLoughlin, *Cherokees and Missionaries, 1789–1839* (New Haven CT, 1984); *Cherokee Renascence in the New Republic* (Princeton NJ, 1986); *The Cherokee Ghost Dance: Essays on the Southeastern Indians, 1789–1861* (Macon GA, 1986); *Champions of the Cherokees: Evan and John B. Jones* (Princeton NJ, 1993); *After the Trail of Tears: The Cherokees' Struggle for Sovereignty, 1839–1880* (Chapel Hill NC, 1993). For a knowledgeable assessment of McLoughlin's Cherokee studies, see Theda Perdue's review article in *Ethnohistory* 42 (fall 1995): 651–57.

24. J. Leitch Wright Jr., *The Only Land They Knew: The Tragic Story of the American Indians in the Old South* (New York, 1981); *Creeks and Seminoles: The Destruction and Regeneration of the Muscogulge People* (Lincoln NE, 1986).

25. The major books on postremoval Indians of the South written over the past

quarter-century, in order of publication years, are: W. McKee Evans, *To Die Game: The Story of the Lowry Band, Indian Guerrillas of Reconstruction* (Baton Rouge LA, 1971); Harry A. Kersey Jr., *Pelts, Plumes, and Hides: White Traders among the Seminole Indians, 1870–1930* (Gainesville FL, 1975); Walter L. Williams, ed., *Southeastern Indians since the Removal Era* (Athens GA, 1979); Karen I. Blu, *The Lumbee Problem: The Making of an American Indian People* (Cambridge MA, 1980); Kendall Blanchard, *The Mississippi Choctaws at Play: The Serious Side of Leisure* (Urbana IL, 1981); John R. Finger, *The Eastern Band of Cherokees, 1819–1900* (Knoxville TN, 1984); Samuel J. Wells and Roseanna Tubby, eds., *After Removal: The Choctaw in Mississippi* (Jackson MS, 1986); Fred B. Kniffen, Hiram F. Gregory, and George A. Stokes, *The Historic Indian Tribes of Louisiana: From 1542 to the Present* (Baton Rouge LA, 1987); Patti Carr Black, ed., *Persistence of Pattern in Mississippi Choctaw Culture* (Jackson MS, 1988); Kersey, *The Florida Seminoles and the New Deal, 1933–1942* (Gainesville FL, 1989); E. Stanly Godbold Jr. and Mattie U. Russell, *Confederate Colonel and Cherokee Chief: The Life of William Holland Thomas* (Knoxville TN, 1990); Helen C. Rountree, *Pocahontas's People: The Powhatan Indians of Virginia through Four Centuries* (Norman OK, 1990); Russell Thornton, *The Cherokees: A Population History* (Lincoln NE, 1990); Finger, *Cherokee Americans: The Eastern Band of Cherokees in the Twentieth Century* (Lincoln NE, 1991); Sharlotte Neely, *Snowbird Cherokees: People of Persistence* (Athens GA, 1991); J. Anthony Paredes, ed., *Indians of the Southeastern United States in the Late 20th Century* (Tuscaloosa AL, 1992); Gerald Sider, *Lumbee Indian Histories: Race, Ethnicity and Indian Identity in the Southern United States* (Cambridge MA, 1993); Clara Sue Kidwell, *Choctaws and Missionaries in Mississippi, 1818–1918* (Norman OK, 1995); Kersey, *An Assumption of Sovereignty: Social and Political Transformation among the Florida Seminoles, 1953–1979* (Lincoln NE, 1996).

26. For assessments of American Indian and African-American studies, respectively, for the colonial period, see James H. Merrell, "Some Thoughts on Colonial Historians and American Indians," *William and Mary Quarterly*, 3d ser., 46 (January 1989): 94–119, and Donald R. Wright, *African Americans in the Colonial Era: From African Origins through the American Revolution* (Arlington Heights IL, 1990), 153–75.

27. For examples of this new scholarship, see Patricia K. Galloway, ed., *La Salle and His Legacy: Frenchmen and Indians in the Lower Mississippi Valley* (Jackson MS, 1982); Richard White, *The Roots of Dependency: Subsistence, Environment, and Social Change among the Choctaws, Pawnees, and Navajos* (Lincoln NE, 1983); Karen Ordahl Kupperman, *Roanoke: The Abandoned Colony* (Totowa NJ, 1984); J. Frederick Fausz, "Present at the 'Creation': The Chesapeake World that Greeted the Maryland Colonists," *Maryland Historical Magazine* 79 (spring 1984): 7–20; Fausz, "Middlemen in Peace and War: Virginia's Earliest Indian Interpreters, 1608–1632," *Virginia Maga-*

zine of History and Biography 95 (January 1987): 41–64; Jeffrey P. Brain, *Tunica Archaeology* (Cambridge MA, 1988); James Merrell, *The Indians' New World: Catawbas and Their Neighbors from European Contact through the Era of Removal* (Chapel Hill NC, 1989); Helen C. Rountree, *The Powhatan Indians of Virginia: Their Traditional Culture* (Norman OK, 1989); Peter H. Wood, Gregory A. Waselkov, and M. Thomas Hatley, eds., *Powhatan's Mantle: Indians in the Colonial Southeast* (Lincoln NE, 1989); Michael James Foret, "War or Peace? Louisiana, the Choctaws, and the Chickasaws, 1733–1735," *Louisiana History* 31 (summer 1990): 272–93; Timothy Silver, *A New Face on the Countryside: Indians, Colonists, and Slaves in South Atlantic Forests, 1500–1800* (Cambridge MA, 1990); Joel W. Martin, *Sacred Revolt: The Muskogees' Struggle for a New World* (Boston, 1991); Edward J. Cashin, *Lachlan McGillivray, Indian Trader: The Shaping of the Southern Colonial Frontier* (Athens GA, 1992); Daniel H. Usner Jr., *Indians, Settlers, and Slaves in a Frontier Exchange Economy: The Lower Mississippi Valley before 1783* (Chapel Hill NC, 1992); John A. Walthall and Thomas E. Emerson, eds., *Calumet and Fleur-de-Lys: Archaeology of Indian and French Contact in the Midcontinent* (Washington DC, 1992); Kathryn E. Holland Braund, *Deerskins and Duffels: Creek Indian Trade with Anglo-America, 1685–1815* (Lincoln NE, 1993); Douglas J. Deal, *Race and Class in Colonial Virginia: Indians, Englishmen, and Africans on the Eastern Shore during the Seventeenth Century* (New York, 1993); M. Thomas Hatley, *The Dividing Paths: Cherokees and South Carolinians through the Era of Revolution* (New York, 1993); Stephen R. Potter, *Commoners, Tribute, and Chiefs: The Development of Algonquian Culture in the Potomac Valley* (Charlottesville VA, 1993); Patricia Galloway, *Choctaw Genesis, 1500–1700* (Lincoln NE, 1995); F. Todd Smith, *The Caddo Indians: Tribes at the Convergence of Empires, 1542–1854* (College Station TX, 1995); Gregory A. Waselkov and Kathryn E. Holland Braund, eds., *William Bartram on the Southeastern Indians* (Lincoln NE, 1995); J. Russell Snapp, *John Stuart and the Struggle for Empire on the Southern Frontier* (Baton Rouge LA, 1996); James Axtell, *The Indians' New South: Cultural Change in the Colonial Southeast* (Baton Rouge LA, 1997); Frederic W. Gleach, *Powhatan's World and Colonial Virginia: A Conflict of Cultures* (Lincoln NE, 1997). Also see Gregory Evans Dowd, *A Spirited Resistance: The North American Indian Struggle for Unity, 1745–1815* (Baltimore, 1992), and Colin G. Calloway, *The American Revolution in Indian Country: Crisis and Diversity in Native American Communities* (Cambridge MA, 1994) for studies of broader geographical scope that include important analysis of southern Indians.

28. Robert S. Weddle, *Spanish Sea: The Gulf of Mexico in North American Discovery, 1500–1685* (College Station TX, 1985); Paul E. Hoffman, *A New Andalucia and a Way to the Orient: The American Southeast during the Sixteenth Century* (Baton Rouge LA, 1990); Hudson, *Juan Pardo Expeditions* and *Knights of Spain*; Patricia Gal-

loway, ed., *The Hernando de Soto Expedition: History, Historiography, and "Discovery"
in the Southeast* (Lincoln NE, 1997). Carl O. Sauer's *Sixteenth Century North America:
The Land and the People as Seen by the Europeans* (Berkeley CA, 1971) and *Seventeenth
Century North America* (Berkeley CA, 1980) and David B. Quinn's *North America
from Earliest Discovery to First Settlements: The Norse Voyages to 1612* (New York, 1977)
are important earlier works that revealed the extent and impact of European contact
with American Indians in the sixteenth- and early-seventeenth-century South.

29. George R. Milner, "Epidemic Disease in the Postcontact Southeast: A Reap-
praisal," *Midcontinental Journal of Archaeology* 5 (1980): 39–56; Henry F. Dobyns,
*Their Number become Thinned: Native American Population Dynamics in Eastern North
America* (Knoxville TN, 1983); Ann F. Ramenofsky, *Vectors of Death: The Archaeology
of European Contact* (Albuquerque, 1987); Marvin T. Smith, *Archaeology of Aboriginal
Culture Change in the Interior Southeast: Depopulation during the Early Historic Period*
(Gainesville FL, 1987).

30. The major books in this area include Amy Turner Bushnell, *Situatdo and
Sabana: Spain's Support System for the Presidio and Mission Provinces of Florida* (Athens
GA, 1995); Kathleen Deagan, *Spanish St. Augustine: The Archaeology of Colonial Creole
Community* (New York, 1983); John H. Hann, *Apalachee: The Land between the
Rivers* (Tallahassee FL, 1988); Hann, *A History of the Timucua Indians and Missions*
(Gainesville FL, 1996); Jerald T. Milanich, *Florida Indians and the Invasion from Eu-
rope* (Gainesville FL, 1995); Milanich, *The Timucua* (Cambridge MA, 1996); and
Brent Richards Weisman, *Excavations on the Franciscan Frontier: Archaeology at the
Fig Springs Mission* (Gainesville FL, 1992). For significant path-breaking works on
early Spanish Florida, see Eugene Lyon, *The Enterprise of Florida: Pedro Menéndez de
Avilés and the Spanish Conquest of 1565–1568* (Gainesville FL, 1976); Lyon, "Spain's
Sixteenth-Century North American Settlement Attempts: A Neglected Aspect,"
Florida Historical Quarterly 59 (January 1981): 275–91; and David Hurst Thomas,
Grant D. Jones, Roger S. Durham, and Clark Spencer Larsen, *The Anthropology of St.
Catherines Island: 1. Natural and Cultural History,* Anthropological Papers of the
American Museum of Natural History (New York, 1978), 55(2):155–248.

31. Charles Hudson and Carmen Chaves Tesser, eds., *The Forgotten Centuries: Indians and Europeans in the American South, 1521–1704* (Athens GA, 1994).

32. For examples of publications sponsored by Mississippi Choctaws, see Wil-
liam Brescia, ed., *Tribal Government: A New Era* (Philadelphia MS, 1982); Carolyn
Keller Reeves, ed., *The Choctaw before Removal* (Jackson MS, 1985); Wells and Tubby,
After Removal; and Black, *Persistence of Pattern in Mississippi Choctaw Culture.*

33. Peter H. Wood, "When Old Worlds Meet," *Southern Exposure* 20 (spring
1992): 14–45; Mary Ann Wells, *Native Land: Mississippi, 1540–1798* (Jackson MS,
1994).

34. Frederick E. Hoxie, "The Problems of Indian History," *Social Science Journal* 25, no. 4 (1988): 389–99; Merrell, "Some Thoughts on Colonial Historians and American Indians"; Daniel K. Richter, "Whose Indian History?" *William and Mary Quarterly*, 3d ser., 50 (April 1993): 379–93.

35. Peter Wood has laid important groundwork at the regional level in "The Changing Population of the Colonial South: An Overview by Race and Region, 1685–1790," in *Powhatan's Mantle*, 35–103.

36. Helen Hornbeck Tanner, ed., *Atlas of Great Lakes Indian History* (Norman OK, 1987).

37. See, for excellent examples, M. Thomas Hatley, "The Three Lives of Keowee: Loss and Recovery in Eighteenth-Century Cherokee Villages," and Patricia Galloway, "'The Chief Who Is Your Father': Choctaw and French Views of the Diplomatic Relation," in *Powhatan's Mantle*, 223–48, 254–78. For a promising effort to focus analysis on a particular Indian community during the colonial period, see Joshua Piker, "'Peculiarly Connected': The Creek Town of Oakfuskee and the Study of Colonial American Communities, 1708–1785" (Ph.D. diss., Cornell University, 1998).

38. Nancy Shoemaker, ed., *Negotiators of Change: Historical Perspectives on Native American Women* (New York, 1995), captures the depth and breadth of current studies.

39. Braund, *Deerskins and Duffels*; Hatley, *Dividing Paths*. Also see Braund, "Guardians of Tradition and Handmaidens to Change: Women's Roles in Creek Economic and Social Life during the Eighteenth Century," *American Indian Quarterly* 14 (summer 1990): 239–58.

40. Theda Perdue, *Cherokee Women: Gender and Culture Change, 1700–1835* (Lincoln NE, 1998).

41. For a variety of recent works that reveal the importance of the early national period in southern Indian history, with varying degrees of emphasis on Indian experiences, see Frank Lawrence Owsley Jr., *Struggle for the Gulf Borderlands: The Creek War and the Battle of New Orleans, 1812–1815* (Gainesville FL, 1981); John D. W. Guice, "Face to Face in Mississippi Territory, 1798–1817," in *Choctaw before Removal*, 157–80; Samuel J. Wells, "Federal Indian Policy: From Accommodation to Removal," in *Choctaw before Removal*, 181–213; William S. Coker and Thomas D. Watson, *Indian Traders of the Southeastern Spanish Borderlands: Panton, Leslie & Company and John Forbes & Company, 1783–1847* (Pensacola FL, 1986); Florette Henri, *The Southern Indians and Benjamin Hawkins, 1796–1816* (Norman OK, 1986); Wright, *Creeks and Seminoles*; Martin, *Sacred Revolt*. For promising new approaches to this period that focus sharply on Indian agency, see James Taylor Carson, "Searching for the Bright Path: The Mississippi Choctaws from Contact to Removal" (Ph.D. diss.,

University of Kentucky, 1996) and Markusz Claudio Saunt, "A New Order of Things: Creeks and Seminoles in the Deep South Interior, 1733–1816" (Ph.D. diss., Duke University, 1996).

2. FRENCH-NATCHEZ BORDERLANDS

1. Beginning with John R. Swanton, "Ethnological Position of the Natchez Indians," *American Anthropologist*, n.s., 9 (July–September 1907): 513–28, there is a long list of essays that address Natchez social and political organization.

2. Swanton, *Indian Tribes of the Lower Mississippi Valley and Adjacent Coast of the Gulf of Mexico*, Smithsonian Institution, Bureau of American Ethnology Bulletin 43 (Washington DC, 1911), 2, 257.

3. For interesting attempts to make sense of Louisiana's apparently unusual situation in comparison with other colonies, see David C. Rankin, "The Tannenbaum Thesis Reconsidered: Slavery and Race Relations in Antebellum Louisiana," *Southern Studies* 18 (spring 1979): 5–31, and Joseph Zitomersky, "The Form and Function of French-Native American Relation in Early Eighteenth-Century French Colonial Louisiana," in *Proceedings of the Fifteenth Meeting of the French Colonial Historical Society*, ed. Patricia Galloway and Philip P. Boucher (Lanham MD, 1992), 154–77.

4. Major works in the historiography of Natchez-French relations include Swanton, *Indian Tribes of the Lower Mississippi Valley*; Andrew C. Albrecht, "Indian-French Relations at Natchez," *American Anthropologist*, n.s., 48 (July–September 1946): 321–54; Patricia D. Woods, "The French and the Natchez Indians in Louisiana: 1700–1731," *Louisiana History* 19 (fall 1978): 413–35; Woods, *French-Indian Relations on the Southern Frontier, 1699–1762* (Ann Arbor MI, 1980); Ian W. Brown, "An Archaeological Study of Culture Contact and Change in the Natchez Bluffs Region," in *La Salle and His Legacy*, 176–93; Marcel Giraud, *The Company of the Indies, 1723–1731*, trans. Brian Pearce, vol. 5 of *A History of French Louisiana* (Baton Rouge LA, 1991).

5. Renato Rosaldo, *Culture and Truth: The Remaking of Social Analysis* (Boston, 1989), 28–30.

6. See Neal Salisbury, "The Indians' Old World: Native Americans and the Coming of Europeans," *William and Mary Quarterly*, 3d ser., 53 (July 1996): 435–58, for a general discussion of this point and Galloway, *Choctaw Genesis*, for a specific analysis closely related to the Natchez case.

7. While framing these questions, I have been especially impressed with such notable works on native resistance and adaptation in the Spanish colonial world as Nancy M. Farriss, *Maya Society under Colonial Rule: The Collective Enterprise of Survival* (Princeton NJ, 1984); Karen Spalding, *Huarochirí: An Andean Society under Inca and Spanish Rule* (Stanford CA, 1984), and Steve J. Stern, ed., *Resistance, Rebel-*

lion, and Consciousness in the Andean Peasant World, 18th to 20th Centuries (Madison WI, 1987). Meanwhile, important works on Indian-colonial relations in North America have also advanced my understanding. See especially Merrell, *Indians' New World*; Richard White, *The Middle Ground: Indians, Empires, and Republics in the Great Lakes Region, 1650–1815* (New York, 1991); and Daniel K. Richter, *The Ordeal of the Longhouse: The Peoples of the Iroquois League in the Era of European Colonization* (Chapel Hill NC, 1992).

8. Jeffrey P. Brain, "La Salle at the Natchez: An Archaeological and Historical Perspective," in *La Salle and His Legacy*, 49–59.

9. Antoine Le Page du Pratz, *The History of Louisiana*, ed. Joseph Tregle Jr. (1774; Baton Rouge LA, 1975), 327–33; Andrew C. Albrecht, "Ethical Precepts among the Natchez Indians," *Louisiana Historical Quarterly* 31 (July 1948): 581, 586–88.

10. Mallory McCane O'Connor, *Lost Cities of the Ancient Southeast* (Gainesville FL, 1995), 92–97.

11. Le Page du Pratz, *History of Louisiana*, 346–47; Swanton, *Indian Tribes of the Lower Mississippi*, 107.

12. Mary Haas, "Natchez and Chitimacha Clans and Kinship Terminology," *American Anthropologist* 41 (October–December 1939): 602; Charles Hart, "A Reconsideration of the Natchez Social Structure," *American Anthropologist* 45 (July–September 1943): 374–87; George Quimby Jr., "Natchez Social Structure as an Instrument of Assimilation," *American Anthropologist* 48 (January–March 1946): 134–36; Elizabeth Tooker, "Natchez Social Organization," *Ethnohistory* 10 (fall 1963): 358–72; John Fischer, "Solutions for the Natchez Paradox," *Ethnology* 3 (January 1964): 53–65; Jeffrey P. Brain, "The Natchez 'Paradox,'" *Ethnology* 10 (April 1971): 215–22; Douglas R. White, George P. Murdock, and Richard Scaglion, "Natchez Class and Rank Reconsidered," *Ethnology* 10 (October 1971): 369–88; Ian W. Brown, "Natchez Indians and the Remains of a Proud Past," in *Natchez before 1830*, ed. Noel Polk (Jackson MS, 1989), 8–28.

13. "Memoir Sent in 1693, on the Discovery of the Mississippi and the Neighboring Nations by M. de La Salle, from the Year 1678 to the time of his death, and by the Sieur de Tonty to the Year 1691," in *Historical Collections of Louisiana*, ed. B. F. French (New York, 1846–53), 1:62–65.

14. Ruth Lapham Butler, trans., *Journal of Paul Du Ru (February 1 to May 8, 1700) Missionary Priest to Louisiana* (Chicago, 1934), 38–39.

15. "Relation or Journal of the voyage of Father Gravier, of the Society of Jesus, in 1700, from the Country of the Illinois to the Mouth of the Mississippi River . . . 16th of February, 1701," in *The Jesuit Relations and Allied Documents: Travels and Explorations of the Jesuit Missionaries in New France, 1610–1710*, ed. Reuben Gold Thwaites (Cleveland, 1900), 65:142–45.

16. *Journal of Paul Du Ru*, 39, 42; "Relation . . . of Father Gravier," 145.

17. Richebourg Gaillard McWilliams, ed., *Fleur de Lys and Calumet: Being the Pénicaut Narrative of French Adventure in Louisiana* (Baton Rouge LA, 1953), 92–96, cited hereafter as *Pénicaut Narrative*.

18. "Memoir Sent in 1693," 62; "Relation . . . of Father Gravier," 139.

19. "Letter from Father Le Petit, Missionary, to Father d'Avaugour, Procurator of the Missions in North America. At New Orleans, July 12, 1730," in *Jesuit Relations*, 68:139–41.

20. *Pénicaut Narrative*, 86–87.

21. Richard Switzer, *Chateaubriand* (New York, 1971), 43–49, 80–87; Letha Wood Audhuy, "Natchez in French Louisiana and Chateaubriand's Epic, *The Natchez*," in *Natchez before 1830*, 29–42.

22. *Mississippi Provincial Archives: French Dominion*, vols. 1–5, ed. Dunbar Rowland and Albert Godfrey Sanders (Jackson MS, 1929–1932), vols. 4–5, rev. and ed. Patricia Kay Galloway (Baton Rouge LA, 1984), 2:20–29, 58–59, 3:35–36, cited hereafter as *MPAFD*; Giraud, *The Reign of Louis XIV, 1698–1715*, trans. Joseph C. Lambert, vol. 1 of *A History of French Louisiana* (Baton Rouge LA, 1974), 76–79, 99–101.

23. *Pénicaut Narrative*, 162–63.

24. *MPAFD*, 3:208–14; *Pénicaut Narrative*, 180; Albrecht, "Relations at Natchez," 333–34.

25. *MPAFD*, 3:210.

26. *MPAFD*, 2:9–18, 31–32, 167.

27. *MPAFD*, 2:58–59, 211–19.

28. *MPAFD*, 2:247.

29. *Pénicaut Narrative*, 80–83.

30. *MPAFD*, 2:58–59, 211–19; Pierre François Xavier de Charlevoix, *Journal of a Voyage to North America* (London, 1761), 2:267; "Letter from Father Le Petit," 141–43; *Pénicaut Narrative*, 87; Le Page du Pratz, *History of Louisiana*, 328, 343.

31. François Le Maire, "Memoir on Louisiana," 1714–1717, Works Progress Administration (WPA) typescript copy, Manuscript Department, Perkins Library, Duke University, 5, 20.

32. *Pénicaut Narrative*, 237–39.

33. "Historical Memoirs of M. Dumont," in *Historical Collections*, 5:31–32; Charlevoix, *Journal*, 2:255–58.

34. "Excerpt from a letter written by M. Faucond du Manoir, Director General of the Colony of Ste Catherine, July 18, 1721," *Louisiana Historical Quarterly* 2 (April 1919): 164–69; Le Page du Pratz, *History of Louisiana*, 305–6; Swanton, *Indian Tribes*

of the Lower Mississippi, 40. See chapter 3 for analysis of decline and other forms of population change among all Lower Mississippi Valley Indians.

35. "Historical Memoirs of M. Dumont," 32; Jean-Baptiste Bernard de La Harpe, *The Historical Journal of the Establishment of the French in Louisiana*, trans. Joan Cain and Virginia Koenig, ed. and annot. Glenn R. Conrad (Lafayette LA, 1971), 98; Le Page du Pratz, *History of Louisiana*, 35–36, 375. Samuel Wilson Jr., "French Fortification at Fort Rosalie, Natchez," in *La Salle and His Legacy*, 194–210.

36. Le Maire, "Memoir on Louisiana," 11; Le Page du Pratz, *History of Louisiana*, 29, 35, 48, 248–53.

37. Le Page du Pratz, *History of Louisiana*, 329.

38. La Harpe, *Journal*, 216–17; MPAFD, 3:360; "Narrative of the Hostilities Committed by the Natchez Against the Concession of St. Catherine, 1722," *Journal of Mississippi History* 7 (January 1945): 3–10; Joe Wilkins, "'The French Have Two Hearts': Bienville and the Natchez, 1715–1723: A Prelude to the Natchez Revolt of November 28, 1729" (paper presented at the French Colonial Historical Society, Cleveland, 28 May 1994).

39. MPAFD, 2:374, 396–99, 3:366–77; Le Page du Pratz, *History of Louisiana*, 38–39; "Historical Memoirs of M. Dumont," 47–50.

40. MPAFD, 3:385–71.

41. "Historical Memoirs of M. Dumont," 56; MPAFD, 3:381. For a comparative discussion of colonial policies regarding Indian-black relations, see William Willis Jr., "Divide and Rule: Red, White, and Black in the Southeast," *Journal of Negro History* 48 (July 1963): 157–76; James H. Merrell, "The Racial Education of the Catawba Indians," *Journal of Southern History* 50 (August 1984): 363–84.

42. Charlevoix, *Journal*, 2:280. For a discussion of tension within the Natchez belief system, see Albrecht, "Ethical Precepts," 591, and his "Indian-French Relations at Natchez," 341.

43. "Journal of Diron d'Artaguette, Sept. 1, 1722–Sept. 10, 1723," in *Travels in the American Colonies*, ed. Newton Mereness (New York, 1916), 90–91; "Historical Memoirs of M. Dumont," 59–61; Le Page du Pratz, *History of Louisiana*, 44–45.

44. MPAFD, 1:128; "Historical Memoirs of M. Dumont," 61–63.

45. Le Page du Pratz, *History of Louisiana*, 78–81.

46. Le Page du Pratz, *History of Louisiana*, 81–84.

47. Le Page du Pratz, *History of Louisiana*, 370–73; "Letter from Father Le Petit," 143–47. For analysis of the use of emetics in southeastern Indian rituals, see Hudson, *Black Drink*.

48. MPAFD, 1:54, 58, 62–63, 76; "Historical Memoirs of M. Dumont," 77; Giraud, *Company of the Indies*, 392–98.

49. *MPAFD*, 1:64–65, 71.

50. *MPAFD*, 1:68–69, 79–80; "Letter from Father Le Petit," 189, 197–98; Giraud, *The Company of the Indies*, 399–425.

51. *MPAFD*, 4:57–58, 79, 102–5; John A. Green, "Governor Périer's Expedition Against the Natchez Indians, December, 1730-January, 1731," *Louisiana Historical Quarterly* 19 (July 1936), 547–77.

52. *MPAFD*, 1:196–99, 234–35, 3:530–31, 622–25, 4:73, 77–79, 102–3, 111–13.

53. "Historical Memoires of M. Dumont," 5:96.

54. Giraud, *Company of the Indies*, 425–27.

55. *MPAFD*, 1:196–99, 234–35, 3:530–31, 622–25, 4:73, 77–79, 102–3, 111–13, 5:48–49, 76; Foret, "War or Peace?" 275–79.

56. *MPAFD*, 5:48–49, 76.

57. Virginia Pounds Brown, ed., *Creek Indian History: A Historical Narrative of the Genealogy, Traditions and Downfall of the Ispocoga or Creek Indian Tribe of Indians by One of the Tribe, George Stiggins (1788–1845)* (Birmingham AL, 1989), 14–19, 33–42; Swanton, *Indian Tribes of the Lower Mississippi*, 251–57.

58. "Journal of Antoine Bonnefoy," in *Early Travels in the Tennessee Country, 1540–1800*, ed. Samuel Cole Williams (Johnson City TN, 1928), 158.

59. James Mooney, "The End of the Natchez," *American Anthropologist*, n.s., 1 (July 1899): 510–21.

60. Robert K. Thomas, "The Redbird Smith Movement," in *Symposium on Cherokee and Iroquois Culture*, ed. William N. Fenton and John Gulick, Smithsonian Institution, Bureau of American Ethnology Bulletin 180 (Washington DC, 1961), 164; Emanuel J. Drechsel, "The Natchez Way," *Chronicles of Oklahoma* 65 (summer 1987): 174–81.

61. *MPAFD*, 4:39–40.

62. "Letter from Father Le Petit," 195.

3. POPULATION HISTORY IN THE LOWER MISSISSIPPI VALLEY

1. Russell Thornton, *American Indian Holocaust and Survival: A Population History since 1492* (Norman OK, 1987). Douglas H. Ubelaker provides a succinct history of population studies for North American Indians in "North American Indian Population Size: Changing Perspectives," in *Disease and Demography in the Americas*, ed. John W. Verano and Douglas H. Ubelaker (Washington DC, 1992), 169–76.

2. David Henige, "If Pigs Could Fly: Timucuan Population and Native American Historical Demography," *Journal of Interdisciplinary History* 16 (spring 1986): 701–20; Henry F. Dobyns, "More Methodological Perspectives on History Demography," with rejoinders by Dean R. Snow, Kim M. Lanphear, and David Henige, *Eth-*

nohistory 36 (summer 1989): 285–307; John D. Daniels, "The Indian Population of North America in 1492," *William and Mary Quarterly*, 3d ser., 49 (April 1992): 298–320.

3. For a sample of approaches in archaeology, physical anthropology, ethnohistory, and related disciplines, see Verano and Ubelaker, *Disease and Demography in the Americas*, and Clark Spencer Larsen and George R. Milner, eds., *In the Wake of Contact: Biological Responses to Conquest* (New York, 1994).

4. Sherburne F. Cook's path-breaking works on the Indian population of California were collected in a single volume published shortly after his death, *The Conflict between the California Indian and White Civilization* (Berkeley CA, 1976). The most provocative analysis of precontact, protohistoric, and historic Indian populations within a colonial region is Dobyns's study of the Timucuan chiefdom in Florida, *Their Number become Thinned*. The latest advances in the history of Indian depopulation during the colonial era are represented in Daniel T. Reff, *Disease, Depopulation, and Culture Change in Northwestern New Spain, 1518–1764* (Salt Lake City, 1991). For exemplary assessments of Indian populations in other colonial regions, see Arthur J. Ray, *Indians in the Fur Trade: Their Role as Hunters, Trappers, and Middlemen in the Lands Southwest of Hudson Bay, 1660–1870* (Toronto, 1974), esp. 94–116, 182–94; Neal Salisbury, *Manitou and Providence: Indians, Europeans, and the Making of New England, 1500–1643* (New York, 1982), 22–30, 101–5; Gary Clayton Anderson, *Kinsmen of Another Kind: Dakota-White Relations in the Upper Mississippi Valley, 1650–1862* (Lincoln NE, 1984), 14–28; and Colin G. Calloway, "Green Mountain Diaspora: Indian Population Movements in Vermont, c. 1600–1800," *Vermont History* 54 (fall 1986): 197–228.

5. Ramenofsky, *Vectors of Death*, 51–67.

6. Smith, *Archaeology of Aboriginal Culture in the Interior Southeast*, 54–142.

7. For learning the utility of subdividing a study area into smaller population units, I am grateful to Peter H. Wood. In "The Changing Population of the Colonial South: An Overview by Race and Region, 1685–1790," in *Powhatan's Mantle*, 35–103, he delineates ten subregions of the entire South for the sake of analyzing population change among both native and colonial groups. My subregions of the Lower Mississippi Valley do not exactly correspond to his because I am focusing on a smaller region's Indian population, but we strive for the same degree of local specificity in order to understand better general processes of change.

8. A general populace-to-warrior ratio of 3.5:1 is derived from "Colonel Bull's map of the Florida frontier, 1738," MS, Colonial Office Series, Public Record Office, London, reproduced in Verne E. Chatelain, *The Defenses of Spanish Florida 1565 to 1763* (Washington DC, 1941), map 8. Ratios of 2.9:1 for the Creeks, 3.2:1 for the Choctaws, and 3.9:1 for the Chickasaws are indicated in cartographer Joseph Pur-

cell's 1780 figures, cited in *Collections of the Massachusetts Historical Society*, 1st ser. (Boston, 1795), 4:99–100. The Spanish census of the Choctaws in 1795 has been published in Jack D. L. Holmes, "The Choctaws in 1795," *Alabama Historical Quarterly* 30 (spring 1968): 33–49. A ratio of 3.5:1 was used by Swanton in *Indian Tribes of the Lower Mississippi Valley*, 43.

9. This summary of the characteristics of smallpox transmission and infection is based on discussions in Arthur J. Ray, "Diffusion of Diseases in the Western Interior of Canada, 1830–1850," *Geographical Review* 66 (April 1976): 139–57; Clyde D. Dollar, "The High Plains Smallpox Epidemic of 1837–38," *Western Historical Quarterly* 8 (January 1977): 15–38; and Peter H. Wood, "The Impact of Smallpox on the Native Population of the 18th Century South," *New York State Journal of Medicine* 87 (January 1987): 30–36.

10. Russell Thornton, Tim Miller, and Jonathan Warren, "American Indian Population Recovery Following Smallpox Epidemics," *American Anthropologist* 93 (March 1991): 28–45. For access to the literature on disease among Indian peoples, see Henry F. Dobyns, *Native American Historical Demography: A Critical Bibliography* (Bloomington IN, 1976), and Pauline A. Keehn, *The Effect of Epidemic Diseases on the Natives of North America* (London, 1978). A convenient overview of diseases transmitted across the oceans can be found in William H. McNeill, *Plagues and Peoples* (Garden City NY, 1976), 199–234.

11. Milner, "Epidemic Disease in the Postcontact Southeast; Smith, *Archaeology of Aboriginal Culture Change in the Interior Southeast*, 86–112.

12. Richebourg Gaillard McWilliams, trans. and ed., *Iberville's Gulf Journals* (University AL, 1981), 140–41, 169.

13. *MPAFD*, 3:537. Early epidemics around Mobile Bay are discussed in Howard L. Holley, *The History of Medicine in Alabama* (Birmingham AL, 1982), 15–21.

14. *Iberville's Gulf Journals*, 140; La Harpe, *Journal*, 22–23; *MPAFD*, 3:535–37.

15. The journal of Levasseur's expedition up the Mobile River is translated and ethnographically analyzed in Vernon J. Knight Jr. and Sheree L. Adams, "A Voyage to the Mobile and Tomeh in 1700, with Notes on the Interior of Alabama," *Ethnohistory* 28 (spring 1981): 179–94. Cf. *Iberville's Gulf Journals*, 141, and La Harpe, *Journal*, 23.

16. *MPAFD*, 3:26–27, 136.

17. *MPAFD*, 3:535–37; Albert S. Gatschet, *A Migration Legend of the Creek Indians* (Philadelphia, 1884), 33–34, 109–12.

18. Le Page du Pratz, *History of Louisiana*, 308–9; Giraud, *La Louisiane apres le systeme de Law (1721–1723)*, vol. 4 of *Histoire de la Louisiane Française* (Paris, 1974), 421–22.

19. *MPAFD*, 1:167–78, 4:161, 5:224–25. The proximity of these and other Indian communities in the Lower Mississippi Valley to colonial posts is discussed in terms

of comparative settlement patterns in Zitomersky, "Form and Function of French-Native American Relations."

20. Missionary efforts among Indians in the Lower Mississippi Valley were negligible, in contrast to French Canada. The Jesuits and Capuchins who served in Louisiana concentrated their energies on the settler and slave populations. See Jean Delanglez, S.J., *The French Jesuits in Lower Louisiana (1700–1763)* (Washington DC, 1935), 96, 420–90, and Claude L. Vogel, O.M.Cap., *The Capuchins in French Louisiana (1722–1766)* (New York, 1928), 60–64, 122.

21. The figure of 250 warriors is from "Memoir on the state of the Colony of Louisiana in 1746," Archives des Colonies, Paris, Series C13A, 30:259–60. By the middle of the century the Tohomés were absorbed, as distinct villages, into the Choctaw nation. *MPAFD*, 4:313, 315.

22. A copy of this village-by-village list of the number of households was later made by geographer Claude Delisle and has been found in the Archives Hydrographiques, Paris. Its publication in the *Louisiana Historical Quarterly* revealed that the actual totals from the census differed slightly from those specified in Iberville's journal (George Kernion, trans., "Documents Concerning the History of the Indians of the Eastern Region of Louisiana," *Louisiana Historical Quarterly* 8 [January 1925]: 38–39). It is possible that not all of the Choctaw villages were represented at this meeting, since most estimates exceeded fifty in number. On 29 April 1700 the Pascagoulas told Iberville that more than six thousand men lived in fifty different Choctaw villages. *Iberville's Gulf Journals*, 141.

23. *Iberville's Gulf Journals*, 172. South Carolina's Indian agent, who visited the Chickasaws in 1708, reported that "The Chicasaw Tribe at present consists of 700 men Devided in 8 Villages." Alexander Moore, ed., *Nairne's Muskhogean Journals: The 1708 Expedition to the Mississippi River* (Jackson MS, 1988), 36.

24. The list compiled by Levasseur is printed in Knight and Adams, "A Voyage to the Mobile and Tomeh in 1700," 181, 189–92. For Iberville's 1701 estimate see Jay Higginbotham, *Old Mobile: Fort Louis de la Louisiane, 1702–1711* (Mobile AL, 1977), 117–18, n. 14.

25. *MPAFD*, 3:536–37.

26. *MPAFD*, 1:150–54.

27. *MPAFD*, 3:796, 4:81.

28. "Letter from Father Le Petit," 195–97. The effects of disease upon the Choctaw population during these years can be traced in Archives des Colonies C13A, 13:173–78, 18:153v–56; *MPAFD*, 4:58–60, 313.

29. *MPAFD*, 1:183–84, 4:58–60, 313.

30. "Relation de la Louisiane" [c. 1735], anonymous MS, Edward E. Ayer Collection, Newberry Library, Chicago, 117–18, 164–65, 170–72.

31. *MPAFD*, 3:773–74, 4:105, 172.

32. *MPAFD*, 1:146; Lawrence Kinnaird, trans. and ed., *Spain in the Mississippi Valley, 1765–1794* (Washington DC, 1946–49), 1:419.

33. Bernard Romans, *A Concise Natural History of East and West Florida* (1775; reprint, New Orleans, 1961), 55.

34. *MPAFD*, 4:146, 5:47. In addition to the cultural disorientation caused by inexplicable diseases and by other foreign pressures, all of which could themselves drive people to drunkenness, a genetically transmitted biological process might also have been operating to the disadvantage of Indian drinkers. The very metabolic mechanism within their bodies that efficiently converted corn, beans, and other items in their traditional diet into glucose and other sources of energy made Indians extremely vulnerable to refined sugar and distilled alcohol. Unable to metabolize or break down such foodstuffs as rapidly as Europeans, their increasing exposure to cheap rum, manufactured principally for the Indian trade, caused rapid inebriation and chronic alcoholism. Summaries of cultural and biological aspects of alcoholism among Indians are available in Wilcomb E. Washburn, *The Indian in America* (New York, 1975), 107–10, and Dobyns, *Native American Historical Demography*, 27–33. The complex history of alcohol use among American Indians in the British colonial world is skillfully examined in Peter C. Mancall, *Deadly Medicine: Indians and Alcohol in Early America* (Ithaca NY, 1995).

35. Speech of Mingo Emmitta at a Congress of the Principal Chiefs and warriors of the Chickasaw and Choctaw Nations held at Mobille, 2 January 1772, *Publications of the Mississippi Historical Society: Centenary Series* (Jackson MS, 1925), 5:148.

36. "Ress en Sement Des Villages Sauvages de la Poste des Alybamons," enclosed in Major Farmar's letter of 24 January 1764, in *Mississippi Provincial Archives, 1763–1766: English Dominion*, comp. and ed. Dunbar Rowland (Nashville, 1911), 1:94–97. For the immigration of the Shawnees, see *MPAFD*, 4:222, 5:48–49. Also see Wilbur R. Jacobs, ed., *The Appalachian Indian Frontier: The Edmund Atkin Report and Plan of 1755* (Lincoln NE, 1967), 42.

37. Archives des Colonies C13A, 35:384; *Edmund Atkin Report*, 42.

38. The *Pennsylvania Gazette* reported that fifteen hundred Choctaws and three hundred Chickasaws died during the smallpox epidemic of 1763–64. Cited in John Duffy, *Epidemics in Colonial America* (Baton Rouge LA, 1953), 98.

39. Purcell's population figures are quoted in "Observations on the Indians in the Southern Parts of the United States in a Letter from the Hon. Dr. Ramsay, Corresponding Member of the Historical Society, March 10, 1795," *Collections of the Massachusetts Historical Society*, 1st ser. (Boston, 1795), 4:99–100. For discussion of growth and other demographic changes among the Creeks into the nineteenth century, see J. Anthony Paredes and Kenneth J. Plante, "A Reexamination of Creek In-

dian Population Trends: 1738–1832," *American Indian Culture and Research Journal* 6, no. 4 (1982): 3–28.

40. La Harpe, *Journal*, 23–24; Tonti to his brother, 4 March 1700, in "Documents: Tonti Letters," *Mid-America* 21 (July 1939): 223–24; *MPAFD*, 3:527. Tonti's figure of 250 men for the three villages that he visited below the Bayogoulas – Ouacha, Chitimacha, Quisitou – is used here as a rough estimate for the little known Ouachas and Chaouachas. Referring to the Ouachas only in 1726, Bienville recalled an earlier population of "two hundred men fit to bear arms."

41. *Iberville's Gulf Journals*, 63. On his first visit to the Bayogoula village in March 1699, Iberville counted 107 cabins and 2 temples with 200–250 men. His brother later recalled that "they were still of the number of more than two hundred and fifty warriors as laborious as they were brave." *MPAFD*, 3:528. In 1700 Tonti estimated a population of 180 men. "Documents: Tonti Letters," 225–26.

42. Jay Higginbotham, trans. and ed., *The Journal of Sauvole: Historical Journal of the Establishment of the French in Louisiana by M. de Sauvole* (Mobile AL, 1969), 31; *Iberville's Gulf Journals*, 111.

43. *Iberville's Gulf Journals*, 63.

44. *Journal of Paul Du Ru*, 19–22, 52–53.

45. *MPAFD*, 3:38–39, 115–16, 529.

46. The Atakapas included in this study because of their interaction with colonial Louisiana are ethnologically referred to as the Atakapas proper. Three other Atakapan-speaking groups – the Bidais, Akokisas, and Deadoses – lived west of the Sabine River, and by the 1750s their activities centered around Spanish missions and forts in Texas. Elizabeth A. H. John, *Storms Brewed in Other Men's Worlds: The Confrontation of Indians, Spanish, and French in the Southwest, 1540–1795* (College Station TX, 1975), 349–50; Lawrence Aten, *Indians of the Upper Texas Coast* (New York, 1983), 44–64.

47. *MPAFD*, 3:528–29.

48. *Journal of Paul Du Ru*, 65–66.

49. *Iberville's Gulf Journals*, 69, 122; *Journal of Paul Du Ru*, 28–29.

50. La Harpe, *Journal*, 76; *Pénicaut Narrative*, 146.

51. *MPAFD*, 3:527–29, 535–36.

52. Charlevoix, *Journal of a Voyage*, 2:279–80. The rich archaeological and documentary data available for the Tunicas have been compiled in Jeffrey P. Brain, *Tunica Treasure* (Cambridge MA, 1979).

53. *MPAFD*, 3:528–35; Charlevoix, *Journal*, 2:285. The participation of these villagers in the local food market is further discussed in chapter 4.

54. *MPAFD*, 5:212–13. According to Kerlérec's report the Tunicas numbered sixty warriors, the Houmas sixty, the Chitimachas eighty, and the Chaouachas ten to

twelve. Other valuable descriptions of these villages during this period can be found in "Letter from Father du Poisson, Missionary to the Akensas . . . 3rd of October, 1727," in *Jesuit Relations*, 67:276–325, and "Journal of the Chickasaw War, 1739," trans. in J. F. H. Claiborne, *Mississippi, as a Province, Territory and State, with Biographical Notices of Eminent Citizens* (Jackson MS, 1880), 66–67.

55. Carl A. Brasseaux, trans. and annot., *A Comparative View of French Louisiana, 1699 and 1762: The Journals of Pierre Le Moyne d'Iberville and Jean-Jacques-Blaise d'Abbadie* (Lafayette LA, 1979), 100–12; Kinnaird, *Spain in the Mississippi Valley*, 2:14.

56. List of the Several Tribes of Indians inhabiting the banks of the Mississippi, Between New Orleans and Red River, with their number of gun men and places of residence, January 1, 1773, William Haldimand Papers, British Museum (microfilm, Louisiana Division, New Orleans Public Library). A census by Spanish officials indicates a warrior population of 402 among these *petites nations* (Census of Indian Villages and Tribes taken in 1766, *Some Late Eighteenth-Century Louisianians: Census Records of the Colony, 1758–1796*, trans. and comp. Jacqueline K. Voorhies [Lafayette LA, 1973], 164–65). Another English list of "the small Tribes of Indians on the Mississippi who were settled there when this Province was Ceded to His Majesty" shows a total of 237 warriors. *Mississippi Historical Society: Centenary Series*, 5:97.

57. Kinnaird, *Spain in the Mississippi Valley*, 2:65. For information about the twenty thousand or so American Indians presently living in the state of Louisiana, see Kniffen, Gregory, and Stokes, *Historic Indian Tribes of Louisiana*, and Hiram F. Gregory, "The Louisiana Tribes: Entering Hard Times," in *Indians of the Southeastern United States in the Late 20th Century*, 162–82.

58. The Quapaws, a Siouan-speaking people also known as the Arkansas, had been seriously neglected by scholars until W. David Baird, *The Quapaw Indians: A History of the Downstream People* (Norman OK, 1980). See pp. 21–46 of Baird's tribal history for his summary of their relations with European colonies during the period under discussion here. For some of the latest inquiries into the Quapaws during the colonial period, see Jeannie Whayne, comp., *Cultural Encounters in the Early South: Indians and Europeans in Arkansas* (Fayetteville AR, 1995), especially Willard H. Rollings, "Living in a Graveyard: Native Americans in Colonial Arkansas," 38–60.

59. "Relation . . . of Father Gravier," 113–17; "Documents: Tonti Letters," 228–29; *Pénicaut Narrative*, 34–35.

60. "Relation . . . of Father Gravier," 135–37.

61. In 1700 Tonti wrote to his brother that the Taensas numbered more than four hundred men. During the spring of that year Iberville visited them and figured that after several years of decimation "there are not more than 300 men." Twenty-five years after his own visit to the Taensas, Bienville recalled that they were as numerous as the Natchez, whom he estimated had twelve hundred warriors. "Documents:

Tonti Letters," 227; *Iberville's Gulf Journals*, 125; MPAFD, 3:532, 536; Tristram R. Kidder, "Ceramic Chronology and Culture History of the Southern Ouachita River Basin: Coles Creek to the Early Historic Period," *Midcontinental Journal of Archaeology* 15, no. 1 (1990): 51–99.

62. *Journal of Paul Du Ru*, 34–37; "Relation . . . of Father Gravier," 141–43.

63. "Documents: Tonti Letters," 226–27; MPAFD, 3:530–31; Swanton, *Indian Tribes of the Lower Mississippi Valley*, 334–36. Also see chapter 2.

64. MPAFD, 3:530–31. Bienville stated that the Tunicas had "more than five hundred warriors . . . at the time of our exploration." In January 1699 missionary M. de Montigny had visited the Tunicas and estimated that "they make about 2,000 souls." John Gilmary Shea, trans. and ed., *Early Voyages Up and Down the Mississippi, by Cavelier, St. Cosme, Le Seur, Gravier, and Guignas* (Albany NY, 1861), 76.

65. Shea, *Early Voyages*, 80–81. Also see "Relation . . . of Father Gravier," 133.

66. "Letter from Father du Poisson," 319; La Harpe, *Journal*, 202; MPAFD, 3:531–32, 4:316.

67. MPAFD, 3:531. In 1721 Charlevoix observed that in a "fine meadow" one league above the fort on the Yazoo River, there is "a village of the Yasous, mixed with the Couroas and Ofogoulas, who altogether may send about two hundred fighting men into the field." *Journal of a Voyage*, 2:250–51.

68. MPAFD, 3:530–31, 4:73, 77–79, 102–3, 111–13; Gatschet, *Migration Legend of the Creek Indians*, 97–100.

69. According to an anonymous military officer who participated in the campaign against the Chickasaws in 1739, the Quapaws were able to furnish four hundred warriors (Claiborne, *Mississippi*, 71). But by 1758 Governor Kerlérec estimated "about 160 men" for the Quapaws. He also reported then that fifteen warriors comprised the Ofogoula village at the Natchez post (MPAFD, 5:210, 212, 226). The only other major group known still to occupy this area by midcentury was a village of Chachiumas, "about One hundred and fifty Men, living near the Head of the Yasou River, about 60 Miles either from the Choctaw, or the Chickasaw Nation" (*Edmund Atkin Report*, 44). For my 1750 approximation of nineteen hundred Indians in this area, the 1739 estimate of the Quapaws and Atkin's estimate of the Chachiumas were combined.

70. For the details of this attack and an exploration into its wider significance, see Michael James Foret, "Blood on the Bayou: A Black Legend in French Colonial Louisiana?" *Revue Francophone de Louisiane* 2 (spring 1987): 57–63.

71. MPAFD, 4:122–23, 250, 338, 5:62–63; H. B. Cushman, *History of the Choctaw, Chickasaw and Natchez Indians* (Greenville TX, 1899), 242–45; Henry S. Halbert, "The Small Tribes of Mississippi," *Publications of the Mississippi Historical Society*, 5 (1903): 303–4.

72. Philip Pittman, *The Present State of the European Settlements on the Mississippi*, ed. Robert Rea (Gainesville FL, 1973), 40. Also see Robin Fabel, "The Letters of R: The Lower Mississippi in the Early 1770s," *Louisiana History* 24 (fall 1983): 422–23.

73. *MPAFD*, 3:529–30. Our understanding of Caddo history from the late seventeenth century to the mid–nineteenth century has been significantly advanced in Smith, *Caddo Indians*. For his treatment of population changes over the eighteenth century, see pp. 8–9, 22, 37, 54–55, 65, 74–75. Also see Timothy K. Perttula, *The Caddo Nation: Archaeological and Ethnohistoric Perspectives* (Austin TX, 1992).

74. Pierre Margry, comp. and ed., *Découvertes et etablissements des Français dans l'ouest et dans le sud de l'Amerique septentrionale (1614–1754): Mémoires et documents originaux* (Paris, 1876–86), 5:316.

75. Fray Isidro Felis de Espinosa, "Descriptions of the Tejas or Asinai Indians, 1691–1722," trans. Mattie Austin Hatcher, *Southwestern Historical Quarterly* 31 (October 1927): 150–80; Herbert Eugene Bolton, *The Hasinais: Southern Caddoans as Seen by the Earliest Europeans*, ed. with an introduction by Russell M. Magnaghi (Norman OK, 1987); Daniel A. Hickerson, "Historical Processes, Epidemic Disease, and the Formation of the Hasinai Confederacy," *Ethnohistory* 44 (winter 1997): 31–52.

76. *MPAFD*, 3:529–30. The Caddos, Nasonis, Nacogdoches, and Nanatshohos Kichais (Kadohadacho confederacy) numbered two hundred warriors, the Yatasis, Doustionis, and Natchitoches (Natchitoches confederacy) eighty, the Adaes one hundred, and Avoyelles forty.

77. Le Page du Pratz, *Histoire de la Louisiane* (Paris, 1758), 1:297–98, 2:241–42; *MPAFD*, 5:213.

78. La Harpe, *Journal*, 134; De Mézières to Luis de Unzaga, 10 January 1776, *Athanase de Mézières*, 2:120.

79. *Athanase de Mézières*, 2:83.

80. Kinnaird, *Spain in the Mississippi Valley*, 1:156. This westward migration marks the beginning of a strategic movement of several Indian groups across the Mississippi River during the late eighteenth and early nineteenth centuries, which is discussed in chapter 6.

81. *Athanase de Mézières*, 2:83; Bolton, *Texas in the Middle Eighteenth Century*, 312, 379. Site locations and changes among the Caddos are discussed in Clarence H. Webb and Hiram F. Gregory, *The Caddo Indians of Louisiana* (Baton Rouge LA, 1978), 24–32.

82. *Athanase de Mézières*, 2:173, 231–32; John Duffy, ed., *The Rudolph Matas History of Medicine in Louisiana* (Baton Rouge LA, 1958–62), 1:198–201.

83. The effects of this epidemic on other villages in eastern Texas were recorded

by Fray Juan Agustin de Morfi in *History of Texas, 1673–1779*, trans. and annot. Carlos Eduardo Castañeda (Albuquerque, 1935), 1:79–88. For more demographic information about late-eighteenth-century Texas, see John C. Ewers, "The Influence of Epidemics on the Indian Populations and Cultures of Texas," *Plains Anthropologist* 18 (May 1973): 104–15, and Alicia V. Tjarks, "Comparative Demographic Analysis of Texas, 1777–1793," *Southwestern Historical Quarterly* 77 (January 1974): 291–338.

4. AMERICAN INDIANS IN A FRONTIER EXCHANGE ECONOMY

1. Merrell, *Indians' New World*; Peter C. Mancall, *Valley of Opportunity: Economic Culture along the Upper Susquehanna, 1700–1800* (Ithaca NY, 1991); White, *Middle Ground*; Ramon A. Gutiérrez, *When Jesus Came, the Corn Mothers Went Away: Marriage, Sexuality, and Power in New Mexico, 1500–1846* (Stanford CA, 1992).

2. Martin, *Sacred Revolt*; Dowd, *Spirited Resistance*.

3. Usner, *Indians, Settlers, and Slaves*.

4. These works include Carol A. Smith, ed., *Regional Analysis*, 2 vols. (New York, 1976); James C. Scott, *The Moral Economy of the Peasant: Rebellion and Subsistence in Southeast Asia* (New Haven CT, 1976); Stephen Gudeman, *The Demise of a Rural Economy: From Subsistence to Capitalism in a Latin American Village* (London, 1978); Gerald M. Sider, *Culture and Class in Anthropology and History: A Newfoundland Illustration* (Cambridge MA, 1986); and Richard Hodges, *Primitive and Peasant Markets* (New York, 1988).

5. Our understanding of Indian-colonial relations in the upper Mississippi Valley has been advanced by Anderson, *Kinsmen of Another Kind*; Carl J. Ekberg, *Colonial Ste. Genevieve: An Adventure on the Mississippi Frontier* (Gerald MO, 1985); White, *Middle Ground*; Willard H. Rollings, *The Osage: An Ethnohistorical Study of Hegemony on the Prairie-Plains* (Columbia MO, 1992); and R. David Edmunds and Joseph L. Peyser, *The Fox Wars: The Mesquakie Challenge to New France* (Norman OK, 1993).

6. *MPAFD*, 2:81–89, 129–32, 232, 3:177–78. The early dependence on trade with Indians was first emphasized in Giraud, *The Reign of Louis XIV, 1698–1715*, and then closely detailed in Higginbotham, *Old Mobile*. For analysis of France's mercantile policy at the time of Louisiana's beginnings, see Mathé Allain, *"Not Worth a Straw": French Colonial Policy and the Early Years of Louisiana* (Lafayette LA, 1988).

7. *MPAFD*, 3:183, 187–88, 193–94, 198, 213; La Harpe, *Journal*, 91–98. For an overview of the pan-Indian war against English Carolina and the shift toward the French in Louisiana, see Crane, *The Southern Frontier, 1670–1732*, 162–86. Important recent discussions of the Yamassee War can be found in Merrell, *Indians' New World*, 66–91, and Braund, *Deerskins and Duffels*, 30–37.

8. *MPAFD*, 3:314–15, 515; La Harpe, *Journal*, 130–42. See also Mildred Mott

Wedel, *La Harpe's 1719 Post on Red River and Nearby Caddo Settlements* (Austin TX, 1978); Smith, *Caddo Indians*, 40–42; and Morris S. Arnold, *Colonial Arkansas, 1686–1804: A Social and Cultural History* (Fayetteville AK, 1991), 9–12.

9. Charles R. Maduell Jr., comp. and trans., *The Census Tables for the French Colony of Louisiana from 1699 through 1732* (Baltimore, 1972), 113, 123; Salmon to Maurepas, 12 May 1732, Archives des Colonies C13A, Correspondance Générale Louisiane, 15:105. See chapter 3 for my calculation of changes in the Indian population.

10. Jacqueline K. Voorhies, trans. and comp., *Some Late Eighteenth-Century Louisianians: Census Records, 1758–1796* (Lafayette LA, 1973), 103–5; Katherine Bridges and Winston DeVille [trans.], "Natchitoches in 1766," *Louisiana History* 4 (spring 1963): 156–59.

11. *MPAFD*, 2:23–24, 3:52, 575–76. Gift-giving and other forms of exchange are examined within the historical context of interplay between native and colonial societies in Nicholas Thomas, *Entangled Objects: Exchange, Material Culture, and Colonialism in the Pacific* (Cambridge MA, 1991).

12. For recent studies of the English trade system that operated among Creeks and Chickasaws through the eighteenth century, see Cashin, *Lachlan McGillivray, Indian Trader*, and Braund, *Deerskins and Duffels*.

13. For a comprehensive and outstanding study of Louisiana slavery during these years and throughout the eighteenth century, see Gwendolyn Midlo Hall, *Africans in Colonial Louisiana: The Development of Afro-Creole Culture in the Eighteenth Century* (Baton Rouge LA, 1992).

14. Patricia Kay Galloway, "Choctaw Factionalism and Civil War, 1746–1750," *Journal of Mississippi History* 44 (November 1982): 289–327; White, *Roots of Dependency*, 34–68; Michael James Foret, "On the Marchlands of Empire: Trade, Diplomacy, and War on the Southeastern Frontier, 1733–1763" (Ph.D. diss., College of William and Mary, 1990), 131–208.

15. Gilbert C. Din, "Early Spanish Colonization Efforts in Louisiana," *Louisiana Studies* 11 (spring 1972): 31–49; Din, "Spain's Immigration Policy and Efforts during the American Revolution," *Louisiana Studies* 14 (fall 1975): 241–57. For thorough studies of the major groups of immigrants and imported slaves, see Carl A. Brasseaux, *The Founding of New Acadia: The Beginnings of Acadian Life in Louisiana, 1765–1803* (Baton Rouge LA, 1987); Din, *The Canary Islanders of Louisiana* (Baton Rouge LA, 1988); and Hall, *Africans in Colonial Louisiana*.

16. Census of Louisiana in the year 1785, *American State Papers: Miscellaneous* (Washington DC, 1834), 1:381. For information about migration into West Florida during these years, see J. Barton Starr, *Tories, Dons, and Rebels: The American Revolution in British West Florida* (Gainesville FL, 1976), 230–40, and Robin F. A. Fabel, *The Economy of British West Florida, 1763–1783* (Tuscaloosa AL, 1988), 6–21.

17. See chapters 5–8.

18. Usner, *Indians, Settlers, and Slaves*, passim.

19. *MPAFD*, 3:303.

20. *MPAFD*, 2:613–14.

21. *MPAFD*, 1:261–63, 3:497, 4:39, 208–9.

22. *MPAFD*, 2:647–48, 3:565.

23. *MPAFD*, 3:596, 651–52.

24. "Relation de la Louisiane," 158–159.

25. *MPAFD*, 1:21, 86, 95, 103, 3:303–4, 4:13–16.

26. *MPAFD*, 4:17–19, 170–71.

27. *MPAFD*, 4:196, 198, 285, 5:89–93, 97–104.

28. Kinnaird, *Spain in the Mississippi Valley*, 2:137, 143–47; Juan de la Villebeuvre, List of the Choctaw Towns and Traders, 24 November 1787, Legajo 200, Papeles Procedentes de Cuba, Archivo General de Indias, Seville, Spain.

29. Cushman, *History of Choctaw, Chickasaw and Natchez Indians*, 386–403; Alexander Spoehr, "Changing Kinship Systems: A Study in the Acculturation of the Creeks, Cherokee, and Choctaw," Field Museum of Natural History, *Anthropological Series* (Chicago, 1947), 33:153–235.

30. "Relation de la Louisiane," 125; Dumont de Montigny, *Mémoires Historiques sur la Louisiane* (Paris, 1753), 1:181–82.

31. Le Page du Pratz, *Histoire de la Louisiane*, 2:242. For major contributions to our understanding of Mobilian, see James M. Crawford, *The Mobilian Trade Language* (Knoxville TN, 1978); Emanuel Johannes Drechsel, "Mobilian Jargon: Linguistic, Sociocultural, and Historical Aspects of an American Indian Lingua Franca" (Ph.D. diss., University of Wisconsin, Madison, 1979); and Drechsel, "Towards an Ethnohistory of Speaking: The Case of Mobilian Jargon, an American Indian Pidgin of the Lower Mississippi Valley," *Ethnohistory* 30, no. 3 (1983): 165–76.

32. Le Page du Pratz, *Histoire*, 1:347; "Records of the Superior Council," published intermittently in the *Louisiana Historical Quarterly*, vols. 1–22 (1918–39), 3:74.

33. Talk of Captain Ouma of Seneacha, Mobile, 2 January 1772, *Mississippi Historical Society: Centenary Series*, 5:150–51; Romans, *Concise Natural History*, 56; Kinnaird, *Spain in the Mississippi Valley*, 2:150–51. For the best analysis of alcohol use in Indian-colonial relations, see Mancall, *Deadly Medicine*.

34. "Records of the Superior Council," 18:705, 708; Villebeuvre and Pedro Chabert vs. Simon Favre, late interpreter for the Indians, 20 October 1783, Spanish Judicial Records, Louisiana Historical Center, New Orleans.

35. Amos Stoddard, *Sketches, Historical and Descriptive, of Louisiana* (Philadelphia, 1812), 445.

36. Margaret Fisher Dalrymple, ed., *The Merchant of Manchac: The Letterbooks of John Fitzpatrick, 1768–1798* (Baton Rouge LA, 1978), 287–88.

37. "Spanish Judicial Records," published intermittently in the *Louisiana Historical Quarterly*, vols. 6–25 (1923–42), 14:608–10.

38. *Iberville's Gulf Journals*, 78, 170; MPAFD, 2:13; *Pénicaut Narrative*, 98–103.

39. MPAFD, 2:32–34, 52–53.

40. MPAFD, 3:64. The conflict between the pro–Le Moyne and anti–Le Moyne factions, much of which centered on distribution of food supplies, is thoroughly explored in Charles Edwards O'Neill, *Church and State in French Colonial Louisiana: Policy and Politics to 1732* (New Haven CT, 1966), 44–47. For the regulation of food marketing in the ancien régime, see Steven L. Kaplan, *Bread, Politics and Political Economy in the Reign of Louis XV* (The Hague, 1976), 1:65–68.

41. MPAFD, 3:326; Archives des Colonies C13A, 11:174–76, 19:142, 44:21–22.

42. MPAFD, 2:232; William M. Carroll, *Beranger's Discovery of Aransas Pass. A Translation of Jean Beranger's French Manuscript* (Corpus Christi TX, 1983), 33.

43. Dumont de Montigny, *Mémoires Historiques*, 2:41–42; Glenn R. Conrad, trans. and ed., *Immigration and War: Louisiana, 1718–1721. From the Memoir of Charles Le Gac* (Lafayette LA, 1970), 1–8, 30–35; La Harpe, *Journal*, 113, 154, 167–73.

44. MPAFD, 2:347; N. M. Miller Surrey, *The Commerce of Louisiana during the French Régime, 1699–1763* (New York, 1916), 265–66, 291–99; John G. Clark, *New Orleans, 1718–1812: An Economic History* (Baton Rouge LA, 1969), 30, 59–60; Clark, *La Rochelle and the Atlantic Economy during the Eighteenth Century* (Baltimore, 1981), 170–73.

45. MPAFD, 3:423, 535–36; Heloise H. Cruzat, trans., "Louisiana in 1724: Banet's Report to the Company of the Indies, Dated Paris, December 20, 1724," *Louisiana Historical Quarterly* 12 (1929): 126.

46. Romans, *Concise Natural History*, 57; Romans, "An Attempt towards a Short Description of West Florida," in *Notes on the Life and Work of Bernard Romans,* ed. P. Lee Phillips (Gainesville FL, 1924), 120.

47. MPAFD, 3:535–36; Le Page du Pratz, *History of Louisiana*, 202, 233, 2262–63. For the changing locations and populations of these Indian communities, see chapter 3.

48. English Provincial Records, 1763–1783, 3:94–95, 4:20–21, transcripts from the Colonial Office Records, British Public Record Office, in the Mississippi Department of Archives and History, Jackson; Pittman, *Present State of the European Settlements*, 22–35; Romans, *Concise Natural History*, 71.

49. "Relation de la Louisiane," 198; Seymour Feiler, trans. and ed., *Jean-Bernard Bossu's Travels in the Interior of North America, 1751–1762* (Norman OK, 1962), 146; Romans, *Concise Natural History*, 56, 202–19.

50. *MPAFD*, 2:594; Surrey, *Commerce of Louisiana*, 251–54; John, *Storms Brewed in Other Men's Worlds*, 165–95, 338–44. In their proficient participation in the formative livestock trade of the Lower Mississippi Valley, these Indians resembled indigenous peoples in other frontier regions. See S. Daniel Neumark, *Economic Influences on the South African Frontier, 1652–1836* (Stanford CA, 1957), 94–107, and Silvio R. Duncan Taretta and John Markoff, "Civilization and Barbarism: Cattle Frontiers in Latin America," *Comparative Studies in Society and History* 20 (October 1978): 587–620.

51. Charlevoix, *Journal of a Voyage*, 2:280; Le Page du Pratz, *Histoire*, 1:297–98, 2:241–42.

52. *Athanase de Mézières*, 1:179, 2:105–6, 242; Lauren C. Post, "The Old Cattle Industry of Southwest Louisiana," *McNeese Review* 9 (winter 1957): 43–55; Post, "Some Notes on the Attakapas Indians of Southwest Louisiana," *Louisiana History* 3 (summer 1962): 221–42.

53. Peter H. Wood, *Black Majority: Negroes in Colonial South Carolina from 1670 through the Stono Rebellion* (New York, 1974); T. H. Breen and Stephen Innes, *"Myne Owne Ground": Race and Freedom on Virginia's Eastern Shore, 1640–1676* (New York, 1980).

54. Tariff for Trade with the Chickasaw, Choctaw and Alibamon Nations Established at a Congress in Mobile, 22–23 June 1784, Papers of Panton, Leslie and Company, University of West Florida Library, Pensacola.

55. Kinnaird, *Spain in the Mississippi Valley*, 2:232–33; Manuel Gayoso de Lemos to Juan Ventura Morales, 7 February 1799, trans. D. C. Corbitt, *Georgia Historical Quarterly* 35 (1941): 164–69; Paul C. Phillips, *The Fur Trade* (Norman OK, 1961), 2:184–222; Coker and Watson, *Indian Traders of the Southeastern Borderlands*, 15–92.

56. Kinnaird, *Spain in the Mississippi Valley*, 2:59; Villebeuvre to Francisco Luis Hector de Carondelet, 30 March 1793, *East Tennessee Historical Society Publications*, 3 (1958): 101–2. For closer scrutiny into the deteriorating economic position of the Choctaws, see White, *Roots of Dependency*, 97–146.

57. See, for example, Mancall, *Valley of Opportunity*; Braund, *Deerskins and Duffels*; and Hatley, *Dividing Paths*.

5. AMERICAN INDIANS AND THE EARLY COTTON ECONOMY

1. Michael M. Edwards, *The Growth of the British Cotton Trade, 1780–1815* (Manchester, 1967), 75–106; Paul W. Gates, *The Farmer's Age: Agriculture, 1815–1860* (New York, 1960), 1–21. On the shift to cotton cultivation in the Natchez area, see Jack D. L. Holmes, *Gayoso: The Life of a Spanish Governor in the Mississippi Valley, 1789–1799* (Baton Rouge LA, 1965), 96–101, and D. Clayton James, *Antebellum Natchez* (Baton Rouge LA, 1968), 48–53.

2. These subsequent forces, as experienced by the Choctaws, are examined closely

in Arthur H. DeRosier Jr., *The Removal of the Choctaw Indians* (Knoxville TN, 1970), and Kidwell, *Choctaws and Missionaries in Mississippi*.

3. My estimate of an Indian population of at least 30,000 includes 15,160 Creeks, 11,447 Choctaws, and 2,400 Chickasaws. These tribal counts do not include separate Indian communities such as the Chickamauga Cherokees in the Tennessee Valley. Kinnaird, *Spain in the Mississippi Valley*, 3:229–33; Holmes, "Choctaws in 1795"; *American State Papers: Indian Affairs* (Washington DC, 1832–48), 1:39; Census of the District of Mobile, 1 January 1787, Favrot Papers, Louisiana Historical Center; Holmes, *Gayoso*, 115.

4. Holmes, *Gayoso*, 23–24; James, *Antebellum Natchez*, 41–42; Schedule of the Whole Number of Persons in the Mississippi Territory, 1801, Mississippi Territorial Census Returns, Territorial Governor Record Group 2, Mississippi Department of Archives and History, Jackson; C. Richard Arena, "Land Settlement Policies and Practices in Spanish Louisiana," *The Spanish in the Mississippi Valley, 1762–1804*, ed. John Francis McDermott (Urbana IL, 1974), 51–60. On political relations among the United States, Spain, and the Indian nations, see Arthur Preston Whitaker, *The Mississippi Question, 1795–1803: A Study in Trade, Politics, and Diplomacy* (New York, 1934), esp. 51–97, and Thomas P. Abernethy, *The South in the New Nation, 1789–1819* (Baton Rouge LA, 1961), 43–101, 169–216.

5. Dunbar Rowland, ed., *The Mississippi Territorial Archives, 1798–1803: Executive Journals of Governor Winthrop Sargent and Governor William Charles Cole Claiborne* (Nashville, 1905), 148–49.

6. Clarence Edwin Carter, ed., *The Territorial Papers of the United States*, vol. 5: *The Territory of Mississippi, 1798–1817* (Washington DC, 1937), 58, 146; W. C. C. Claiborne to Silas Dinsmoor, 28 January 1803, Indian Department Journal, 1803–1808, Territorial Governor Record Group 2, Mississippi Department of Archives and History, Jackson. For general discussions of the implementation of U.S. Indian policy in the Mississippi Territory, see Martin Abbott, "Indian Policy and Management in the Mississippi Territory, 1798–1817," *Journal of Mississippi History* 14 (July 1952): 153–69; Joseph T. Hatfield, *William Claiborne: Jeffersonian Centurion in the American Southwest* (Lafayette LA, 1976), 41–66; and Guice, "Face to Face in Mississippi Territory."

7. Ora Brooks Peake, *A History of the United States Indian Factory System, 1795–1822* (Denver, 1954), 11–15; Aloysius Plaisance, "The Choctaw Trading House – 1803–1822," *Alabama Historical Quarterly* 16 (fall–winter 1954): 393–423; Nella J. Chambers, "The Creek Indian Factory at Fort Mitchell," *Alabama Historical Quarterly* 21 (1959): 15–53; Choctaw Factory Daybooks, 1808–1819, Records of the Office of Indian Trade, Record Group 75, National Archives.

8. Choctaw Factory Daybooks, Records of the Office of Indian Trade; Peake,

History of the United States Indian Factory System, 204–56; Herman J. Viola, *Thomas L. McKenney: Architect of America's Early Indian Policy, 1816–1830* (Chicago, 1974), 47–70.

9. *American States Papers: Indian Affairs*, 1:669.

10. Andrew A. Lipscomb and Albert Ellery Bergh, eds., *The Writings of Thomas Jefferson* (Washington DC, 1903–4), 17:373–74.

11. Claiborne to Samuel Mitchell, 23 March 1803, Indian Department Journal; *American State Papers: Indian Affairs*, 1:697; "John Forbes & Co., Successors to Panton, Leslie & Co., vs. the Chickasaw Nation: A Journal of an Indian Talk, July, 1805," *Florida Historical Quarterly* 8 (January 1930): 131–42.

12. Gayoso to Conde de Santa Clara, 24 September 1797, Papeles Procedentes de Cuba transcripts, North Carolina State Archives, Raleigh; Panton to Hawkins, 11 June 1799, Papers of Panton, Leslie and Company. For the definitive study of this important business, see Coker and Watson, *Indian Traders of the Southeastern Spanish Borderlands*.

13. Carter, *Territorial Papers*, 5:189.

14. Kirby to Thomas Jefferson, 20 April 1804, Kirby to Albert Gallatin, 1 July 1804, Ephraim Kirby Papers, Manuscript Department, Perkins Library, Duke University, Durham NC.

15. *American State Papers: Indian Affairs*, 1:748, 750; Carter, ed., *Territorial Papers of the United States*, vol. 6: *The Territory of Mississippi, 1798–1817*, 123; Memorial of John Forbes & Co. to the President of the United States, 1807, Papers of Panton, Leslie and Company; David H. White, "The John Forbes Company: Heir to the Florida Indian Trade, 1801–1819" (Ph.D. diss., University of Alabama, 1973), 64–77. For details about the diplomacy behind this treaty, see Samuel J. Wells, "International Causes of the Treaty of Mount Dexter, 1805," *Journal of Mississippi History* 48 (August 1986): 177–85.

16. *American State Papers: Indian Affairs*, 1:748–49, 751–52; Carter, *Territorial Papers*, 5:434, 6:123; DeRosier, *Removal of the Choctaw Indians*, 29, 32; Coker and Watson, *Indian Traders of the Southeastern Spanish Borderlands*, 243–72.

17. *American State Papers: Public Lands* (Washington DC, 1860–61), 3:461–62; "A List of Individual debts Due to the Chaktaw Trading House, March 31st 1822," Choctaw Factory Miscellaneous Accounts, 1803–1825, Records of the Office of Indian Trade. For summaries of Creek, Choctaw, and Chickasaw treaties with the United States during the Mississippi territorial period, see Green, *Politics of Indian Removal*, 36–73; DeRosier, *Removal of the Choctaw Indians*, 27–52; and Arrell M. Gibson, *The Chickasaws* (Norman OK, 1971), 80–105.

18. Chapter 6 explores these and other Indians' economic activities in the Orleans Territory.

19. Choctaw Factory Daybooks and Choctaw Factory Miscellaneous Accounts, Records of the Office of Indian Trade.

20. Fortescue Cuming, *Cuming's Tour to the Western Country (1807–1809)*, vol. 4 of *Early Western Travels, 1748–1846*, ed. Reuben Gold Thwaites (1810; reprint, Cleveland, 1904), 351–52.

21. John A. Watkins, "Choctaw Indians," John A. Watkins Manuscripts, Howard-Tilton Memorial Library, Tulane University, New Orleans; John McKee to Andrew Jackson, 19 November 1814, Andrew Jackson Papers, Library of Congress, Washington DC.

22. Dominique Rouquette, "The Choctaws," typescript of MS written in 1850, Louisiana Historical Center, 37–43; Walter Pritchard, Fred B. Kniffen, and Clair A. Brown, eds., "Southern Louisiana and Southern Alabama in 1819: The Journal of James Leander Cathcart," *Louisiana Historical Quarterly* 28 (July 1945): 850–51. For examples of horses being purchased from Choctaws at Mobile, see transactions of 7 October and 15 November 1814, in Panton, Leslie & Company Receipt Book, Papers of Panton, Leslie and Company.

23. Rowland, *Mississippi Territorial Archives*, 223–24; Rowland, ed., *Official Letter Books of W. C. C. Claiborne, 1801–1816* (Jackson MS, 1917), 1:13–14, 22–23, 69–70, 120–21, 202–4.

24. Watkins, "Choctaw Indians," John A. Watkins Manuscripts; Claiborne to Mitchell, 29 April 1803, Claiborne to Ochchummey, 17 May 1803, Indian Department Journal.

25. Rowland, *Official Letter Books of W. C. C. Claiborne*, 1:67–68; Carter, *Territorial Papers of the United States*, 6:69–70; Claiborne to Henry Dearborn, 28 June 1803, 2 June 1804, Indian Department Journal.

26. Holmes to William Eustis, 12 December 1812, Correspondence and Papers of Governor David Holmes, Territorial Governor Record Group 2.

27. *Cuming's Tour*, 320–21; Estwick Evans, *A Pedestrious Tour of Four Thousand Miles, through the Western States and Territories, during the Winter and Spring of 1818*, vol. 8 of *Early Western Travels, 1748–1846*, ed. Reuben Gold Thwaites (Cleveland, 1904–7), 324; Howard Corning, ed., *Journal of John James Audubon Made during His Trip to New Orleans in 1820–1821* (Boston, 1929), 92; Thomas Nuttall, *A Journal of Travels into the Arkansas Territory during the Year 1819*, ed. Savoie Lottinville (Norman OK, 1980), 258–60.

28. Christian Schultz Jr., *Travels on an Inland Voyage through the States of New-York, Pennsylvania, Virginia, Ohio, Kentucky and Tennessee, and through the Territories of Indiana, Louisiana, Mississippi, and New-Orleans: Performed in the Years 1807 and 1808* (New York, 1810), 2:140–43.

29. Benjamin Hawkins, "A Sketch of the Creek Country in the Years 1798 and

1799," in *Collections of the Georgia Historical Society*, vol. III, pt. 1 (Savannah GA, 1848), 26–66, esp. 32–33.

30. *Mississippi Herald and Natchez City Gazette*, 15 June 1804; Dinsmoor to Cato West, 10 June, 15 June 1804, Indian Department Journal; Jesse D. Jennings, ed., "Nutt's Trip to the Chickasaw Country," *Journal of Mississippi History* 9 (January 1947): 40–45, 60–61.

31. *American State Papers: Indian Affairs*, 1:659; Claiborne to Mitchell, 29 April 1803, Indian Department Journal; James L. Watkins, *King Cotton: A Historical and Statistical Review, 1790 to 1908* (New York, 1908), 164.

32. Albert James Pickett, *History of Alabama, and Incidentally of Georgia and Mississippi, from the Earliest Period* (Charleston, 1851), 2:189–90.

33. Pickett, *History of Alabama*, 2:123–35; Hawkins, "Sketch of the Creek Country," 26–48; Jennings, "Nutt's Trip to the Chickasaw Country," 41–44; Bonds of Tax Collectors, Sheriffs and Indian Traders, 1802–1817, Territorial Governor Record Group 2; Dawson A. Phelps, "Stands and Travel Accommodations on the Natchez Trace," *Journal of Mississippi History* 11 (January 1949): 1–54; Phelps, ed., "Excerpts from the Journal of the Reverend Joseph Bullen, 1799 and 1800," *Journal of Mississippi History* 17 (October 1955): 262–63, 273; Receipts, 15 July, 6 October 1803, 9 March 1807, Choctaw Factory Miscellaneous Accounts, Records of the Office of Indian Trade; Rowland, *Mississippi Territorial Archives*, 164–65, 233–34; Jack D. L. Holmes, "The Role of Blacks in Spanish Alabama: The Mobile District, 1780–1813," *Alabama Historical Quarterly* 37 (spring 1975): 5–18.

34. Rowland, *Official Letter Books of W. C. C. Claiborne*, 1:219; Carter, *Territorial Papers*, 5:192–205, esp. 203; Malcolm J. Rohrbough, *The Land Office Business: The Settlement and Administration of American Public Lands, 1789–1837* (New York, 1968), esp. 26–70.

35. Carter, *Territorial Papers*, 5:279–87; Benjamin Horace Hibbard, *A History of the Public Land Polices* (New York, 1924), 75; Rohrbough, *Land Office Business*, 35–59; Frederick Kimball to Nephew and Niece, 23 May 1808, Frederick Kimball Letters, Louisiana and Lower Mississippi Valley Collections, Louisiana State University, Baton Rouge; Flower & Faulkner to John Pintard, 20 May 1809, John M. Pintard Papers, Louisiana and Lower Mississippi Valley Collections, Louisiana State University; *Louisiana Gazette*, 30 August 1805, 26 August 1806, 30 June 1807; *Louisiana Gazette and New Orleans Daily Advertiser*, 21 June 1808, 1 September 1809. Uncertainty over land titles and animosity toward land speculators were greatly exacerbated in the Mississippi Territory by claims to the Yazoo River valley sold by the Georgia state legislature. See Abernethy, *South in the New Nation*, 136–68, and Peter Magrath, *Yazoo: Law and Politics in the New Republic: The Case of Fletcher v. Peck* (Providence RI, 1966).

36. Carter, *Territorial Papers*, 6:226.

37. Frank Lawrence Owsley, *Plain Folk in the Old South* (Baton Rouge LA, 1949), esp. 1–90; Gavin Wright, *The Political Economy of the Cotton South: Households, Markets, and Wealth in the Nineteenth Century* (New York, 1978), 69–74. For a view of important directions in recent scholarship on the origins and evolution of the southern yeomanry, see Steven Hahn, *The Roots of Southern Populism: Yeoman Farmers and the Transformation of the Georgia Upcountry, 1850–1890* (New York, 1983); J. William Harris, *Plain Folk and Gentry in a Slave Society: White Liberty and Black Slavery in Augusta's Hinterlands* (Middleton CT, 1985); Grady McWhiney, *Cracker Culture: Celtic Ways in the Old South* (Tuscaloosa AL, 1988); Lacy K. Ford Jr., *Origins of Southern Radicalism: The South Carolina Upcountry, 1800–1860* (New York, 1988); and John Solomon Otto, *The Southern Frontiers, 1607–1860: The Agricultural Evolution of the Colonial and Antebellum South* (Westport CT, 1989). Christopher Morris's *Becoming Southern: The Evolution of a Way of Life, Warren County and Vicksburg, Mississippi, 1770–1860* (New York, 1995) is a path-breaking study that traces precisely how a particular section of Mississippi passed through stages of transformation.

38. John Mills to cousin Gilbert, 19 May 1807, John Mills Letters, Department of Archives and History, Louisiana State University, Baton Rouge; U.S. Census Bureau, *Aggregate Amount of Each Description of Persons within the United States of America and the Territories thereof, agreeable to actual enumeration made according to law, in the year 1810* (Washington DC, 1811), 83. On changing life on the cotton frontier, see Ulrich Bonnell Phillips, *Life and Labor in the Old South* (Boston, 1929), esp. 95–111, 274–304; Malcolm J. Rohrbough, *The Trans-Appalachian Frontier: People, Societies, and Institutions, 1775–1850* (New York, 1978), 93–114, 192–217; William B. Hamilton Jr., "American Beginnings in the Old Southwest: The Mississippi Phase" (Ph.D. diss., Duke University, 1938); and Hamilton, "Mississippi 1817: A Sociological and Economic Analysis," *Journal of Mississippi History* 29 (November 1967): 270–92.

39. Ira Berlin and Philip D. Morgan, eds., *Cultivation and Culture: Labor and the Shaping of Slave Life in the Americas* (Charlottesville VA, 1993); Mary Turner, ed., *From Chattel Slaves to Wage Slaves: The Dynamics of Labour Bargaining in the Americas* (Bloomington IN, 1995).

40. On slavery in the Indian nations of the Mississippi Territory, see Wyatt F. Jeltz, "The Relations of Negroes and Choctaw and Chickasaw Indians," *Journal of Negro History* 33 (January 1948): 24–37; Arthur H. DeRosier Jr. "Pioneers with Conflicting Ideals: Christianity and Slavery in the Choctaw Nation," *Journal of Mississippi History* 21 (July 1959): 174–89; Michael F. Doran, "Negro Slaves of the Five Civilized Tribes," *Annals of the Association of American Geographers* 68 (September 1978): 335–50; and Daniel F. Littlefield Jr., *Africans and Creeks: From the Colonial Pe-*

riod to the Civil War (Westport CT, 1979), 26–109. For a provocative explanation of the biological and cultural significance of Indian-black interaction, see Wright, *The Only Land They Knew*, 248–78.

41. Archives of the Spanish Government of West Florida, 1782–1810, WPA typescript translations, Louisiana Historical Center, 4:165, 7:345–80; Gilbert Russell to Governor Holmes, 30 April 1811, Dinsmoor to Holmes, 4 May 1811, John Pitchlynn to Dinsmoor, 30 May 1811, Correspondence and Papers of Governor David Holmes; Dinsmoor to Secretary of War William Eustis, 27 September 1812, Andrew Jackson Papers.

42. Horace Mann Bond, "Two Racial Islands in Alabama," *American Journal of Sociology* 36 (January 1931): 552–67; J. Anthony Paredes, "Back from Disappearance: The Alabama Creek Indian Community," in *Southeastern Indians since the Removal Era*, 123–41; Darrell A. Posey, "Origin, Development and Maintenance of a Louisiana Mixed-Blood Community: The Ethnohistory of the Freejacks of the First Ward Settlement," *Ethnohistory* 26 (spring 1979): 177–92.

43. For examples of licenses issued and of violations penalized, see Bonds of Tax Collectors, Territorial Governor Record Group 2; and West to John Kincaid, 15 February 1805, Indian Department Journal.

44. Rowland, *Mississippi Territorial Archives*, 82; William D. McCain, ed., *Laws of the Mississippi Territory, May 27, 1800* (Beauvoir Community MS, 1948), 237–40.

45. *Statutes of the Mississippi Territory* (Natchez, 1816), 384, 388–89.

46. McCain, *Laws of the Mississippi Territory*, 237–40; *Statutes of the Mississippi Territory*, 385–86, 393.

47. Rowland, *Mississippi Territorial Archives*, 311–12; Rowland, *Official Letter Books of W. C. C. Claiborne*, 1:39. It is important to note that the expansion of cotton agriculture in the Lower Mississippi Valley coincided with a tightening of slave codes and a heightening of racial barriers across the South that reflected in large part a reaction to the contagion of rebellion among blacks in the Americas sparked by the slave revolution in St. Domingo. Many historians, however, neglected or downplayed the authenticity of this spreading rebelliousness and thereby missed its influence on the renewed codification of race relations that occurred during the early nineteenth century. Important exceptions include Vincent Harding, *There Is a River: The Black Struggle for Freedom in America* (New York, 1981), 46–74, and Merton L. Dillon, *Slavery Attacked: Southern Slaves and Their Allies, 1819–1865* (Baton Rouge LA, 1990), 45–129.

48. John Hope Franklin, *The Militant South, 1800–1861* (Cambridge MA, 1956), 25–32; Tommy R. Young II, "The United States Army and the Institution of Slavery in Louisiana, 1803–1815," *Louisiana Studies* 13 (fall 1974): 201–22; James H. Dor-

man, "The Persistent Specter: Slave Rebellion in Territorial Louisiana," *Louisiana History* 18 (fall 1977): 389–404.

49. Rowland, *Official Letter Books of W. C. C. Claiborne*, 1:42–43; Carter, *Territorial Papers*, 5:217, 6:298–99, 301, 328–29.

50. Owsley, *Struggle for the Gulf Borderlands*; Green, *Politics of Indian Removal*; Wright, *Creeks and Seminoles*; Martin, *Sacred Revolt*; Dowd, *Spirited Resistance*; Braund, *Deerskins and Duffels*.

51. John Forbes's record of his talks with chiefs of Creek, Cherokee, Choctaw, and Chickasaw tribes, held at Hickory Ground, 27 May–3 June 1803, concerning Indian debts, Manuscripts Division, Howard-Tilton Memorial Library, Tulane University; Account of trip made into the Indian Country by John Innerarity, 14 October–1 November 1812, Papers of Panton, Leslie and Company.

52. Green, *Politics of Indian Removal*, 39–42; Martin, *Sacred Revolt*; Braund, *Deerskins and Duffels*.

53. H. S. Halbert and T. H. Ball, *The Creek War of 1813 and 1814* (Chicago, 1895), 125–76; Owsley, *Struggle for the Gulf Borderlands*, 30–41.

54. Halbert and Ball, *Creek War of 1813 and 1814*, 177–286; Michael Paul Rogin, *Fathers and Children: Andrew Jackson and the Subjugation of the American Indian* (New York, 1975), 149–64; Owsley, *Struggle for the Gulf Borderlands*, 42–94.

55. Thomas Perkins Abernethy, *The Formative Period in Alabama, 1815–1828* (University AL, 1965), 34–71; Charles S. Davis, *The Cotton Kingdom in Alabama* (Montgomery AL, 1939), 25–32; Rohrbough, *Land Office Business*, 97–126; J. Mills Thornton III, *Politics and Power in a Slave Society: Alabama, 1800–1860* (Baton Rouge LA, 1978).

56. U.S. Department of Commerce, *Historical Statistics of the United States: Colonial Times to 1970* (Washington DC, 1975), 1:24, 30; John R. Swanton, *Early History of the Creek Indians and Their Neighbors* (Washington DC, 1922), 443–52.

57. This suggestion defies a general impression, produced by some removal historiography, that proponents of change within Indian societies tended to accept removal. Alignment in favor of removal treaties, however, did not automatically form around people of mixed ancestry who practiced commercial agriculture. For a revised understanding, see Young, *Redskins, Ruffleshirts, and Rednecks*, 3–46; White, *Roots of Dependency*, 110–46; and Kidwell, *Choctaws and Missionaries in Mississippi*, 92–146.

58. William Faulkner, *Go Down, Moses and Other Stories* (New York, 1942), 254.

6. ECONOMIC STRATEGIES IN LOUISIANA

1. See, for example, White, *Roots of Dependency*; Albert L. Hurtado, *Indian Survival on the California Frontier* (New Haven CT, 1988); Daniel L. Boxberger, *To Fish*

in Common: The Ethnohistory of Lummi Indian Salmon Fishing (Lincoln NE, 1989); David Rich Lewis, *Neither Wolf nor Dog: American Indians, Environment, and Agrarian Change* (New York, 1994); and Melissa L. Meyer, *The White Earth Tragedy: Ethnicity and Dispossession at a Minnesota Anishinaabe Reservation, 1889–1920* (Lincoln NE, 1994).

2. Theda Perdue, *Slavery and the Evolution of Cherokee Society, 1540–1866* (Knoxville TN, 1979); McLoughlin, *Cherokee Renascence.*

3. In this respect, Indian responses to outside economic pressures resemble strategies used by various European and non-European societies to influence and interpret change. See, for example, Bonham C. Richardson, *Caribbean Migrants: Environment and Human Survival on St. Kitts and Nevis* (Knoxville TN, 1983); James C. Scott, *Weapons of the Weak: Everyday Forms of Peasant Resistance* (New Haven CT, 1985); Rhoda H. Halperin, *The Livelihood of Kin: Making Ends Meet "The Kentucky Way"* (Austin TX, 1990); and Stuart Woolf, ed., *Domestic Strategies: Work and Family in France and Italy, 1600–1800* (Cambridge MA, 1991).

4. Gerald Sider, "When Parrots Learn to Talk, and Why They Can't: Domination, Deception, and Self-Deception in Indian-White Relations," *Comparative Studies in Society and History* 29 (January 1987): 3–23; Scott Rushforth, "Political Resistance in a Contemporary Hunter-Gatherer Society: More About Bearlake Athapaskan Knowledge and Authority," *American Ethnologist* 21 (May 1994): 335–52; Chase Hensel, *Telling Our Selves: Ethnicity and Discourse in Southwestern Alaska* (New York, 1996).

5. Brooke Larson and Olivia Harris with Enrique Tandeter, eds., *Ethnicity, Markets, and Migration in the Andes: At the Crossroads of History and Anthropology* (Durham NC, 1995).

6. Rowland, *Mississippi Territorial Archives*, 210–12.

7. Carter, *Territorial Papers*, 5:177; James Wilkinson to Claiborne, 13 April 1803, Indian Department Journal; Pierre-Clément de Laussat, *Memoirs of My Life to My Son during the Years 1803 and After, Which I Spent in Public Service in Louisiana as Commissioner of the French Government for the Retrocession to France of That Colony and for Its Transfer to the United States*, trans. Sister Agnes-Josephine Pastwa, ed. Robert D. Bush (Baton Rouge LA, 1978), 39. Jefferson's "a light French breeze" is quoted from his 15 February 1803 letter to Dearborn in Mary P. Adams, "Jefferson's Reaction to the Treaty of San Ildefonso," *Journal of Southern History* 21 (May 1955): 183.

8. P. L. Ford, ed., *The Writings of Thomas Jefferson* (New York, 1892–99), 8:249; Carter, *Territorial Papers*, 9:212–13; Adams, "Jefferson's Reaction to the Treaty of San Ildefonso," 182–83.

9. Kirby to Gallatin, 1 July 1804, Ephraim Kirby Papers.

10. Daniel Clark, "An Account of the Indian Tribes in Louisiana," in Carter, *Ter-*

ritorial Papers, 9:62–63; John Sibley, "Historical sketches of the several Indian Tribes in Louisiana, south of the Arkansas river, and between the Mississippi and river Grand," *Annals of the Congress of the United States*, 9th Cong., 2d sess., 1 December 1806–3 March 1807 (Washington DC, 1852), 1086–88; Henry Adams, ed., *Writings of Albert Gallatin* (Philadelphia, 1879), 1:233; Christian Schultz Jr., *Travels on an Inland Voyage through the States of New-York, Pennsylvania, Virginia, Ohio, Kentucky and Tennessee, and through the Territories of Indiana, Louisiana, Mississippi, and New-Orleans: Performed in the Years 1807 and 1808* (New York, 1810), 2:158, 220–21. See chapter 3 for background information on population changes over the eighteenth century.

11. Carter, *Territorial Papers*, 9:63, 75–76, 271–73, 336; Rowland, *Official Letter Books of W. C. C. Claiborne*, 4:2–4, 161, 254–55; Dan L. Flores, *Jefferson & Southwestern Exploration: The Freeman & Custis Accounts of the Red River Expedition of 1806* (Norman OK, 1984), 24–38, 68–90, 159–72. For a perceptive analysis of the long-neglected Caddos during this period, see Smith, *Caddo Indians*, 84–102.

12. Daniel H. Usner Jr., "An American Indian Gateway: Some Thoughts on the Migration and Settlement of Eastern Indians around Early St. Louis," *Gateway Heritage* 11 (winter 1990–91): 42–51.

13. Clark, "An Account of the Indian Tribes in Louisiana," 64; *Cuming's Tour*, 285–86; Henry Kerr, *Travels through the Western Interior of the United States from the Year 1808 up to the year 1816* (Elizabethtown NJ, 1816), 40; Watkins, "Choctaw Indians," John A. Watkins Manuscripts; Nuttall, *Journal of Travels into the Arkansas Territory*, 49–50, 60, 63–65, 70, 252; Schultz, *Travels on an Inland Voyage*, 183.

14. Mary A. M. O'Callaghan, "An Indian Removal Policy in Spanish Louisiana," in *Greater America: Essays in Honor of Herbert Eugene Bolton*, ed. Adele Ogden and Engel Sluiter (Berkeley CA, 1945), 281–94; Lawrence and Lucia B. Kinnaird, "Choctaws West of the Mississippi, 1766–1800," *Southwestern Historical Quarterly* 83 (April 1980): 349–70.

15. Ernest Russ Williams, "Jean Baptiste Filhiol and the Founding of the Poste du Ouachita," in *North Louisiana*, vol. 1: *To 1865, Essays on the Region and Its History*, ed. B. H. Gilley (Ruston LA, 1984), 16–17.

16. Carter, *Territorial Papers*, 9:63, 224; Sibley, "Historical sketches," 1086–87; Charles César Robin, *Voyage to Louisiana, 1803–1805*, trans. Stuart O. Landry Jr. (New Orleans, 1966), 128–29, 147, 154–55; *American State Papers: Public Lands*, 2:802–3.

17. Clark, "An Account of the Indian Tribes in Louisiana," 63; Sibley, "Historical sketches," 1085–86; Flores, *Jefferson & Southwestern Exploration*, 146–57; Dan L. Flores, "The Red River Branch of the Alabama-Coushatta Indians: An Ethnohistory," *Southern Studies* 16 (spring 1977): 55–72.

18. Rowland, *Official Letter Books of W. C. C. Claiborne*, 2:2; Carter, *Territorial Papers*, 9:387.

19. Carter, *Territorial Papers*, 9:212–13, 514–15; Rowland, *Official Letter Books of W. C. C. Claiborne*, 2:72–73, 128–29, 5:275, 322–23.

20. Natchitoches Day Book, 1806–1812, Records of the Office of Indian Trade.

21. Robin, *Voyage to Louisiana, 1803–1805*, 129.

22. Sibley, "Historical sketches," 1085–86.

23. Rowland, *Official Letter Books of W. C. C. Claiborne*, 4:223–24.

24. Sibley, "Historical sketches," 1086; James Pitot, *Observations on the Colony of Louisiana from 1796 to 1802*, trans. Henry C. Pitot (Baton Rouge LA, 1979), 128.

25. Pritchard, Kniffen, and Brown, "Southern Louisiana and Southern Alabama in 1819," 760–61, 780–82.

26. Historians are just beginning to recognize the participation of small American Indian groups in local markets for some duration after the non-Indian population outnumbers them and dispossesses them of their land. For comparable settings, see Donna Keith Baron, J. Edward Hood, and Holly V. Izard, "They Were Here All Along: The Native American Presence in Lower-Central New England in the Eighteenth and Nineteenth Centuries," *William and Mary Quarterly*, 3d ser., 53 (July 1996): 561–86, and Susan E. Gray, *The Yankee West: Community Life on the Michigan Frontier* (Chapel Hill NC, 1996), 67–79.

27. John Sibley, *A Report from Natchitoches in 1807*, ed. Annie Heloise Abel (New York, 1922), 29–30. For more information about this sport, see chapter 7.

28. Daniel H. Usner Jr., "American Indians in Colonial New Orleans," in *Powhatan's Mantle*, 104–27.

29. Spanish Colonial Land Grant Papers, The Historic New Orleans Collection, New Orleans; Francis P. Burns, "The Spanish Land Laws of Louisiana," *Louisiana Historical Quarterly* 11 (October 1928): 565–66.

30. Winston DeVille, *Calender–St. Landry Parish* (Baton Rouge LA, 1965), pt. 1, p. 24; DeVille, *Opelousas: The History of a French and Spanish Military Post in America, 1716–1803* (Cottonport LA, 1973), 15; *American State Papers: Public Lands*, 3:111, 113; Post, "Some Notes on the Attakapas Indians of Southwest Louisiana," 239–40.

31. *American State Papers: Public Lands*, 2:789–90, 796–97, 802–3; Henry P. Dart, "Louisiana Land Titles Derived from Indian Tribes," *Louisiana Historical Quarterly* 4 (January 1921): 134–44; Saucier, *History of Avoyelles Parish*, 458, 460, 522. Many non-Indians in Louisiana, especially small farmers along the Mississippi, were losing land similarly through indebtedness to merchants and planters. See James H. Dorman, *The People Called Cajuns: An Introduction to an Ethnohistory* (Lafayette LA, 1983), 25–30. The relationship between patron-client trade and land speculation

needs to be examined more closely before a better understanding of these and other land cessions can be reached.

32. Jedidiah A. Morse, *Report to the Secretary of War of the United States, on Indian Affairs* (New Haven CT, 1822), 257.

33. Rowland, *Official Letter Books of W. C. C. Claiborne*, 2:72–73; François-Xavier Martin, ed., *A General Digest of the Acts of the Legislatures of the Late Territory of Orleans and the State of Louisiana* (New Orleans, 1816), 1:648–50, 2:434, 438.

34. Sibley, *Report from Natchitoches*, 12–15, 19–20; Rowland, *Official Letter Books of W. C. C. Claiborne*, 4:21–22; Carter, *Territorial Papers*, 9:758.

35. Rowland, *Official Letter Books of W. C. C. Claiborne*, 4:183, 185–87, 238; *American State Papers: Indian Affairs*, 2:755–56.

36. Rowland, *Official Letter Books of W. C. C. Claiborne*, 4:185–86.

37. Julia Kathryn Garrett, ed., "Doctor John Sibley and the Louisiana-Texas Frontier, 1803–1814" [letters and documents], *Southwestern Historical Quarterly* 45–49 (January 1942–April 1946), 48:67–68.

38. Linnaird to John Mason, 15 December 1813, Fowler to Thomas McKenney, 8 April 1817, 9 May 1817, Letterbook of the Natchitoches-Sulphur Fork Factory, 1809–1821, Records of the Office of Indian Trade.

39. This account was written by "a lady of respectability and piety, who was an eye witness to a part of what she relates" in a letter initialized M. C. and dated New Haven, July 1822. Jedidiah Morse included it in his *Report to the Secretary of War* as appendix F, pp. 260–63.

40. Pedro de Nava to Juan Bautista Elguezabal, 10 November 1800, Nemesio Salcedo to Antonio Cordero, 16 August 1806, Bexar Archives, University of Texas, Austin.

41. Garrett, "Doctor John Sibley," 49:403–5, 601–3, 611; Juan Antonio Padilla, "Texas in 1820: Report of the Barbarous Indians of the Province of Texas, by Juan Antonio Padilla, Made December 27, 1819," trans. Mattie Austin Hatcher, *Southwestern Historical Quarterly* 23 (July 1919): 47–53; J. Villasana Haggard, "The House of Barr and Davenport," *Southwestern Historical Quarterly* 49 (July 1945): 71; Flores, "Red River Branch of the Alabama-Coushatta Indians," 68–72; William B. Gannett, "The American Invasion of Texas, 1820–1845: Patterns of Conflict between Settlers and Indians" (Ph.D. diss., Cornell University, 1984), 274–307.

42. *American State Papers: Indian Affairs*, 2:542, 546. For the latest overview of Louisiana Indians since the early nineteenth century, see Kniffen, Gregory, and Stokes, *Historic Indian Tribes of Louisiana*.

43. Carter, *Territorial Papers*, 9:421–22; *American State Papers: Indian Affairs*, 2:810–11.

44. *American State Papers: Indian Affairs*, 2:230; DeRosier, *Removal of the Choc-*

taw Indians, 46–69; White, *Roots of Dependency*, 113–16. Among the Cherokees, U.S. officials were using individuals who had already migrated westward to promote removal of the entire nation. McLoughlin, *Cherokee Renascence*, 209, 268.

7. AMERICAN INDIANS IN NINETEENTH-CENTURY NEW ORLEANS

1. Russell Thornton, Gary D. Sandefur, and Harold G. Grasmick, *The Urbanization of American Indians: A Critical Bibliography* (Bloomington IN, 1982).

2. Important contributions to our understanding of the pre–World War II urban experiences of American Indians include Jacqueline Peterson, "'Wild Chicago': The Formation and Destruction of a Multiracial Community on the Midwestern Frontier, 1816–1837," in *The Ethnic Frontier: Essays in the History of Group Survival in Chicago and the Midwest*, ed. Melvin G. Holi and Peter d'A. Jones (Grand Rapids MI, 1977), 25–71; George Harwood Phillips, "Indians in Los Angeles, 1781–1875: Economic Integration, Social Disintegration," *Pacific Historical Review*, 49 (August 1980): 427–51; Bruce Katzer, "The Caughnawaga Mohawks: The Other Side of Ironwork," *Journal of Ethnic Studies* 15 (winter 1988): 39–55; and Russel Lawrence Barsh, "Puget Sound Indian Demography, 1900–1920: Migration and Economic Integration," *Ethnohistory* 43 (winter 1996): 65–97.

3. Usner, "American Indians in Colonial New Orleans."

4. The few references to Indians in nineteenth-century New Orleans found in secondary literature tend to be incidental and to mimic the image created by bourgeois observers. See, for example, Reginald Horsman, *The Frontier in the Formative Years, 1783–1815* (New York, 1970), 60, and Liliane Crété, *Daily Life in Louisiana, 1815–1830*, trans. Patrick Gregory (Baton Rouge LA, 1981), 53–54, 290–92.

5. For notable examples of scholarship that explore the less pathological and more adaptive dimensions of Indian urbanization, see Henry F. Dobyns, Richard W. Stoffle, and Kristine Jones, "Native American Urbanization and Socio-Economic Integration in the Southwestern United States," *Ethnohistory*, 22 (spring 1975): 155–79, and James Nwannukwu Kerri, "The Economic Adjustment of Indians in Winnipeg, Canada," *Urban Anthropology* 5 (winter 1976): 351–65.

6. Kinnaird, *Spain in the Mississippi Valley*, 2:185, 258, 3:141–43, 151–52; Miro to Luis de las Casas, 10 September, 26 December 1790, 28 June 1791, Dispatches of the Spanish Governors of Louisiana, 1766–1792, WPA typescript, Louisiana Historical Center; Villebeuvre to Carondelet, 16 January, 7 February, 30 March 1793, *East Tennessee Historical Society Publications* 29 (1957): 142–43, 152; 30 (1958): 101–2.

7. Laussat to Minister of Navy, Paris, 27 September 1802, Claude Perrin Victor Papers, Historic New Orleans Collection; Wilkinson to Claiborne, Fort Adams, 13 April 1803, Indian Department Journal: "I have received the following information from a confidential source in New Orleans, viz.: 'Mingo poos Coos has been here,

and thro the Interpreter has been invited to bring his people to meet their old friends the French, the Indians are daily comeing in, and the Interpreter has gone over the lake (Pontchartrain) to provide for their accommodation.'"

8. Rowland, *Official Letter Books of W. C. C. Claiborne*, 5:275, 322–23; Jan Curry, "A History of the Houma Indians and Their Story of Federal Nonrecognition," *American Indian Journal* 5 (February 1979): 8–28.

9. *New Orleans Deutsche Zeitung*, 4 November 1849, 13 December 1857, 15 May 1858; *New Orleans Picayune*, 18 March 1838, 19 January 1860.

10. *Picayune*, 17, 18 October 1837. For details about the Seminole War and removal, see Edwin C. McReynolds, *The Seminoles* (Norman OK, 1957), 159–242.

11. *Picayune*, 15, 17, 21, 25 August, 3 November 1837; C. B. Clark, "'Drove Off Like Dogs'—Creek Removal," *Indians of the South: Past and Present*, ed. John K. Mahon (Pensacola FL, 1975), 118–24; Kenneth L. Valliere, "The Creek War of 1836: A Military History," *Chronicles of Oklahoma* 57 (winter 1979–80): 463–85. Joy Harjo's poem "New Orleans" poignantly represents the Creek memory of this and other tragic episodes of removal. *Words in the Blood: Contemporary Indian Writers of North and South America*, ed. Jamake Highwater (New York, 1984), 212.

12. Watkins, "Choctaw Indians," John A. Watkins Manuscripts; *Cuming's Tour*, 351–52. For comparable forms of economic adjustment among other Indians, see L. F. S. Upton, *Micmacs and Colonists: Indian-White Relations in the Maritimes, 1713–1867* (Vancouver, 1979), 127–30, 172–73; Merrell, *Indians' New World*, 226–33.

13. Howard Corning, ed., *Journal of John James Audubon Made during His Trip to New Orleans in 1820–1821* (Boston, 1929), 170.

14. John Francis McDermott, ed., *Tixier's Travels on the Osage Prairies* (Norman OK, 1940), 55–59, 81–82. Also see J. Hanno Deiler, *The Settlement of the German Coast of Louisiana and the Creoles of German Descent* (Philadelphia, 1909), 62; Meloncy C. Soniat, "The Tchoupitoulas Plantation," *Louisiana Historical Quarterly* 7 (April 1924): 309–10.

15. Pierre-Louis Berquin-Duvallon, *Travels in Louisiana and the Floridas, in the Year, 1802, Giving a Correct Picture of those Countries*, trans. John Davis (New York, 1806), 96–99; Christian Schultz Jr., *Travels on an Inland Voyage through the States of New-York, Pennsylvania, Virginia, Ohio, Kentucky and Tennessee, and through the Territories of Indiana, Louisiana, Mississippi and New-Orleans* (New York, 1810), 2:198; Rowland, *Official Letter Books of W. C. C. Claiborne*, 3:50–51.

16. John Adams Paxton, *The New Orleans Directory and Register* (New Orleans, 1822), 37; Edna B. Freiberg, *Bayou St. John in Colonial Louisiana 1699–1803* (New Orleans, 1980), 5–15.

17. *Cuming's Tour*, 365–66; James A. Robertson, ed., *Louisiana under the Rule of Spain, France, and the United States, 1785–1807* (Cleveland, 1911), 2:81–83.

18. *New Orleans Times*, 6 June 1867; Henry C. Castellanos, *New Orleans as It Was: Episodes of Louisiana Life*, ed. George F. Reinecke (1895; reprint, Baton Rouge LA, 1978), 339; *The WPA Guide to New Orleans: The Federal Writers' Project Guide to 1930s New Orleans with a New Introduction by the Historic New Orleans Collection* (New York, 1983), 255.

19. Rosetta Ryan Lambert, taped interview, 19 July 1976, Friends of the Cabildo History Project, Manuscripts Division, Tulane University Library, New Orleans.

20. McDermott, *Tixier's Travels*, 57.

21. Wells and Tubby, *After Removal*; Kniffen, Gregory, and Stokes, *Historic Indian Tribes of Louisiana*.

22. Rouquette, "The Choctaws," 11–12.

23. Both historians and anthropologists have been slow to interpret the marketing activities of American Indians as partly a means of expressing their separate identity in day-to-day interaction with others. For notable exceptions, see David H. Snow, "Some Economic Considerations of Historic Rio Grande Pueblo Pottery," *The Changing Ways of Southwestern Indians: A Historic Perspective*, ed. Albert H. Schroeder (Glorieta NM, 1973), 57; James A. Clifton, *The Pokagons, 1683–1983: Catholic Potawatomi Indians of the St. Joseph River Valley* (Lanham MD, 1984), 116–17; Merrell, *Indians' New World*, 267–71. Sarah H. Hill's *Weaving New Worlds: Southeastern Cherokee Women and Their Basketry* (Chapel Hill NC, 1997) is a pathbreaking historical study of the importance of making and trading baskets for one American Indian society.

24. Tyrone Power, *Impressions of America during the Years 1833, 1834, and 1835* (Philadelphia, 1836), 2:145, 147.

25. Walt Whitman, *Prose Works, 1892*, ed. Floyd Stovall (New York, 1964), 2:606.

26. Overshadowed in the scholarly literature by long-term changes and continuities in the imagery of American Indians, different perceptions within a single region and short span of time shaped by the relative positions of Indian groups can be very informative. See, for example, Robin Fisher, *Contact and Conflict: Indian-European Relations in British Columbia, 1774–1890* (Vancouver, 1977), 73–94, and James J. Rawls, *Indians of California: The Changing Image* (Norman OK, 1984).

27. Earl F. Niehaus, *The Irish in New Orleans 1800–1860* (Baton Rouge LA, 1965); John W. Blassingame, *Black New Orleans 1860–1880* (Chicago, 1973). See John M. Merriman's *Margins of City Life: Explorations on the French Urban Frontier, 1815–1851* (New York, 1991) for an innovative study of the geographical, economic, and cultural dimensions of marginality in rapidly changing cities.

28. For a comparative pattern of Indian evasion and white observation in twentieth-century settings, see Neils Winther Braroe, *Indian and White: Self-Image and Interaction in a Canadian Plains Community* (Stanford CA, 1975), 102–8; Hugh Brody, *Maps and Dreams* (New York, 1981), 143–44.

29. *Cuming's Tour*, 365–66; Benjamin Henry Boneval Latrobe, *Impressions Respecting New Orleans: Diary and Sketches 1818–1820*, ed. Samuel Wilson Jr. (New York, 1951), 75–76; *Daily Picayune*, 2 April 1839; Rouquette, "The Choctaws," 56.

30. Castellanos, *New Orleans as It Was*, 221–22. When Henry David Thoreau met his guide, Louis Neptune and three other Penobscots on one of his journeys through Maine, he jumped to a revealing conclusion: "Met face to face, these Indians in their native woods looked like the sinister and slouching fellows whom you meet picking up strings and paper in the streets of a city. There is, in fact, a remarkable and unexpected resemblance between the degraded savage and the lowest classes in a great city. The one is no more a child of nature than the other. In the progress of degradation the distinction of races is soon lost." *The Maine Woods* (1864; New York: Thomas Y. Crowell, 1961), 101–3.

31. Roy Harvey Pearce, *Savagism and Civilization: A Study of the Indian and the American Mind*, rev. ed. (Berkeley CA, 1988), 58–66; Richard Drinnon, *Facing West: The Metaphysics of Indian-Hating and Empire-Building* (Minneapolis, 1980), 160–61.

32. Edouard de Montulé, *Travels in America, 1816–1817*, trans. Edward D. Seeber (Bloomington IN, 1951), 84–85; Latrobe, *Impressions*, 76.

33. Stewart A. Stehlin, trans. and ed., *Sketches of Urban and Cultural Life in North America by Friedrich Ratzel* (New Brunswick NJ, 1988), 198.

34. Latrobe, *Impressions*, 77; Rouquette, "The Choctaws," 50, 57.

35. *Picayune*, 6 April 1837; Latrobe, *Impressions*, 77–78; Castellanos, *New Orleans as It Was*, 222–24. For more information on crime and punishment in Choctaw society, see John R. Swanton, *Source Material for the Social and Ceremonial Life of the Choctaw Indians* (Washington DC, 1931), 104–15.

36. Castellanos, *New Orleans as It Was*, 328–29. For the importance of Congo Square in the cultural life of working-class New Orleanians, see Jerah Johnson, "New Orleans's Congo Square: An Urban Setting for Early Afro-American Culture Formation," *Louisiana History* 32 (spring 1991): 117–57.

37. Laussat, *Memoirs of My Life to My Son*, 53–54; Rouquette, "The Choctaws," 51–54; George W. Cable, "The Dance in Place Congo," *Century Magazine* 31 (February 1886): 518–19; Elise Kirsch, *"Downtown" New Orleans in the Early "Eighties": Customs and Characters of Old Robertson Street and Its Neighborhoods* (New Orleans, 1951), 6.

38. Steward Culin, *Games of the North American Indians*, Smithsonian Institution, Twenty-fourth Annual Report of the Bureau of American Ethnology (Washington

DC, 1907), 604–5. Blanchard, *Mississippi Choctaws at Play*, 24–43, is an illuminating analysis of *toli* in the wider cultural and historical context of Choctaw sports. For an informative overview of this ball game among many different Indian societies, see Thomas Vennum Jr., *American Indian Lacrosse: Little Brother of War* (Washington DC, 1994).

39. Castellanos, *New Orleans as It Was*, 298–300.

40. WPA *Guide to New Orleans*, 84–85. The popularity of raquettes in nineteenth-century New Orleans was uncovered in Dale A. Somers's scholarly *Rise of Sports in New Orleans 1850–1900* (Baton Rouge LA, 1972), 71–72, 208–9.

41. *Daily Picayune*, 4 August 1882, 21 December 1890; John Dimitry, "Chahta Ima – Father Rouquette," *Harper's Weekly* 21 (30 July 1887): 537–38; David I. Bushnell Jr., *The Choctaw of Bayou Lacomb, St. Tammany Parish, Louisiana* (Washington DC, 1909), 1–16; Susan Blanchard Elder, *Life of the Abbe Adrien Rouquette* (New Orleans, 1913), 142–45.

42. *Daily Picayune*, 22 September 1882.

43. Adrien Rouquette to John Dimitry, New Orleans, 12 December 1884, Adrien Emmanuel Rouquette Transcripts, Manuscripts Division, Howard-Tilton Memorial Library, Tulane University. The fullest biography of Adrien Rouquette is Dagmar Renshaw LeBreton, *Chahta-Ima: The Life of Adrien-Emmanuel Rouquette* (Baton Rouge LA, 1947), but also see Elder, *Life of the Abbe Adrien Rouquette*; Eleanor Van Trump, "Calendar of the Rouquette Material in the Archdiocesan Archives of New Orleans" (M.A. thesis, Tulane University, 1942); Blaise C. D'Antoni, *Chahta-Ima and St. Tammany's Choctaws* (Mandeville LA, 1986); and Dominic Braud, "Père Rouquette, Missionaire Extraordinaire: Father Adrien Rouquette's Mission to the Choctaw," *Cross, Crozier and Crucible: A Volume Celebrating the Bicentennial of a Catholic Diocese in Louisiana*, ed. Glenn R. Conrad (New Orleans, 1993), 314–27.

44. Rouquette to Dimitry, New Orleans, 1 December 1884, 12 December 1884, Rouquette Transcripts; LeBreton, *Chahta-Ima*, 223–24, 238–55.

45. *Daily Picayune*, 4 August 1882; Rouquette to Dimitry, New Orleans, 12 December 1884, Rouquette Transcripts.

46. *Daily Picayune*, 4 August 1882, 17 February 1893; Rouquette to Dimitry, New Orleans, 12 December 1882, Rouquette Transcripts. The ethnography on Choctaw burial practices is in Swanton, *Source Material for the Social and Ceremonial Life of the Choctaw Indians*, 170–94.

47. Rouquette, "The Choctaws," 50; *Daily Picayune*, 4 August 1882, 1 July 1888; Castellanos, *New Orleans as It Was*, 146–47.

48. "Pictures of the South. The French Market, New Orleans," *Harper's Weekly* 10 (18 August 1866): 517, 527. For pictorial illustrations of Choctaw women in the market, see chapter 8.

49. John R. Kemp, ed., *Martin Behrman of New Orleans: Memoirs of a City Boss* (Baton Rouge LA, 1977), 1–2.

50. *Historical Sketch Book and Guide to New Orleans and Environs, Edited and Compiled by Several Leading Writers of the New Orleans Press* (New York, 1885), 169, 258. Also see James S. Zacherie, *The New Orleans Guide and Exposition Handbook* (New Orleans, 1885), 95–96, 101–3. For one tourist's reaction to Indian women at the New Orleans market, see Frederic Trautmann, "New Orleans, the Mississippi, and the Delta through a German's Eyes: The Travels of Emile Derkert," *Louisiana History* 25 (winter 1984): 86–87.

51. William E. Deahl Jr., "Buffalo Bill's Wild West Show in New Orleans," *Louisiana History* 16 (summer 1975): 289–98. The image of American Indians projected at international exhibitions throughout this period is examined in Robert W. Rydell, *All the World's a Fair: Visions of Empire at American International Expositions, 1876–1916* (Chicago, 1984). Also see Raymond D. Fogelson, "The Red Man in the White City," in *Columbian Consequences*, vol. 3: *Perspective*, ed. David Hurst Thomas (Washington DC, 1991), 73–90.

52. Alice Dunbar-Nelson, "A Carnival Jangle," in *Violets and Other Tales* (Boston, 1895), 80–81.

53. Jason Berry, Jonathan Foose, and Tad Jones, *Up from the Cradle of Jazz: New Orleans Music since World War II* (Athens GA, 1986), 210–14; George Lipsitz, *Time Passages: Collective Memory and American Popular Culture* (Minneapolis, 1990), 233–53; Samuel Kinser, *Carnival, American Style: Mardi Gras at New Orleans and Mobile* (Chicago, 1990), 151–94; Michael P. Smith, "New Orleans' Carnival Culture from the Underside," in *Plantation Society in the Americas* (New Orleans, 1990), 11–32; Reid Mitchell, *All on a Mardi Gras Day: Episodes in the History of New Orleans Carnival* (Cambridge MA, 1995), 113–30; Joseph Roach, *Cities of the Dead: Circum-Atlantic Performance* (New York, 1996), 179–211; interview with eighty-year-old Robert "Robbie" Lee, *New Orleans Times-Picayune*, 24 March 1996.

54. Marcus Bruce Christian, Manuscript for a Black History of Louisiana, typescript in Marcus Bruce Christian Collection, chap. 42, pp. 5–6, Archives and Manuscripts Department, Earl K. Long Library, University of New Orleans.

55. James Owen Dorsey, "The Biloxi Indians of Louisiana," in *Proceedings of the American Association for the Advancement of Science for the Forty-second Meeting* (Salem MA, 1894); Oliver LaFarge, "A Lesson from the Mighty Choctaws of Louisiana," *New Orleans Morning-Tribune*, 6 June 1906; M. Raymond Harrington, "Among Louisiana Indians," *Southern Workman* 37 (December 1908): 656–61; Bushnell, *Choctaw of Bayou Lacomb*; David I. Bushnell Jr., "The Chitimacha of Bayou LaFourche, Louisiana," *Journal of the Washington Academy of Sciences* 7 (19 May 1917), 301–7.

56. *Daily Picayune*, 17 February 1893, 2 October 1898, 3 April 1910; *New Orleans Times-Democrat*, 12 May 1893.

57. Charles Roberts, "The Second Choctaw Removal, 1903," in *After Removal: The Choctaws in Mississippi*, 94–111. For a good profile of the Louisiana Choctaws at the time of this emigration, see John H. Peterson Jr., "Louisiana Choctaw Life at the End of the Nineteenth Century," in *Four Centuries of Southern Indians*, 101–12. Studies that document the endurance of Choctaw people in the area over the twentieth century include Dennis A. Booker, "Indian Identity in Louisiana: Two Contrasting Approaches to Ethnic Identity" (M.A. thesis, Louisiana State University, 1973); Ewell P. Roy and Don Leary, "Economic Survey of American Indians in Louisiana," *American Indian Journal* 3 (January 1977): 11–16; Darrell A. Posey, "Origin, Development and Maintenance of a Louisiana Mixed-Blood Community: The Ethnohistory of the Freejacks of the First Ward Settlement," *Ethnohistory* 26 (spring 1979): 177–92. Also see Kniffen, Gregory, and Stokes, *Historic Indian Tribes of Louisiana*, passim.

58. Williams, *Southeastern Indians since the Removal Era*; Frank W. Porter III, ed., *Strategies for Survival: American Indians in the Eastern United States* (Westport CT, 1986).

59. The role of dress, language, music, sports, and crafts in preserving ethnic identity among the Choctaws in Mississippi has been recently noted in James H. Howard and Victoria Lindsay Levine, *Choctaw Music and Dance* (Norman OK, 1990), 5. Also see Blanchard, *Mississippi Choctaws at Play*.

8. IMAGES OF LOWER MISSISSIPPI VALLEY INDIANS

1. Rosaldo, *Culture and Truth*, 68–73.

2. George Catlin, *North American Indians*, ed. Peter Matthiessen (New York: Penguin Books), 4; Brian W. Dippie, *Catlin and His Contemporaries: The Politics of Patronage* (Lincoln NE, 1990), 16–18, 41, 186–87.

3. John Francis McDermott, *Seth Eastman: Pictorial Historian of the Indian* (Norman OK, 1961), 32–62; McDermott, *Seth Eastman's Mississippi: A Lost Portfolio Recovered* (Urbana IL, 1973), 25.

4. William Cronon, "Telling Tales on Canvas: Landscapes of Frontier Change," in *Discovered Lands, Invented Pasts: Transforming Visions of the American West*, Jules David Prown, Nancy K. Anderson, Brian Dippie, William Cronon, Martha A. Sandweiss, Susan Schoelwer, and Howard Lamar (New Haven CT, 1992), 64–67.

5. Francis Parkman, *The Jesuits in North America in the Seventeenth Century*, vol. 1 of *France and England in North America*, ed. David Levin (New York, 1983), 702.

6. Ray Allen Billington, *The Genesis of the Frontier Thesis: A Study in Historical Creativity* (San Marino CA, 1971), 12.

7. *Cuming's Tour*, 285–86.

8. R. W. G. Vail, "The American Sketchbook of a French Naturalist, 1816–1837: A Description of the Charles Alexandre Lesueur Collection, with a Brief Account of the Artist," *Proceedings of the American Antiquarian Society* 48 (April 1938): 49–155.

9. David C. Hunt and Marsha V. Gallagher, eds., *Karl Bodmer's America* (Omaha NE, 1984), 109, 111–12, 119–20.

10. Joseph Holt Ingraham, *The Southwest. By a Yankee* (New York, 1835), 1:24–26.

11. Theda Perdue, "Southern Indians and the Cult of True Womanhood," in *The Web of Southern Social Relations: Women, Family, and Education*, ed. Walter J. Fraser Jr., Frank Saunders Jr., and Jon L. Wakelyn (Athens GA, 1985), 35–51.

12. Berquin-Duvallon, *Travels*, 103.

13. Harriet Martineau, *Society in America*, ed. Seymour Martin Lipset (Garden City NY, 1962), 148–49.

14. Berquin-Duvallon, *Travels*, 96–99; *Cuming's Tour*, 286; Robertson, *Louisiana under the Rule of Spain, France, and the United States*, 2:81–83.

15. For a description of Choctaw buildings and shelters outside New Orleans based on documentary, pictorial, and archaeological evidence, see Bushnell, *Native Villages*, 64–65.

16. Miriam J. Shillingsburg, "The Maturing of Simms's Short Fiction: The Example of 'Oakatibbe,'" *Mississippi Quarterly* 38 (spring 1985): 99–117. In a short story set in his home state of South Carolina, "Caloya; or, the Loves of the Driver" (1842), Simms builds the plot around his childhood memory of the seasonal travels of Catawbas to Charleston in order to sell pottery and other goods. Both "Oakatibbe" and "Caloya" can be found in Simms's *Wigwam and the Cabin* (New York, 1856).

17. Alfred Mercier, *L'Habitation Saint-Ybars, ou Matres et esclaves en Louisiane: Récit social* (New Orleans, 1881); George Reinecke, "Alfred Mercier, French Novelist of New Orleans," in *In Old New Orleans*, ed. W. Kenneth Holditch (Jackson MS, 1983), 145–76.

18. Louis Moreau Gottschalk, *Notes of a Pianist*, ed. Jeanne Behrend (New York, 1964), 291–92; Vernon Loggins, *Where the World Ends: The Life of Louis Moreau Gottschalk* (Baton Rouge LA, 1958), 20–25.

19. Grace King and John R. Ficklen, *A History of Louisiana* (New York, 1893), 165. For a study of basketry made by Choctaws to the present, see Marshall Gettys, "Choctaw Baskets," in *Basketry of Southeastern Indians*, ed. Gettys (Idabel OK, 1984), 35–42.

20. Per Seyersted, ed., *The Complete Works of Kate Chopin* (Baton Rouge LA,

1969), 1:506. "Nég Créol" originally appeared in the July 1897 issue of *Atlantic-Monthly* magazine.

21. George Washington Cable, *Old Creole Days* (New York, 1879).

22. Richardson Cox, "Up the Mississippi," *Putnam's Monthly* 5 (October 1857): 438.

23. Charles Joseph Latrobe, *The Rambler in North America* (London, 1836), 2:334.

Index

In the Indians of the Southeast series

WILLIAM BARTRAM ON THE SOUTHEASTERN INDIANS
Edited and annotated by Gregory A. Waselkov and
Kathryn E. Holland Braund

DEERSKINS AND DUFFELS
The Creek Indian Trade with Anglo-America, 1685–1815
By Kathryn E. Holland Braund

SEARCHING FOR THE BRIGHT PATH
The Mississippi Choctaws from Prehistory to Removal
By James Taylor Carson

DEMANDING THE CHEROKEE NATION
Indian Autonomy and American Culture, 1830–1900
By Andrew Denson

CHEROKEE AMERICANS
The Eastern Band of Cherokees in the Twentieth Century
By John R. Finger

CREEKS AND SOUTHERNERS
Biculturalism on the Early American Frontier
By Andrew K. Frank

CHOCTAW GENESIS, 1500–1700
By Patricia Galloway

THE SOUTHEASTERN CEREMONIAL COMPLEX
ARTIFACTS AND ANALYSIS
The Cottonlandia Conference
Edited by Patricia Galloway
Exhibition Catalog by David H. Dye and Camille Wharey

The Invention of the Creek Nation, 1670–1763
By Steven C. Hahn

AN ASSUMPTION OF SOVEREIGNTY
*Social and Political Transformation among
the Florida Seminoles, 1953–1979*
By Harry A. Kersey Jr.

THE CADDO CHIEFDOMS
Caddo Economics and Politics, 700–1835
By David La Vere

KEEPING THE CIRCLE
American Indian Identity in Eastern North Carolina, 1885–2004
Christopher Arris Oakley

CHOCTAWS IN A REVOLUTIONARY AGE, 1750–1830
By Greg O'Brien

CHEROKEE WOMEN
Gender and Culture Change, 1700–1835
By Theda Perdue

THE BRAINERD JOURNAL
A Mission to the Cherokees, 1817–1823
Edited and introduced by Joyce B. Phillips and Paul Gary Phillips

THE CHEROKEES
A Population History
By Russell Thornton

BUFFALO TIGER
A Life in the Everglades
By Buffalo Tiger and Harry A. Kersey Jr.

AMERICAN INDIANS IN THE LOWER MISSISSIPPI VALLEY
Social and Economic Histories
By Daniel H. Usner Jr.

POWHATAN'S MANTLE
Indians in the Colonial Southeast
Edited by Peter H. Wood, Gregory A. Waselkov, and M. Thomas Hatley

CREEKS AND SEMINOLES
The Destruction and Regeneration of the Muscogulge People
By J. Leitch Wright Jr.